AF557750

GLOBALISATION AND THE PROSPECTS FOR CRITICAL REFLECTION

GLOBALISATION AND THE PROSPECTS FOR CRITICAL REFLECTION

Edited by
Jung Min Choi and John W. Murphy

GLOBALISATION AND THE PROSPECTS FOR CRITICAL REFLECTION

Ed. by Jung Min Choi and John W. Murphy

First Indian Edition 2009

ISBN 978-81-89833-98-5 (Hb)

Published by

AAKAR BOOKS

28 E Pocket IV, Mayur Vihar Phase I, Delhi-110 091

Phone : 011-2279 5505 Telefax : 011-2279 5641

aakarbooks@gmail.com; www.aakarbooks.com

Printed at

Arpit Printographers

E-mail: arpitprinto@yahoo.com

To *Camilo Jin Suh*
and
other future revolutionaries

Preface

Modern globalization is sustained by realism. In this context, realism signals that this economic trend is thought by most persons to be natural and inevitable. Of course, the media and schools foster this portrayal. Globalization, nonetheless, is described to be the product of long-term economic cycles that cannot be reversed. Hence informed persons do not lament this change and try to return to the halcyon days of Keynesianism and social supports. Such a reaction would only result in slowing economic growth and undermine the future.

On the other hand, realism supports the neo-liberal claim that markets are the only reliable means to regulate an economy and, presumably, a society. After all, markets are touted to be rational and universal, and thus the only reliable mechanism to coordinate buying and selling and arbitrate competing claims. Consistent with realism, markets are autonomous and transcend politics. Any outside intervention into the operation of these devices, moreover, compromises their efficiency and effectiveness.

The general results of realism, accordingly, are very pragmatic assessments of globalization, at least from the mainstream quarters of society. Most often persons learn simply to adapt to the problems spawned by globalization and hope to find a niche at the marketplace and manage to survive. As part of this process, they are expected to recognize the benefits of globalization or risk marginalization and impoverishment.

But many critics around the globe are chanting that another world is both necessary and possible. Their survey of the current economic situation reveals that since 1980—roughly the onset of widespread neo-liberalism—only a few countries such as China have improved their standard of living. And in these places, incomes remain exceedingly low.

The rest of the world has witnessed a race to the bottom, as corporations scour the world for the cheapest labor. Consequently, in countries throughout Latin America and Africa the gap between the rich and poor has widened, with the vast majority of their populations living in dire poverty. And even the United States and Europe have been shaken by what President Obama calls the failed economic, i.e., laissez-faire, policies of the past.

These protestors, therefore, desire a new economic orientation that is less dependent on markets and reject the accompanying internecine rivalries. Their hope is that an alternative world can be created where emphasis is placed on justice, solidarity, and cooperation and mutual aid. In such a community, the deep divisions that characterize present societies would be overcome, so that racism, poverty, and other forms of discrimination are challenged and eliminated. In this sense, a more humane and enlightened world might be promoted.

But before this reorientation can occur, a break must be made with realism. Critics must not be afraid to engage in utopian thought, and propose ideas that currently may be dismissed automatically by realists as beyond the pale or unworkable. Particularly important, for example, a serious reassessment must be made of the claim that a functional economy can only be organized around markets. But in general, critics must not remain trapped within outmoded social or economic paradigms by the fear of being labeled irrational, idealistic, or radical. At this juncture of history, bold strokes are needed to invent a new economic reality that is less exploitative and more inclusive.

The aim of this book is to engage in some utopian thinking. Instead of reifying globalization, the point is to reveal the values, biases, and commitments that sustain this trend. In this way, to borrow from Marx, readers should not simply interpret but reassess the current state of the world. The analyses provided are not designed to help persons adapt to and work more efficiently in a globalized world, but to illustrate that this economic and social reality can be re-conceptualized and significantly changed. Such change, moreover, does not violate some basic social mores or human nature, but represents the ability of persons to respond to one another in respectful and constructive ways.

Following such criticism, globalization is revealed to be a social invention that serves particular interests. Certain so-called economic realities are proposed as necessary that, in fact, conceal malevolent political motives and the interests of particular powerful groups. The goal of utopian planning, therefore, should be to invent institutions such as the economy that reflect the widest possible range of interests and foster the common weal. Indeed, only a world predicated on solidarity can promote widespread prosperity and peace. Hopefully, this book can contribute, in some small way, to the development of this new world.

Jung Min Choi
John W. Murphy

Acknowledgments

There are many people who made this project possible. John Murphy and I thank K K and Rahul Saxena at Aakar Books for being patient with this project and seeing it to its fruition. We also thank the graduate students (Soo Mee Kim and Jerry Flores) who helped out in tracking down partial citations in several different languages. In particular, I thank Paul Cortopassi, my graduate assistant, who worked weekends and nights and read the entire manuscript multiple times to make sure our edits made sense.

List of Contributors

Steven Arxer (Ph.D.) is an assistant professor of sociology at Belmont Abbey College. He received his Ph.D. from the University of Florida and has published several papers on globalization, education, postmodernism, and aging. He is currently interested in the role of civil society in Latin America and has conducted qualitative research on the identity work of NGO members in Colombia.

Amy Berberi teaches at Ashford University. Her areas of interest are sociology of media, globalization, and sociological theory.

Vicente Berdayes (Ph.D.) is Professor of Communication Studies at Saint Mary's College, Notre Dame, Indiana. His research interests are in the areas of communication theory, intercultural communication, and organizational communication. His recent publications include the edited volumes *Computers, Human Interaction and Organizations: Critical Issues* (with John Murphy), Greenwood Press, 2000, and The *Body in Human Inquiry: Interdisciplinary Explorations of Embodiment* (with Luigi Esposito and John W. Murphy), Hampton Press, 2004.

Jung Min Choi (Ph.D.) is Associate Professor of Sociology at San Diego State University. He has published books and articles on various topics, including education, globalization, race/ ethnicity, and theory. His recent interest lies in the implementation of imagination into formal education.

Manuel Caro (Ph.D.) is currently working at the Fundación Andaluza Fondo de Formación y Empleo in Spain. His areas of interests are criminological and sociological theory.

Luigi Esposito (Ph.D.) is Associate Professor of Sociology at Barry University in Miami Shores, FL. He teaches various courses in sociology and criminology, and has published several articles on issues related to globalization, race relations, methodology, ethics, and democracy.

Heather Gautney (Ph.D.) is an assistant professor at Fordham University, Lincoln Center in the Department of Sociology and Anthropology, where she teaches courses on Social Movements, Social Theory and political sociology. She recently completed a book on contemporary transnational movements called *When the Empire Falls* and is co-editor of *Implicating Empire: Globalization and Resistance in the 21st Century* (Basic Books) and *Democracy, States and the Struggle for Global Justice* (forthcoming on Routledge).

Taesik Kim is a doctoral candidate in communication at the University of Oklahoma. His areas of interest are symbolic violence and nationalism.

Eric Kramer (Ph.D.) is Professor of communication at the University of Oklahoma. He received his graduate degrees in philosophy, sociology, and telecommunications. His areas of interest are myth of rationality, comparative civilizations, and intercultural communication.

Carlos Largacha-Martínez (Ph.D.) is Provost for Research at Universidad EAN in Bogota, Colombia. His main research interest is on quantum humanism and management.

Algis Mickunas (Ph.D.) received his education at various universities including, Chicago, Cologne, and Freiberg. He received his Ph.D. from Emory University and is Professor of Philosophy at Ohio University. His interests include European Philosophy including hermeneutics and semiotics.

John W. Murphy (Ph.D.) is Professor of Sociology at the University of Miami. He received his doctorate degree from Ohio State University. His interests are sociological theory, Latin America, and globalization. His most recent book is with Jung Min Choi and is titled *Globalization with a Human Face.*

Dana Rasch (Ph.D.) is Assistant Professor at Bethune-Cookman University in Daytona Beach, Florida. His areas of interest include social movements in Latin America, service-learning, and race and ethnic relations.

David Reznik is a Ph.D. candidate in sociology at the University of Florida. His interests include critical theory, radical political economy, and social justice.

Michael Roberts (Ph.D.) is an assistant professor of sociology at San Diego State University. He has published articles in the areas of social theory, labor studies and popular culture. His book *Tell*

Tchaikovsky the News: the Problem of Rock and Roll in the Musicians' Union is due out next fall with Duke University Press. He received his Ph.D. from the Graduate Center at the City University of New York.

Tom Semm teaches in the Sociology Department at San Diego State University. His areas of interest are globalization, ethics, and mass media. He is currently working on a paper that deals with globalization and the private military corporations.

Contents

1

Introduction

Jung Min Choi and John W. Murphy

Is Another World Possible?

Nowadays many persons in the anti-globalization movement are wondering if another world is possible. Indeed, globalization has not turned out to be as wonderful as many of its proponents originally thought. Good jobs are not proliferating throughout the world, the environment is suffering, and those who were already rich seem to be getting wealthier. And on the more spiritual side, the lives of persons are becoming cheaper every day. In general, there is a race to the bottom that no one appears to be capable of stopping.

Yet subsequent to the events at Porto Alegre, critics of the economic and cultural trends associated with globalization ask about an alternative world. They declare that another world is needed where justice prevails and persons are treated more humanely. A world-wide community is desired that is inclusive and fosters the well-being of everyone.

Of course such ideals are marvelous and indicative of the most progressive sentiments. The problem is that most of the public has been convinced that proposals about universal justice and equitable social development, for example, are simply utopian and unattainable. In the so-called real world, such dreams can never be realized and should not leave the confines of the classroom or church.

What persons have done, accordingly, is entrusted their futures to fate. But by repressing their dreams, they have ignored a key source of their liberation. In fact, many persons are afraid that such musings are irrational and may jeopardize their current place in the world. The present may be bad, they believe, but something worse may be lurking around the corner.

And in many respects their fears may be well founded. After all, if they are intimidated to act in a proactive manner, someone will likely create a future that is much worse than the present. Although the future is not guaranteed, even if the masses act forcefully, their withdrawal undermines any hope of something occurring that is more positive. Their pessimism may allows their worst fears to be realized.

Trust in Imagination

In a sense, many persons do not trust their imagination.[1] Even worse, their imagination is simply imaginary and pales in comparison to reality. But how has imagination been discredited in this manner?

During the 1960s, for example, graffiti abounded that declared that no one should be intimidated by reality. Surrealist themes became popular that suggested reality is an illusion and standard politics a dead end. Many students, accordingly, engaged in excesses and frivolous activities, but they made a cogent point. That is, reality is a matter of belief and not something that automatically must be taken seriously.

And now globalization represents a reality that is threatening everyone, even those who, at least momentarily, may be benefitting from this trend. At best, persons assume that they have two options. They can either cope with this new reality or discover how to reinvent it. In both cases, however, they have conceded that a reality exists that exceeds the reach of their imagination. They have engaged in what Sartre calls the "serious attitude."[2]

At this juncture is where the power of globalization is revealed—globalization has been given an undeserved status. Globalization, in other words, has become something universal that extends beyond the limiting influence of imagination. In this respect, the dominance of globalization is predicated on a particular philosophical perspective. In a very slick way, realism has been introduced to legitimize the inactivity of persons and the growth of harmful global economic and cultural policies. Accordingly, persons are considered to be rational and intelligent if they recognize the inevitability of globalization and make the proper adjustments. They are rational if they see the wisdom of the market, profit, and the accompanying radical individualism.

Dubious Universals

A particular position on reliable knowledge and order has been at the core of the Western intellectual tradition. This viewpoint, moreover, has made dealing with the claims made regularly about globalization very difficult. Specifically problematic has been the idea that globalization represents a universal trend that supersedes all traditions and cultures. And given this status, globalization is going to unify the world and enrich those who recognize the validity of this sort of development.

Globalization, in this sense, is similar to other myths that have been invoked to substantiate valid knowledge and ethics. Especially noteworthy is that Western philosophy is grounded in the belief that truth, for example, should be based only on an absolute foundation. And in the context, this absolute base is defined as a norm or some other referent that transcends everyday life. Reliable knowledge, in other words, can only survive in a place that is divorced categorically from quotidian concerns and the associated perspectives.

What this belief does is open the possibility of establishing a location that is beyond interpretation and other cultural influences. If persons can be convinced that globalization occupies this space, the resulting policies and practices can be treated as unique. They can be viewed as having their own destiny and demand to be recognized by everyone. Globalization is thus a juggernaut that cannot be stopped by mere mortals. As Heidegger once proclaimed, perhaps now only a God can save humanity.[3]

Within a different milieu, globalization may have an entirely different meaning. For example, claims about the autonomous character of this process would make little sense outside of this absolute domain. Globalization may proceed, but beliefs about inevitability would not have much legitimacy. But within this tradition of indubitable foundations, all discussions about the future must transpire within the parameters associated with globalization. Therefore, globalization is an imposing reality that persons must confront, if they are sufficiently motivated and enlightened.

In this sense, the majority of Westerners have always been realists. They have cherished and sought a base of knowledge and order that they could venerate. But Plato's *Ideas* were not as immediately harmful as globalization. Nonetheless, both required that everyday existence be submitted to a higher authority. The problem is that today this authority is crushing the vast majority of humanity through economic policies that are creating debt, poverty, and dependency.

First Philosophy and Humanity

According to those who engage in such "first philosophy"—by searching for eternal grounds—humanity should not be trusted. In point of fact, humans have been treated traditionally as a source of error or irrationality. In order to know their fate, they must meditate and reflect on a higher reality. In the case of globalization, the laws of economics or the market should be the focus of attention. The point, again, is to anticipate correctly global trends.

No wonder persons are so easily convinced of their impotence with regard to any confrontation with the reality of globalization. Indeed, they are merely fulfilling the role they have been allotted traditionally. Perhaps passivity or withdrawal is all that can be expected, given the ontological status that is linked to globalization. Without a doubt, humans are in no position to challenge such an exalted reality.

But the status of globalization is guaranteed because of a perverse epistemological maneuver. Persons must pretend that the ultimate grounds pursued in "first philosophy" transcend the human condition. After all, the fact is that these norms or laws have a historical origin, cultural significance, and limited importance. They are cultural artifacts, in other words, that are not necessarily absolute or universal. Particularly important is that their reality is assured through self-denial on the part of persons.

In this regard, realism demands a much more fundamental withdrawal even before the reality of globalization is confronted. Specifically, the presence of persons is diminished in the creation of these so-called absolutes. And following this initial debacle, the intimidation wrought by globalization is only natural. When confronted by a true universal, the contingent world must always relent and be given a secondary position.

In this sense, "first philosophy" is inevitably anti-humanistic. What else could be the case, if humanity is an impediment to the discovery of truth and valid ethical norms. Erich Fromm once made this point when he suggested that humanity can only be diminished by these absolutes.[4] Indeed, humanity pales by comparison.

Emerging from the Façade

In order for humanity to become self-directed, persons must emerge from the shadows cast by the traditional absolutes. Only in this way can globalization, not to mention other imperious organizations, be brought under control and made to fulfill human needs. In many respects, however, theses universals are *faux* absolutes, based on a planned escape from everyday experiences.

But such an escape is impossible! Despite a longing for the security provided by these absolutes, their status is fraudulent. They are intimately tied, in other words, to human initiative that attempts to make their identity universal. And thus they are political in the most practical sense, in that they promote one social or cultural end at the expense of others.

The point is that the standard division between universals and particulars represents a false dichotomy. In fact, they are both connected to specific historical conditions and human desires. Therefore, they are both existentially grounded, rather than separated by an ontological chasm. In the end, any absolute must emerge from this existential condition, even if realists want to deny that such a connection exists.

In the absence of this association, these absolutes could not be known. They would be merely a matter of pure speculation, similar to Kant's noumenal realm. But when these absolutes are mediated by experience, they lose their position as inherently universal. They are existential constructs, and nothing more, that are allotted a special or unique status.

Realists are thus correct about one issue: that is, reality has a unique identity. What is noteworthy, however, is not that reality is autonomous, but that a particular existential construction of norms or ideals becomes known as real or the "paramount reality."[5] All the tales about the universal and inevitable nature of globalization, accordingly, are a fabrication. In truth, globalization represents little more than a myth about autonomy and inevitability.

But a lot of effort has been devoted to creating an ideology about the fate of humanity. As Marx declares, the aim of ideology is to generate the illusion that a contingent phenomenon is absolute and, thus, inviolable. Those who champion globalization, accordingly, have used the Western intellectual tradition to propose a mythology about globalization and the resulting future.

The Benefits of Globalization

The question of who benefits from globalization cannot be ignored any longer. Deprived of the space where absolutes used to reside, all claims must emerge from one perspective or another. Absolutes, in other words, must be connected to certain interpretations, ambitions, or desires. And declarations about the fortunes and advantages of globalization are not exempt from this requirement.

Globalization, therefore, reflects certain values, beliefs, and commitments. In other words, someone or some group wants everyone to accept that globalization is part of a universal and natural economic trend that benefits everyone. But philosophically such a proclamation is not obvious or automatically true, due to the absence of a link between globalization and anything absolute. And therefore, in point of fact, globalization reveals a particular perspective on development that is not necessarily shared by a large segment of humanity. Nonetheless, the need for everyone to accept the myth about globalization continues to be fostered.

But without this mythology, claims about globalization certainly can be contested. Minus an absolute justification, globalization does not constitute a reality that can demand legitimately universal recognition. On the other hand, a particular economic or cultural trend could be accorded this status, through informed deliberation and consent, but the result does not represent a traditional absolute. Current globalization, accordingly, could achieve this level of democratic recognition, although this end is unlikely given the configuration of this process. Specifically, most of the world's population has not been allowed to participate in setting global economic and cultural priorities.

A New Future

This introduction began with some speculation about the prospects for creating a new world. Given the mythology about globalization, the ability of persons to invent a new future has been clearly stifled. And all that will likely continue is the usual pragmatic response to global development. Any opposition, simply put, will be treated as immature and little more than fantasy.

With the mythology about globalization existentially grounded, however, the stigma attached to utopianism is no longer valid. Rather than hopeless and hapless dreamers, utopian thinkers refuse to be trapped by a particular rendition of reality. These critics simply recognize the façade of realism and attempt to move the social world in another direction. They see no need to merely cope with a reality based on an outmoded perspective. What is needed nowadays, therefore, is not less but more utopianism.

The key point, accordingly, is that the world can be changed! Another world is certainly possible, without persons having to work within a preconceived reality. The reality imposed by current globalization is nothing special, despite claims made to the contrary by realists. Globalization is simply a perspective on development that many persons consider to be harmful and beyond reform. Change is thus clearly justified!

Contrary to the mythology perpetrated by realism, anything is possible. Nothing is confronted that is autonomous and inevitably dictates the aims of persons. Existence is thus open to a range of possibilities, even entirely new economic or cultural arrangements. How these various perspectives are treated depends on the vision and commitment of persons. If another world is desired, the present reality is not in a position any longer to stifle this option, at least philosophically. Such news should be welcomed by those who oppose the current approach to globalization. All that is needed at this time is the social practice, and the political will, to act in a manner that is consistent with this openness.

NOTES

1. Arjun Appadurai, Modernity at Large, Minneapolis: University of Minnesota Press, 1996.
2. Jean-Paul Sartre, Existentialism and Human Emotions, New York: Philosophical Library, 1957, p. 92.
3. Martin Heidegger, "Only a God can Save Us," in The Heidegger Controversy: A Critical Reader, ed. Richard Wolin, Cambridge, MA: The MIT Press, 1993, pp. 91-116.
4. Erich Fromm, Escape from Freedom, New York: Avon Books, 1969, pp. 208-230.
5. Alfred Schutz, Collected Papers. Vol. I, The Hague: Nijhoff, 1962, pp. 226-234.

2

Diversity as a Threat to Homogenizing Global Culture

Jung Min Choi and Amy N. Berberi

Introduction: Neoliberalism and the Ubiquity of the Market

Let's face it. Globalization is the new juggernaut that is crushing everything in its path in an attempt to homogenize the world. While disagreements abound, both the Right and the Left agree that globalization is here to stay. The world has been compressed and made smaller during the past several decades. Sure, people have always been engaged in the process of globalization for hundreds and thousands of years. People have travelled to different parts of the world and exchanged ideas, cultures, and artifacts with one another.

What is particular about modern-day globalization is the speed at which different parts of the world can be connected. Supposedly, in the new age of globalization, even those in the most remote parts of the world can be connected with people in the metropolis instantaneously. Wireless Internet services have even allowed people to connect while they are "on the move". World events, market fluctuations, natural disasters, even golf scores are readily available to those who are interested. Without moving an inch, persons are able to visit the entire world within the confines of their own rooms. Rather than being uprooted and thrown into a foreign place, places and events are transported into people's living rooms.

Having clear ties with the ever-growing computerization of the world, globalization is viewed as a natural part of the linear progression of history. In a Comtean manner, globalization reflects the pinnacle of the positive stage in human history. For Comte, the rise in scientific inquiry would eventually provide the "common stock" of knowledge for assessing individuals and their relationship with society.[1] True to this world view, globalization has, in fact, pushed its agenda on a universal claim—the Total Market.[2]

To be specific, neoliberalism has been used to justify the homogenizing effects of globalization around the world. The idea is simple and clear: let the market dictate the worth of all commodities in society, including labour, ideas, and human values. In this way, no one is discriminated against on the basis of irrational characteristics such as race, gender, and religion. The market is interested in one major thing: increased profits and decreased costs through efficiency in exchange and production. What can be so bad about this scenario? As long as individuals accept this premise, everyone has a fair shot at succeeding at the market, since all are allowed to compete. No outside forces, such as government mandates and regulations, must retard the efficacy of the market.

Although popular, this is not a novel idea—far from it! Neoliberalism is an extension and revival of the classical economic thought proffered by Adam Smith and his followers, such as David Ricardo and John Stuart Mill. All of them expounded the virtues of entrepreneurialism, free competition, and the rationality of the market in organizing society. In fact, these ideas gave legitimacy to capitalism and paved the way for the dominance of the laissez-faire economy in many parts of Europe subsequent to the industrial revolution.

However, as is widely known, the Great Depression put a screeching halt to the market-led economy. People became painfully aware that an unchecked market *can* and *will* produce extreme inequalities in a society. The "invisible hand" that was to smooth out the differences in wealth, status, and power was never to be found at the market.

It was not surprising, then, that there was a movement away

from laissez-faire to a state-led economy following the Great Depression. This economic model, provided by John Maynard Keynes, spawned the welfare state in Britain and the New Deal in the United States. While robust during its reign, the Keynesian theory of economics would last no more than several decades. By the late1970s and the early 1980s, major changes across the globe were already in motion to usher in neoliberalism—the major oil crises of 1973, 1979; General Pinochet's overthrowing of democratically elected Allende of Chile in 1973;[3] the resurgence of neoliberal intellectualism via Friedrich Von Hayek, Milton Friedman, and Arnold Harberger throughout the 1970s; elections of Margaret Thatcher and Ronald Reagan in the successive years of 1979 and 1980; the deaths of President Roldos of Ecuador and President Torrijos of Panama two months apart in 1981;[4] and the debt crisis of Latin America in the early 1980s where Argentina, Mexico, and Brazil (the three largest economies in Latin America) took out substantial loans from the International Monetary Fund (IMF).[5] Without going into extensive detail, the interconnectedness of these major events precipitated in giving birth to neoliberalism and the rise of the untrammelled market economy that we currently face.

Globalization, Neoliberalism, and the Need for Homogenization

So what is the fallout from globalization? In general, those who support globalization push for standardization of norms. So what's new about this manoeuvre? Standardization of norms has been central to the Western tradition. Major thinkers, like Plato, Aquinas, Hobbes, Locke, and Durkheim argue that society must have ontologically autonomous norms to guide social life. Without such norms, society will collapse into utter chaos.

As mentioned previously, however, standardization of norms in the era of globalization is quite different. Not only are the norms dictated by the market, the spread of these norms is done at an exponential rate across the globe. As argued by Hardt and Negri, the speed at which people are being subsumed under the market rule is astonishing.[6] Unlike the great powers of the past, such as Rome, China, Spain, and Great Britain, where an overt exercise of power and physical colonization was needed, the modern-day empire operates in a manner that is stealthy, efficient, and high-tech.

No longer is domination occurring from a single source or place like the KGB or the United States. Instead, the new form of empire is a conglomeration of power elites who organize and run multinational corporations across the world. In a truly Durkheimean manner, globalization reflects the organic solidarity among the elites where differences of ethnicity, culture, or beliefs become secondary to the mandates of the market.[7]

In a rational manner, globalization through the neoliberal market rule creates a natural hierarchy of values for people throughout the world. Accordingly, the "total market" is touted to be the most egalitarian form of social organization known to date. According to the proponents of globalization, this new form of empire does not discriminate on the basis of race, gender, ethnicity, culture, or any other human traits.

In fact, engaging in such irrational activities as racism or sexism would be counterproductive to the success of the market. Not hiring the best qualified woman or a minority can be detrimental to productivity and optimizing profit. Similarly, debasing certain cultures or religions will eliminate a large number of people from participating in the consumption of goods and services provided by the market. In this sense, the more inclusive the market, the better returns it will have. The better returns it has, the more capital it can invest. The more investments it has, the bigger it will grow. The bigger the market grows, the more it can employ. The more people it employs, the more goods that it can produce. The more goods it produces, the more people it can serve. In this sense, Adam Smith's dream of the market serving everyone has become a reality.

So why would anyone resist globalization? No one is forcing or coercing anyone to work in the market. The market, as shown, welcomes anyone who has talent and is willing to work. The market, as David Ricardo once suggested, is blind to personal differences since even the "wages [are] left to the fair and free competition of the market".[8] To cry foul because one has to submit to the universal and rational principles of the market is absurd.

This world view may be one of the reasons why globalization has been able to continue on its march toward homogenization without major obstacles. And looking at the world scene, homogenization of culture and economy *has* and *continues* to spread very quickly.

One doesn't have to search very hard to see that major cities around the world look like carbon copies of one another. Certain areas of Beijing, Tokyo, Medellin, and Buenos Aires can be mistaken for cities like Los Angeles, New York, London, Paris, or Barcelona. They have similar billboards selling the same products, such as Adidas, Nike, Gucci, Polo, Coke, and of course, McDonalds. Whether you are in Seoul or Guatemala City, these signs are in English and the products are the same. Even intangible products like the news seem to share many similarities across the globe, as local news stations try to imitate and model themselves after corporate giants like CNN, ESPN, FOX, and MSNBC.[9] Nevertheless, no one is restricted to or discriminated against from buying, selling, and consuming these goods and services.

In terms of the economy, globalization has had a major impact on how countries organize their economic structures. With the help of the IMF, World Bank, and the World Trade Organization (WTO)—organizations that support globalization—neoliberals have been able to mandate economic policies to the borrowing countries. For example, under the rubric of structural adjustment, the IMF has been able to influence, and at times set, social policies in countries that borrow money from it.[10] The idea is that as a lending agency, it has the right to mandate social policies that are conducive for the borrowing countries to be able to pay their debt. This doesn't seem to be out of the ordinary since this practice is quite prevalent between lenders and borrowers in modern societies. The lenders have a right to be reimbursed in a timely manner. And as responsible lenders, it is their duty to assist in the economic planning of the borrowers so that people do not default on their loans. Just as a good mortgage loan officer tries to make sure the homeowner does not foreclose or declare bankruptcy, the IMF is interested in the economic well-being of the borrowing countries. And since the IMF's standardized lending policies of "structural adjustment" are in line with the demands of the market economy, there is nothing sinister about the terms of agreement of the loans.

The Truth About Globalization: Wolves in Sheepskins

When seen in this light, globalization seems to be innocuous and even beneficial to everyone. As long as everyone plays by the rules of the market, all is well, right? The answer is No! While globalization seems to be inclusive and egalitarian, it is a mere façade that obfuscates the ghastly unequal distribution of wealth and power, exploitation of labour, repression of differences, and domination of workers all over the world. Those who control the *Empire*, the transnational power elites, have a vested interest in the survival of corporations in the capitalist world market. And under the guise of a global community, they exercise a tremendous amount of power in making economic policies that impact social issues in both the "centre" and "periphery" nations. Most loans to the Third World countries are contingent on the borrowing countries' ability to cut drastically social benefits, repress workers' rights and voices, and expose valuable natural resources (often in virgin territories like the Amazon forests) for foreign investment.[11] Surely, this is not what Marshall McLuhan had in mind when he envisioned his "global village".[12]

Despite claims to the contrary, the market is necessarily based on repression of meaningful differences such as race, gender, ethnicity, class, and culture. This is because the market not only needs standardization for efficiency, but also needs everyone to commit to the basic assumptions of the market exploitation of labour and the manipulation of consumption. So the market is in a perpetual search to locate the most inexpensive method to manufacture goods and services, irrespective of the social costs it produces. This is evident not only in the maquiladoras where sweat shop labour and unconscionable wages are common practice, but also in high-tech industries such as computer tech support where traditional American jobs have moved across continents to India and other Asian countries in favour of cheap labour.

However, because the focus is on the rationality of the market, these issues of social inequality are dissolved into "business as usual". Moreover, because human beings are viewed solely as a "commodity" and an "economic being" by the market, all other human concerns such as dignity, fairness, and equality are pushed to the periphery. And since the market touts itself to be open to all comers and fair competition, structural and institutional discrimination is never challenged. In a Parsonian manner, the market has become the "Ultimate Reality". Challenging the norms set by the market, then, becomes irrational and illogical. Mirroring Talcott Parson's cybernetic hierarchy, human beings, in the modern era of globalization, have become nothing more than energies that need to be directed by the market. Thus, rather than racism, sexism, or classism, failure to compete successfully at the market becomes a reflection of personal shortcomings. Those who are able to adapt to the market will succeed while those who are not capable of such a feat will fail. The market represents the highest form of "natural selection". And who is to challenge natural law and the unfolding of history?

And in terms of consumption, the situation is not much different. As discussed widely by George Ritzer, products and services are becoming increasingly standardized and so is the taste of the consumers.[13] While consumers have seemingly unlimited choices of foods, drinks, clothes, and shoes in a sea of over-produced goods, this is not necessarily true. The variety, in an odd fashion, is quite restricted and limited within the narrow margins of homogenous products. For example, there are hundreds of different athletic shoes made by major corporations like Nike, Adidas, Puma, and Converse. Yet, these shoes don't seem to have significant differences in form and function. This is true of soft drinks and clothes alike. Jean Kilbourne has shown extensively how the entire clothing industry is not geared to making garments for everyone's body shape. Instead, the industry sells images of "normalcy" with respect to the body type and desires.[14] The result of this gambit is the assimilation of consumers to the ideals of fashion set by the industry. The desires of the consumers gradually begin to match the products sold in the stores. Without any overt force, fuss, or mess, the industry has effectively standardized the clothing taste of millions of customers. This, however, is not natural but manipulated by the market through the billion-dollar industry of advertising.[15] Nevertheless, when consumers begin to believe that they are unique and acting on their own accord, even when they are limited to buying "homogeneous" products, social control becomes quite easy and normative. This situation is what Foucault has aptly termed biopolitical power.[16]

Even food doesn't escape this type of standardization. The late Stephen Jay Gould lamented the disappearance of unique regional foods due to the ubiquitous presence of chain restaurants like Chile's, Denny's, and Cheesecake Factory where the food is pre-packaged and cooked the same no matter what city you are in.[17] This is no surprise, given that the success of the market is based on the predictability of guaranteed return on the investment.

But how is this world view of standardization disseminated without much public resistance or ire? According to Chomsky, the media has served as the main conduit in turning the average citizens into busy consumers.[18] Indeed, neoliberalism has benefited greatly from the homogenization of the media over the past two decades. The merging of media corporations into a handful of giant conglomerates has paved a super highway for the consumerization of society that disrupts the people's ability to think critically about their existence. The news has become increasingly sanitized at the political level but sensationalized at the cultural level. So, stories abound on major news networks regarding the death of Hollywood stars like Anna Nicole Smith or Heath Ledger but rarely is there an in-depth reporting on the Blackwater scandal or the impact of neoliberal policies on poor countries around the world. Clearly, the "propaganda model" of media has influenced masses of people into attaining a certain normative world view where consumption is mistaken for freedom. In this scenario, the more you buy, the more freedom you exercise. So a person's "unique" taste in the consumption of food, clothing, even what television programmes she watches, is thought to reflect the wide range of freedom everyone enjoys in societies that employ the market economy.

Accordingly, while the market seems to welcome everyone with his or her idiosyncrasies, it does not truly accept differences or creativity. Why would it support such characteristics that are antithetical to efficiency, standardization, and predictability? On the contrary, the market only "manages" differences so that they do not become a liability and pose a threat to the smooth functioning of the enterprise. And reaping so much success, why would the market ever shed its sheepskin and show its deadly fangs?

Conclusion: What Do We Want? The Death of the Market! When Do We Want it? Now!

This popular slogan, familiar to many North American anti-globalization protestors, is something to behold. It goes straight to the heart of the problem. Because we have been socialized to believe that the most important social structure is the economy, it has become idolized, to borrow from Nietzsche. As a result, most citizens have assigned an autonomous existence to this institution and show an irrational reverence toward it. Even those who are critical of the negative effects of the market believe that it can be fixed with minor adjustments. But, as noted throughout the paper, the market that sustains the current economy of globalization cannot be rehabilitated into a socially responsible institution. The reason is simple: the logic of the market is not designed to benefit everyone and be sensitive to social issues. The market, in a capitalist system, is intentionally programmed to fail the majority. The late Paulo Freire understood this situation quite too well. This is why he refused to accept anything positive in a system that is inherently perverse.[19]

In a ceaseless attempt to accumulate capital, the transnational power elites are pillaging and raping the entire world's resources, including human beings, behind the façade of the neutrality of the market. Furthermore, under the guise of progress, they are pummeling any form of resistance as "irrational and anarchistic". And when such rhetoric falls short, they are not afraid to use force to complete their mission of globalizing the world.[20]

Nevertheless, the best weapon for the capitalists is the "neutrality" of the market. Given this unbiased nature of the market, each person is his or her own responsibility. Portrayed in this manner, human life is reduced to a purely "personal choice". Any type of social concern, then, evaporates into thin air. The ability for social criticism becomes entirely truncated. Consequently, any dialogue of poverty as a social concern is categorically dismissed, while personal charity is applauded. Seen in this light, it becomes clear why charity events for the natural disaster victims (the recent Tsunami, Hurricane Katrina, and the major earthquake in China) are nationally televised during prime time while discussions surrounding world poverty receive little attention. In the midst of over production, where "super sizing" is the norm in the U.S., nearly 36 thousand people per day die of hunger around the world. Something is truly amiss with this scenario. In order to reverse this trend of dehumanizing the world, it is "the market" that needs to die...*now*!

NOTES

1. Auguste Comte, *A General View of Positivism*, trans. J. H. Bridges (Stanford, CA: Academic Reprints, 1953).
2. Alejandro Serrano Caldera, *Los Dilemas de la Democracia* (Managua: Editorial Hispamer, 1995).
3. David Schmitz, *Thank God They're on Our Side: The United States and Right Wing Dictatorships, 1921-1965* (Chapel Hill: University of North Carolina Press, 1999), p. 294.
4. John Perkins, *Confessions of an Economic Hit Man* (New York: Plume Book, 2004), p. 186.
5. Duncan Green, *Silent Revolution* (New York: Monthly Review Press, 2003), pp. 47-49.
6. Michael Hardt and Antonio Negri, *Empire* (Cambridge, MA: Harvard University Press, 2000).
7. Emile Durkheim, *Division of Labor in Society* (New York: Free

Press, 1964).

8. David Ricardo, *On the Principles of Political Economy and Taxation*, in Green's *Silent Revolution*, p. 11.
9. Jung Min Choi and Lawrence Byrne, "Striking Back at Empire: A Postmodern Resistance to Neoliberalism and Globalization," in *Globalization with a Human Face* Westport, CT: Praeger, 2004), pp. 159-170.
10. Joseph Stiglitz, *Globalization and its Discontents* (New York: W. W. Norton and Company, 2002), pp. 195-213.
11. Perkins, *Confessions of an Economic Hitman*, pp. 141-145.
12. Marshall McLuhan, *The Global Village* (New York: Oxford University Press, 1989).
13. Ibid.
14. Jean Kilbourne, *Deadly Persuasion: Why Women and Girls Must Fight the Addictive Power of Advertising* (New York: Free Press, 1999).
15. Ibid.
16. Michel Foucault, *Discipline and Punish: The Birth of the Prison*, trans. Alan Sheridan (New York: Pantheon Books, 1977).
17. Steven J. Gould, *Eight Little Piggies: Reflections in Natural History* (New York: W.W. Norton and Company, 1993).
18. Edward Herman and Noam Chomsky, *Manufacturing Consent: The Political Economy of the Mass Media* (New York: Pantheon Books, 1988).
19. Paulo Freire, *Pedagogy of Indignation* (Boulder, CO: Paradigm Publishers, 2004).
20. Chalmers Johnson, *The Sorrows of Empire: Militarism, Secrecy, and the End of the Republic* (New York: Metropolitan Books, 2004).

3

Human Nature, Freedom, and Neoliberal Rationality

Understanding the Total Market and the Prospects for Global Democratization

Luigi Esposito

INTRODUCTION

When confronted with proposals for radical alternatives to market capitalism, defenders of the marketplace often respond by declaring that this system is an inevitable outgrowth of freedom and human nature.[1] Presupposed by this claim is a particular understanding of people as fundamentally autarkic and rational beings who naturally exercise their liberty by competing with others in a relentless pursuit for private gain that, spontaneously, advances the common good. The market, accordingly, is far more than simply an economic model or cultural formation, and instead constitutes a "beneficent [and rational] order in the natural running of human affairs".[2] In accepting these premises, efforts to develop radical alternatives to the market system will likely seem to be an attack on liberty, a deviation from nature, or an exercise in futility.

The social consequences of these assumptions have been addressed by various writers. In Latin America, for example, critics often talk about a "Total Market" whose basic structures and values (e.g. competition, rugged individualism, materialistic hedonism, etc.) are reified as an "unavoidable fact of life" that shapes social relations and permeates the consciousness of a population.[3] In effect, the market, particularly in the current neoliberal zeitgeist, has gained the status of a reality *tout court* that seeps into every facet of social existence.[4] Values, habits, ambitions, even modes of rebellion are shaped according to a market-based view of the world that defines reality.

This sort of market fundamentalism is even discernible among many so-called "progressives" who vehemently denounce the neoliberal trend to subordinate human needs to corporate profits, yet seem to have a difficult time envisioning a model of living that breaks completely from the market. For example, the majority of those who represent political parties associated with the traditional "left" typically confront issues related to poverty and the erosion of labour rights by proposing reforms such as higher wages and better working conditions, while background assumptions related to people's predisposition toward competition and profit-driven behaviours—all of which substantiate basic capitalist structures and their alleged connection to rationality and human freedom—are assumed to reflect timeless laws of nature that are immune to critical evaluation. Concerns about the abuses of market capitalism, in other words, are not typically directed toward the market itself, but rather addressed via reformist demands that *still* presuppose the market as an inherent feature of a free and rational society which, if properly reformed, will allow persons to maximize their full potential, thereby leading to an ideal society.

Recent research dealing with public attitudes further corroborates this sort of pro-market zeal among the general population. To give one example of this trend, a major scientific poll recently conducted in 20 countries found that while a majority of people agreed on the need for more government regulation of large corporations, there was also "a striking global consensus" that "the free enterprise and free market system is the best system on which to base the future of the world".[5] What these findings suggest is that despite recent discussions about the increasing discontent that exists in various countries with neoliberal policies and financial institutions such as the IMF, the World Bank, and the WTO,[6] most calls for social/economic change are typically based on a very entrenched type of criticism that, here again, focuses on reforms while failing to address the legitimacy of the market system itself. In the end, reformist demands have done very little in terms of posing a serious challenge to the status quo.[7] After all, better wages and stricter business regulations are not synonymous with eradicating completely the structures of exploitation, poverty, and extreme inequality that currently exist in the market-driven world.[8]

A few recent writers have taken these issues into account and argue that effective efforts to challenge the extreme inequality, pandemic destitution, and erosion of democracy associated with unregulated capitalism must address the image of social reality—or specific ontology—that reifies the market itself.[9] One such writer is Franz Hinkelammert, who argues that the legitimacy of market capitalism is tied to a specific version of social reality, and social reality is never "pure and simple"; rather, it is perceived and defined according to particular theoretical categories that make this reality intelligible.[10] Accordingly, challenging the Total Market requires a critical examination of the underlying theoretical categories/assumptions that give coherence to its presumed unassailability—particularly the notion that this system is an inevitable outgrowth of freedom, human nature, and rationality.

DOMINANT CONCEPTIONS OF FREEDOM, PEOPLE, AND AN OPTIMAL SOCIETY IN THE CLASSICAL LIBERAL/NEOLIBERAL TRADITION

For quite some time, supporters of the free market have insisted that this system is synonymous with human freedom. Milton Friedman, for example, suggests that at the heart of all arguments against the free market "is a lack of belief in freedom itself".[11] More recently, the Bush administration, in its National Security Strategy of 2006, declares that efforts to expand free market capitalism constitute a "moral imperative", for the "liberty to create and build, or to buy, sell, and own property is fundamental to *human nature* and foundational to a *free* society".[12] It is no wonder, therefore, that someone like Venezuelan President Hugo Chavez, who publicly questions the sacrosanct status accorded to pro-market policies associated with privatization, deregulation, and liberalization is often labelled by much of the corporate media as an "enemy of freedom".[13]

Far from some pure or ahistorical ideal, however, the freedom that is revered by disciples of the free market is based on specific theoretical assumptions that are associated with the classical liberal tradition. Classical liberalism began as an emancipatory project that broke from abstract structures of authority (e.g. ascribed statuses and a king's divine right to rule), and advanced a novel form of polity where individuals are free from external constraints in pursuing individual desires and interests. This is what Isaiah Berlin refers to as "negative liberty".[14] Freedom, in other words, is the liberty to make choices that will support personal gain without political interferences.

Presupposed by this rendition of freedom is a particular understanding of people as rational and self-serving beings who, unless constrained by tyrannical controls, are naturally driven to compete with others for wealth, resources, recognition, and whatever else they desire. Not surprisingly, therefore, the classical school of economics—an offshoot of classical liberalism—also rested on the presupposition that egotism is an inherent feature of human nature (what the utilitarians often referred to as "hedonistic psychology"). In fact, even the most sanguine of the classical economists, including Adam Smith and John Stuart Mill—who often spoke about the human capacity to sympathize with others —also emphasized a laissez faire approach to commerce and advanced a self-serving image of people that was clearly expressed in their portraits of *homo economicus*.[15] That is, people are understood as reflective and competitive agents making choices "based on a rational calculation of what will serve them best". Thus, human actions are understood as little more than a "mathematical exercise in maximization".[16]

Far from a dangerous condition mandating rigid authoritarianism á la Hobbes, however, most of the classical-liberal economists argued that the self-serving and competitive nature of humans actually benefits the whole of society. Adam Smith in particular, of course, is widely known for his belief that a system of free competition (i.e. a free market) yields "unplanned beneficial effects" that reflect "the wisdom of nature".[17] Specifically, as persons exercise their liberty to pursue private interests in a free market economy, mysterious forces of nature—what Smith famously referred to as an "invisible hand"—automatically organize these individual actions into the common good.[18]

This classical liberal ideal of a free market leading to a prosperous society was seriously challenged during the early decades of the early 20th century, when laissez faire capitalism entered into what is commonly known as the "great depression". As a result of this event, Keynesian economics gained prominence from the 1940s to the 1950s. John M. Keynes broke from the classical liberal ideal of laissez faire by making the point that laws of supply and demand are not always well aligned, and hence prosperity and social well-being could not be guaranteed by the market alone. Accordingly, eschewing economic downfalls requires an interventionist policy whereby governments take fiscal and monetary measures to insure a balanced economy.

By the 1970s, however, there was a revival of the laissez faire model, thus leading to what is known today as "neoliberalism". Broadly regarded as the "defining economic political paradigm of our time", neoliberalism is most commonly associated with prominent neoclassical economists, including Frederick Hayek and Milton Friedman, who espouse many of the aforementioned classical liberal assumptions. Specifically, neoliberals also assume persons to be rational "free agents" driven by self-serving interests, and understand "free societies" as competitive in nature. Furthermore, neoliberals encourage a religious-like faith in the power of the unregulated market to enhance the quality of all products and services, promote consumer choice, motivate people to maximize their potential, and resolve many (if not most) of the world's social problems by allegedly spreading freedom and promoting prosperity.[19]

What distinguishes neoliberalism from its classical liberal heritage, however, is that this perspective encourages a Social Darwinian view of the world that supports what Pope John Paul II denounced as "savage capitalism". Specifically, while Adam Smith and other classical liberals did emphasize a laissez faire approach to trade, they were also widely known for their contempt of corporate monopolies and their insistence that persons are free to pursue their self-interests "as long as [they] do not violate the laws of justice".[20] Neoliberals, on the other hand, advocate a type of unbridled, "gloves off" type of capitalism where corporate monopolies are condoned, and where free competition overshadows any concern for social and economic justice.[21]

Accordingly, consistent with Herbert Spencer's Social Darwinian imagery, neoliberals advance a world view where life is governed by the maxim of "survival of the fittest", and where patterns of extreme inequality and poverty are either accepted as neutral outcomes that reflect differences in people's worth and abilities, or otherwise addressed through what Hinkelammert describes as "una política de más Mercado" (a politics of more market).[22] In other words, because of the unbending faith neoliberals place on the unfettered market to promote an ideal society, any problems that result at the marketplace are simply addressed with even more pro-market policies associated with privatization and deregulation that will restore the natural competitive freedom that presumably eliminates all social ills.

Any resistance to this state of affairs is vilified by neoliberals as tyrannical, irrational, or idealistic. Indeed, this idea of an unmediated market leading to an optimal society that reflects ahistorical features associated with freedom and human nature supports the neoliberal claim that all societies organized around "planned" economies are inherently totalitarian. Specifically, because everything in such societies is typically controlled by a small "planning bureaucracy", life is reduced to a "continual round of abject permissiveness" that undermines the nature of people as rational beings of "volitional consciousness".[23]

Neoliberals, accordingly, are unwavering in their conviction that only free market economies can successfully avoid coercive power and advance a society's full potential by allowing persons the freedom to pursue their preferences, make the best out of their talents, and shape their own destinies.[24]

BEYOND SOCIALIZATION: FREE AGENTS AND THE TOTAL MARKET—THE COLONIZATION OF SOCIAL REALITY

The market image of the individual as a free and rational agent who, driven by a self-serving nature, calculates the costs and benefits of all choices, and acts accordingly, implies that all human actions reflect some "pure" or unmediated self. Indeed, as stated by Ulrich Beck and Elisabeth Beck-Gernsheim, neoliberal economics assumes that "individuals . . .derive and renew their actions from within themselves".[25] All human actions and economic choices, accordingly, are taken to be "rational statements reflecting who we are and what we want in life".[26]

As is well known, this market view of human action, which is advanced in rational choice theory, public choice theory, exchange theory, and other market-based theories about human/social behaviours, has been challenged in a number of different ways. Perhaps one of the most common criticisms of these perspectives is that by explaining all social phenomena in terms of rational calculations made by self-interested individuals, an atomistic conception of the world is presupposed that overlooks the social dimension of human existence. That is, persons are assumed to be self-contained entities driven by essential properties and disconnected from the social or historical context that gives meaning to their actions.

Dennis Wrong, for example, critiques the atomistic, market view of human action by suggesting that any notion of a "rational choice" is never undertaken in a vacuum.[27] Acting rationally involves distinguishing rational from irrational, a distinction that has no inherent meaning but instead is given significance through specific norms and values. Wrong's point is that the rational choices that propel human actions are not simply products of essential properties or some unmediated self, but rather presupposes the prior acquisition of language and a commitment to specific norms—all of which entails a process of socialization.

However, suggesting that market-based perspectives on human behaviour overlook processes of socialization in terms of influencing people's preferences and actions might not be particularly insightful in the current age of neoliberal capitalism. Specifically, while socialization implies teaching persons to accept specific values, norms, and attitudes that sustain one cultural way of life among many others, neoliberalism subsumes all cultural viewpoints into a totalized vision of the world that defines social reality itself. This is what Serrano-Caldera has in mind when he expresses concern about the neoliberal market having taken on the status of an "ontological category".[28] The neoliberal market, in effect, appears to be an ahistorical force that requires no basis for legitimacy outside its own logic.

This reification of the market promotes at least two key outcomes. First, as people accept a market-based reality that appears to be inevitable and even beneficial, structures of power are sustained. Similar to Gramsci's notion of hegemony, the neoliberal Total Market described by Hinkelammert, Serrano-Caldera, and other writers promotes a powerful form of social control that extends throughout the depths of a population's consciousness by shaping all personal fears, desires, and ambitions according to market imperatives that are taken to be inescapable facts of life. Thus, for example, in seeking financial success through hard work, competing with others for all sorts of social and material resources, using education as a means to become "marketable", or evaluating self-worth on the basis of material gain, most persons do not necessarily think they are conforming to specific market values that sustain power, but rather believe they are simply being "rational" and adapting to the real world. As discussed by Hinkelammert, to recognize the market order as synonymous with reality is to be realistic and pragmatic.[29] However, in being "realistic" and adopting these habits, the vast majority of persons inadvertently support the status quo by accommodating to the structures of competition and superfluous consumption that erode communities and promote inequality and injustice.

Second, because one of the primary objectives within the neoliberal market is the smooth flow of capital and goods, principles such as standardization and efficiency are thought of as universal ideals. Diversity, therefore, is an impediment to an efficient order and must be minimized or otherwise made compatible to market demands and standards. The market, in this sense, unifies by homogenizing social existence.[30] Indeed, despite all the neoliberal rhetoric about the market encouraging diversity by affording persons "free choice" and fostering their creative capacities as they naturally compete for self-gain at the marketplace, people's way of life - from Guatemala City to Los Angeles, London to Tokyo, Paris to Bogotá - is becoming increasingly homogenized. As discussed by Choi and Byrne, from the jobs they do, to the clothes they wear, to the movies they watch, to the furniture in their living rooms (including the fact that they even have a "living room"), the neoliberal market has transformed very diverse populations into an interchangeable mass of consumers, all striving to emulate a particular image of an "ideal" global/modern citizen who represents the pinnacle of human development.[31]

On the other hand, with some exceptions, those who reject the market order are typically dismissed by government spokespersons and much of the corporate media as either quixotic or dangerous fanatics. Indeed, whether the opposition comes from Islamists or Western activists, oppositional voices are, most commonly, either shut out completely from the public/political discourse, or otherwise represented as emanating from a blurred and undifferentiated "other" whose anti-market agendas deviate from human nature, freedom, and all standards of rationality.

But exactly what kind of rationality serves to constrain the universe of discourse in such a way that keeps all identities, social ideals, and political orientations that threaten the market order from becoming socially plausible, or even imaginable? The next section addresses this query.

RATIONALITY AS A MORAL UNION BETWEEN INSTRUMENTALISM AND EVANGELICAL METAPHYSICS: NEOLIBERALISM IN THE UNITED STATES

For quite some time, critics of capitalism have theorized about the type of rationality that dominates the marketplace. For example, during the post-World War II era, many writers associated with the Frankfurt School drew from Max Weber and referred to market rationality as "instrumental".[32] Instrumental rationality takes for granted the legitimacy of the objectives that guide human action and instead focuses on the means to achieve pre-established ends. The pervasiveness of instrumental rationality at the marketplace has much to do with the classical liberal/neoliberal presuppositions, previously discussed, about human nature as self-serving and freedom as competitive. In other words, because the "rational" ends/goals of human action are already assumed in the form of wealth, prestige, recognition, or "coming out victorious"—all of which are presumably tied to fundamental human tendencies—rationality simply involves coming up with the most efficient means to fulfill these seemingly natural ends.

The particularly worrying aspect about this type of rationality is that larger questions related to equality, morality, or social justice, are given little (if any) importance. Max Horkheimer, for example, argued that the prevalence of instrumental rationality in modern capitalist societies signified the "eclipse of reason".[33] Specifically, while reason had at one point been predicated on a form of "metaphysical rationality" that concerned itself "with the contemplation of truth and the search for the ultimate goal or meaning in life", including the search for transcendent referents on which to evaluate the moral worth of human actions, modern societies are organized around a much more subjective or instrumental form of reason that concerns itself almost exclusively with how subjects can effectively fulfill their immediate goals. Thus, as argued by Zbigniew Wendland, this latter type of rationality became a purely utilitarian instrument that serves to "count, compare costs and profits, and compute the probability of desired or expected effects at given costs".[34]

It was precisely this type of instrumental rationality or instrumental reason which, according to Horkheimer, Marcuse, and other representatives of the Frankfurt School, bred the sort of passivity that made atrocities such as the Holocaust possible. That is, in focusing exclusively on the efficient fulfilment of tasks, as opposed to larger questions related to the nature of morality and justice, rationality was "transformed from a critical force to one of compliance and adjustment".[35]

Yet, while many Western thinkers conceived of instrumental rationality as a thoroughly secular mode of thought that gave modern capitalism its "means-ends" ethos, thereby breaking from the previous metaphysical rationality that was expressed in Plato's forms, Aristotle's "first substance", or the "divine absolute" advanced by the Christian philosophers, even a cursory epistemological analysis of the neoliberal model dominating the current process of globalization reveals that this paradigm is predicated on a convergence between both instrumentalism and metaphysics. That is to say, not only does rationality within the neoliberal marketplace encourage persons to become "human calculators" as they spend much of their lives—at work, school, the playing field, and home—calculating the costs and benefits of their actions while trying to outdo others in their relentless (and presumably "natural") pursuit for private gain, this state of affairs is also deified by many contemporary neoliberals as constitutive of a truly moral order.[36]

Particularly in the United States, the neoliberal devotion to free markets has, in recent years, taken an evangelical turn.[37] To be sure, it would be inaccurate to suggest that all supporters of neoliberalism are religious, or that all religious persons (particularly evangelical Christians) support the market system. In fact, it is well known that there also exists an "evangelical left" that condemns market capitalism in its totality.[38] Nonetheless, there should be little doubt that within the context of the United States, neoliberal policies are being supported by vast segments of the US population with religious-like zeal.

At the forefront of this trend is the Bush administration.

Indeed, within the current context of the "war against terrorism", this administration has promulgated the spread of free markets not only as an efficient means to promote prosperity, but also as a vital tool in its moral mission to "fight evil".[39] Specifically, the market is touted as the carrier of "godly righteousness" and assumed to unleash the very best of the human spirit, thus quelling social maladies such as terrorism. Despite scholarly claims about a "post-metaphysical" world, therefore, current neoliberal rhetoric, at least as expressed by the neoliberal elite in the United States (i.e. the so-called "Washington consensus"), does indeed emphasize a presumably moral unity between both instrumentalism and evangelical metaphysics.

This sort of unity is easily discernible in the National Security Strategy of the United States (NSSUS), a document that addresses the free market's seminal role in the Bush administration's vision of a peaceful and moral world. For example, in the 2006 version of the NSSUS, the Bush administration claims, "history has judged the market economy as the single most effective economic system".[40] The emphasis on "effectiveness" implies the market's presumed efficiency in terms of allocating resources, thus pointing clearly to the instrumentalist component of neoliberal rationality. The metaphysical component of this rationality is also discernible in claims that the spread of free markets constitutes a "moral imperative" that will free society from terrorism, corruption, totalitarianism, and virtually every other social evil.[41] In this sense, instrumental rationality converges with metaphysical rationality to legitimize a messianic-like mission in which the spread of free markets/pro-market policies become the requisite means to achieve lofty moral objectives (e.g. eradicating evil and promoting freedom).

As might be expected, such assumptions have further reinforced claims that the market is consistent with human nature and freedom, although these features take on a truly divine quality in contemporary neoliberal discourse. Similar to the classical school of economics, the market is assumed to allow people the liberty to exercise their natural drive to pursue their self-interests by promoting competitive relations that nourish "the well springs of initiative and creativity". However, unlike classical economics, evangelical neoliberals also assume that whatever outcomes are produced at the marketplace represent the will of God.

Specifically, by allowing persons to maximize their profit or satisfaction, the market itself will insure that their choices and actions reflect God's will for the world in the form of a moral society in which people's social and economic positions are simply reflections of their morals and God-given talents. In other words, the market is "an unbiased decision-maker, and individuals will eventually get what they deserve". Failure at the marketplace is a clear indication that persons "have not lived a sufficiently moral life".[42] Inequalities at the marketplace are thus thoroughly depoliticized. As discussed by internationally acclaimed theologian Michael Novak, in a system of "democratic capitalism. . .inequalities in wealth and power are not. . . evil in themselves"' rather, they reflect ahistorical forces associated with God and nature.[43]

Clearly, the neoliberal connection between morality and the market has little to do with the "spirit of capitalism" discussed by Max Weber.[44] Specifically, while Weber conceived the capitalist ethos as an outgrowth of Calvinist values (i.e. a "Protestant ethic") that discouraged indulgence in material excess, demanded diligence and self-restraint, and divinized savings as a moral act (all of which promoted the accumulation of capital), the sort of market-driven rationality that underpins neoliberalism legitimizes a very different type of ethic that evaluates morality and self-worth according a person's buying power and ability to consume.

Nowhere is this neoliberal ethic of consumption more visible that in the United States. The North American sociologist George Ritzer, for example, has recently argued, "the United States is increasingly characterized by what could be termed *hyperconsumption*". Americans, he states, consume "far more of virtually everything than people from [any other] nation".[45] Clearly, these trends are predicated on a specific ethos that equates virtue and success with the purchase of fancy cars, big houses, and other expensive commodities. In fact, many persons understand these acquisitions to be fruits of the very "freedom" that is presumably fostered by neoliberal capitalism. Therefore, material consumption, even if excessive, is no longer necessarily regarded as sinful self-indulgence, for the purchase of commodities is not only a rational expression of freedom but also a reflection of a person's diligence, intelligence, and moral worth.

It is also relevant to remind readers at this juncture that soon after the attacks on September 11, 2001 in the United States, evangelical neoliberal George W. Bush urged all Americans to spend in the economy in order to prevent an economic collapse. In doing so, people would be doing their part to "show solidarity and not be defeated by the evil attackers".[46] In other words, consumerism was touted as a way to ward off evil! Clearly, this all presupposes a Manichean view of the world in which the market and its attending values are associated with everything "good" in the world (i.e. morality, freedom, democracy, prosperity, etc.), while anything that deviates from this model is immoral, irrational, and unacceptable.

Here again, the sort of instrumental rationality emphasized by traditional economic theory, which focuses on the most efficient means to achieve desired ends in a competitive market system, takes on a divine-like, universal plan for the world in current neoliberal discourse. What this also suggests is that the highly rational but largely amoral *homo economicus* of the past is elevated to the status of a moral agent who supports freedom and a system that champions "the good".

The evangelical zeal with which these assumptions are defended by various contemporary groups is clearly illustrated in a recent article published by the CATO institute, a prominent think tank headquartered in Washington D.C. that outlines "seven moral arguments for free trade". Their suggestions corroborate the idea that neoliberal rationality is predicated on a fusion between instrumentalism and evangelical metaphysics. The concluding paragraph summarizes the article as follows:

> When all of the arguments are weighed, it should become clear

> that a policy of free trade is moral as well as efficient. Free trade limits the power of the state and enhances freedom, autonomy, and self-responsibility of the individual. It promotes virtuous and responsible personal behavior. . . . it opens the door for ideas and evangelism. It undermines the authority of dictators by expanding the freedom, opportunity, and independence of people they try to control. It promotes peace among nations. It helps the poor to feed and care for themselves and creates a better future for their children. For which of these virtues should we reject free trade?[47]

Here again, the message conveyed is that it would be utterly irrational and immoral to reject free trade, for this system is not only efficient but also constitutes a seemingly inerrant moral force that promotes freedom, peace, opportunity, and, perhaps most important, the actualization of all human potential.

BREAKING FROM THE TOTAL MARKET: TOWARD ALTERNATIVE CONCEPTIONS OF HUMAN NATURE, FREEDOM, AND RATIONALITY

Subsequent to the contributions of critics associated with the Frankfurt School, Liberation Theology, and Cultural Studies, particularly their similar conception of history and social reality as thoroughly political domains, the notion of a self-regulated market that automatically leads to an optimal society is no longer tenable. As opposed to autonomous (as classical liberals and many traditional Marxists had believed), these traditions expose the market and its hierarchical structures as products of particular values, decisions, and commitments. Far from ahistorical, therefore, the connection between human nature, freedom, rationality, and the market is based on politically driven assumptions that, under specific conditions, might become reified to the point of appearing unassailable. Yet, because of their contingent nature, the possibility to challenge and rethink such claims is always available.

The viability and justification for radical social change afforded by these perspectives has inspired various professional and ordinary citizens to engage in efforts to overcome the abuses of neoliberal globalization and inaugurate a "post-capitalist" world.[48] Clearly, this kind of effort, like any other effort devoted to radical social change, requires collective action. What is often overlooked, however, is that the effectiveness of such action depends on formulating a new social vision that breaks completely from the social categories that substantiate prevalent institutional practices, including the underlying assumptions in which these categories are based.[49]

Without making a shift in social imagery, efforts devoted to social change will not likely transcend the sort of reified instrumentalism or neoliberal metaphysics discussed above. In effect, creating an alternative social-political-economic order that benefits everyone as opposed to an elite class of people requires far more than reformist policies, better calculation in public spending, or tinkering with the economy. What is needed, instead, is a paradigmatic shift that redefines root images such as human nature, freedom, and rationality. By giving new meaning to these conceptual foundations that give coherence to the idea that market capitalism represents "the end of history", engaging in efforts to develop alternatives to market-based globalization will no longer seem like a flight of fantasy or a utopian dream, but instead constitute a viable and necessary project to overcome the myriad crises the plague the current world order.

Consistent with these premises, various contemporary critics/activists are inspired by a new social vision in which central categories including human nature, freedom, and rationality are redefined in such a way that benefits democracy and social and economic justice as opposed to the exclusive interests of corporations and wealthy investors.

Human Nature

As discussed, defenders of the marketplace often make the case that the market is an inevitable economic/societal design that results when people are allowed the freedom to act in ways that befit their nature. Yet, for quite some time, various critics associated with the radical left have dismissed the idea of a biologically fixed, universal human nature.[50]

Human behaviours, according to these critics, are not the result of essential properties; rather, they reflect the historical and social circumstances in which people live. Thus, dominant market conceptions of people as egoistical and competitive are little more than social constructions that reflect interest-laden institutional structures as opposed to innate human qualities. To be sure, while many in the radical left hold that humans are driven toward happiness and self-realization, fulfilling these ideals is not only a personal but a social objective. That is to say, outside society, individuality is impossible, since persons need others to "develop, expand, and grow".

What this also suggests is that there is nothing about human nature that impedes people from freely collaborating with one another in such a way that benefits everyone involved. Accordingly, patterns of inequality, domination, or deprivation can no longer be legitimately blamed on essential human traits and made to appear as if they were unavoidable facts of life. Instead, people are now encouraged to focus on challenging the man-made structures, values, and conventions that support these outcomes, and to exercise a creative praxis to do away with them.

These efforts, however, are not based on some sacrosanct altruistic imperative or transcendent metaphysics, but are inspired by the realization that the well-being of society and individuals is one and the same. From these assumptions, it follows that one cannot speak about "human nature" outside the human relations in which people are situated.

Freedom

The understanding of human nature as predicated on "a complex of social relations" as opposed to fixed properties also leads to a radically different understanding of freedom. Unlike neoliberals, who personalize freedom and define this category as the absence of any imposed impediment on people's self-serving actions (irrespective of how these actions affect others), an alternative type of freedom that is conducive to democracy and social/economic justice might be thought of as relational. In effect, freedom is no longer simply equated with policies of deregulation that empower powerful investors to undertake profit-driven activities at the expense of others.

From this perspective, it is absolutely erroneous, and perhaps immoral, to assume that persons who are exploited, illiterate, and hungry are "free". Freedom, therefore, is no longer merely the liberty to compete with others for valued resources, without concern for outcomes, as in neoliberalism. Instead, freedom entails an effort to dislodge human relations from the functional bonds that sustain structures of deprivation and inequality. A genuinely free society, accordingly, is one where people are free to interact without having to abide to rules that encourage egotism and demand predatory competition as a requisite for success. Freedom, in short, cannot coexist with the oppression of others.

At the same time, it is important to understand that calling for this sort of non-repressive freedom is *not* tied to some fundamental moral dictate that rejects self-interests in favour of collective interests, as with various strands of orthodox Marxism. Social interests and self-interests are inextricably linked, although no longer through some abstract, market-based intermediary, as in neoliberalism. For example, if individuals exercise their liberty to exploit and repress others, these persons are complicit in the creation of a social environment in which their own growth as individuals is obstructed.[51] On the other hand, demanding that individuals efface themselves, their aspirations, and desires for the sake of an abstract group that becomes antagonistic to their own individuality is by no means a better alternative. In both cases, freedom is stifled, and both individuals and societies are crippled.[52] For this reason, recent radical thinkers in Latin America contend that genuine freedom requires breaking from both atomized individualism (as in neoliberalism) and blind collectivism (as in various forms of statism).[53]

Rationality

In a recent book, Franz Hinkelammert and Henry Mora Jiménez draw from radical theology and Neo-Marxism to suggest the need for a new type of rationality that understands humans as corporal beings whose very lives depend on satisfying their essential needs. [54] Clearly, the type of neoliberal rationality discussed above does not prioritize human needs and hence human life. The problem is that within the current market order, the sort of means-ends rationality associated with instrumentalism is most commonly predicated on a utility principle that is more concerned with maximizing profits as opposed to securing human needs. Therefore, rather than being used at the service of uplifting the human condition, instrumental rationality is more typically employed for things such as calculating how corporations can maximize the labour output of their workers for the wages that are paid, how to make the most effective weapons of mass destruction, or how to best exploit the natural environment for private gains—all of which are ultimately anathema to human life and social well-being.

Furthermore, the sort of evangelical neoliberal metaphysics in vogue today (particularly in the United States) is also clearly detrimental to human life. Indeed, when rationality involves adherence to the presumed moral wisdom of a market-deity that allegedly rewards "good" behaviour associated with competitiveness, perseverance, and hard-work, and punishes "bad" behaviour associated with dependency, laziness, and irresponsibility, human life is reduced to a privilege as opposed to a right. In other words, those who lose at the marketplace are assumed to be inept, morally deficient, and undeserving of a decent life. Furthermore, as has become abundantly clear in recent years, the sort of market fundamentalism substantiated by this sort of metaphysical neoliberal rationality, which equates the free market with freedom and morality, has perversely rationalized a war of "good versus evil" that is eroding democracy and unleashing remarkable destruction of life—human and otherwise.

As an alternative to these destructive forms of rationality, Hinkelammert and Jiménez propose a radically different variant that they refer to as "reproductive". Reproductive rationality takes as its basis the preservation of the "natural circuit of human life".[55] That is to say, rationality is no longer predicated on hedonistic calculation or abstract metaphysics; instead, it involves creating institutional mechanisms that insure the viability of human life by securing the needs of people—this includes both their internal needs (e.g. food, shelter, education, creativity activities, leisure, spiritual fulfillment), and their external needs (e.g. the need to keep a viable natural environment in which human life can develop).

Because reproductive rationality understands people as corporal beings with essential needs, as opposed to simply creatures of "free choice", issues related to hunger or poverty, for example, cannot be blamed on individualistic explanations such as lifestyle choices, as in current neoliberal rhetoric. As described by Hinkelammert and Jiménez, to "choose" one must first be able to "live",[56] and life itself is something that thousands of people (including children) are denied each day by current structures of poverty and deprivation.

Clearly, a rationality that treats people as corporal beings with essential needs and emphasizes the sustainability of human life, must also prioritize the strengthening of social relations through open dialogue and interpersonal recognition. In other words, this type of rationality seeks to eschew completely the sort of atomism advanced in neoliberalism and recognizes that people need one another in order to attain their essential needs, preserve their environment, and live meaningful lives.[57]

CONCLUSION: THE PROSPECTS OF GLOBAL DEMOCRATIZATION

In recent years, mass mobilizations against neoliberal policies and institutions have been witnessed in various cities throughout the world. A new type of globalization is demanded by these democratic masses—one that prioritizes life as opposed to destruction, citizens as opposed to consumers, and the fulfilment of human needs as opposed bigger corporate profits. According to various commentators, these activist groups are melding into a growing global civil society that, in time, might serve as the basis for all social planning and development.[58]

What is important to understand, however, is that any serious effort to democratize the current process of globalization is not simply technical but paradigmatic. As suggested in this chapter, democratization demands something well beyond reformist agendas. In effect, efforts to build a global civil society that might serve as a catalyst for deep global democratization should be grounded on an alternative social vision that breaks completely from all fundamentalisms—including abstract conceptions of human nature, freedom, and rationality—that support the Total Market and other structures of domination and destruction.

This objective is not new. In their efforts to effect social change, various activist communities have, for quite some time, been calling for a new world devoid of intellectual stagnation, hedonistic materialism, ruthless competition, self-indulgence, fear, war, and violence —all of which are, in one way or another, linked to market conceptions of human nature, freedom, and rationality that uphold the Total Market and the status quo that is structured therein. As alternatives, growing numbers of people within the growing global civil society advocate values associated with generosity, compassion, diversity, sustainable living, and social and economic justice. It is also well known that members of this progressive global community are building countless social spaces that serve as alternatives to prevailing institutions within the neoliberal market system and the corporate elite that benefits from this order.

Renowned activist and author David C. Korten refers to these public spaces as "zones of freedom" which can be "as simple as a local study group, a school to develop inquiring minds. . a socially responsible local business. . a farmer's market. . .or a holistic health clinic". These free zones might also include independent media outlets, cooperatives, and the recent proliferation of organic farms that seek to restore harmony between human needs and environmental well-being. [59] The point is that "no matter how small or isolated such initiatives may originally be, each creates a protected space in which diversity, experimentation, and learning can flourish to create the building blocs of a new culture, politics, and economy".[60]

One strategy toward the objective of democratization, therefore, should be to engage in efforts to organize these "free zones" into an increasing network of communities (i.e. a well organized global civil society) which , together, can exert enough influence to effect wide scale social change. The organizational potential of the emerging global civil society is already discernible in projects such as the World Social Forum, in which thousands of variegated organizations from around the globe are converging under the slogan "another world is possible". It should also be noted that this global civil society has plenty of room for growth, for despite the continued prevalence of the free market myth as the best possible system, public opinion polls have consistently confirmed that the vast majority of the world's people—including the majority of people in the United States—yearn for a "different and better world" bereft of unnecessary wars, corporate domination, environmental erosion, extreme inequality, and coercive power.[61]

Efforts to further expand and solidify this sort of emancipatory consciousness must continue. People throughout the world, especially those living in "core" or affluent regions, must be made aware that they cannot continue to live life as usual while relying on the presumably benevolent forces of the market (i.e. evangelical capitalism) to expand freedom and eradicate poverty—especially in a world where, according to UNICEF, 30,000 children die of poverty-related diseases every day and where close to half of humanity lives on less than three dollars a day.

Indeed, ending poverty and insuring basic human needs would entail far more than simply passing more free trade agreements, or giving more loans, and grants. In fact, such efforts most commonly support local capitalist elites.[62] For this reason, radical communities within the emerging global civil society have been arguing for quite some time that ending poverty and insuring basic human needs would entail addressing the structural conditions that breed poverty in the first place. Specifically, eliminating structures of poverty and deprivation involve, among other things, creating parallel institutions (with attending alternative values) that prioritize human needs over corporate and political interests.

This sort of project is precisely whar Franz Hinkelammert and Henry Mora Jiménez have in mind when they suggest that outside prevailing market structures, an alternative "econonomy of life" *(una economía para la vida)* might be developed where people are no longer understood as simply property owners or abstract competitors who must win over others to attain what they need or desire, but rather as corporal entities with basic needs whose fulfilment must take precedence over any market notion of competition, efficiency, and private property.[63] In this economy of life, the value of human life can no longer be dictated to by the market, nor can persons exonerate themselves of responsibility to others by assuming that the market will insure the common good.

As opposed to relying on ethereal market forces, a culture of responsibility must accompany the creation of a new institutional order. Stated simply, the emerging global civil society must understand that all economic and social arrangements are tied to people's actions or inactions. Only in this manner can a truly responsible form of global society come to fruition. Although some people might take this position to be overwhelmingly burdensome, the implied sense of accountability can also be empowering, as people are no longer spectators of history but rather agents of social change.

In short, those who desire to democratize the current world order must continue building a well-organized global civil society that might serve as a counterforce to the current neoliberal/imperialist forces that are anathema to the well-being of people and planet. This entails working individually and collectively in the advancement of a new worldview devoid of dogmas that would facilitate the redirection of history and put humanity on a path toward social and economic justice, peace, and ecological sustainability. While such a project might sound like a utopian dream to some, it might very well be, as various writers have recently stressed, the key to the very survival of humanity.[64]

NOTES

1. Will Miller. "Social Change and Human Nature," *Monthly Review* 50, no. 9 (1999): 42.
2. Sherwin Klein, "The Natural Roots of Capitalism and its Virtues and Values." *Journal of Business Ethics* 45 (2003): 388.

3. Franz Hinkelammert, *El Capitalismo al Desnudo* (Bogotá, Colombia: Editorial El Buho, 1991), pp. 91-92. See also Alejandro Serrano Caldera, *Los Dilemas de la Democracia* (Managua: Editorial Hispamer, 1995), p. 11.
4. Hinkelammert, *El Capitalismo al Desnudo*, p. 91.
5. This poll, published on January 11, 2006, was conducted by the Program on International Policy Attitudes (PIPA), one of the world's preeminent research institutions devoted to public opinion and headquartered at the University of Maryland. It should also be noted that even among respondents living in countries with relatively high levels of poverty, including China, India, Brazil, Nigeria, Philippines, Kenya, Indonesia, and Mexico, the majority agreed that a free market economy is "the best system on which to base the future of the world". The full report, titled "20 Nation Poll Finds Strong Global Consensus: Support for Fee Market System, But Also More Regulation for Large Companies," is available at http://www.globescan.com/news_archives/pipa_market.html (accessed May 2006).
6. See, for example, Joseph E. Stiglitz, *Globalization and its Discontents* (New York: W.W. Norton and Company, 2002).
7. See Takis Fotopoulos, "Globalisation, the Reformist Left, and the Anti-globalisation Movement," *Democracy and Nature*, 7, no. 1 (2001): 233-280.
8. According to a recent U.N. Human Development Report, "the world's richest 1 percent receive as much income as the poorest 57 percent. The income gap between the richest 20 percent and the poorest 20 percent in the world rose from 30:1 in 1960. . . to 74:1 in 1999, and is projected to reach 100:1 in 2015. In 1999-2000, 2.8 billion people lived on less than $3 a day, 840 million were undernourished, 2.4 billion did not have access to any form of improved sanitation services, and one in every six children in the world of primary school age were not in school. [Furthermore], about 50 percent of the global nonagricultural labor force is estimated to be either unemployed or underemployed." Cited in Henry A. Giroux, *The Terror of Liberalism* (Boulder, CO: Paradigm Publishers, 2004), p. 170.
9. See Franz Hinkelammert, *The Ideological Weapons of Death: a Theological Critique of Capitalism* (New York: Orbis Books, 1985) pp. viii-ix. See also John W. Murphy "The Traditional Ontology of Development, History, and Globalization from Below," in *Globalization with a Human Face*, ed. Jung Min Choi, John W. Murphy, and Manuel J. Caro (Westport, CT: Pareeger, 2004), pp.

11-24.

10. Franz Hinkelammert, *The Ideological Weapons of Death: a Theological Critique of Capitalism* (Maryknoll, New York, USA: Orbis Books, 1986), pp. viii-ix.
11. Milton Friedman, *Capitalism and Freedom* (Chicago: The University of Chicago Press, 1962), p. 15.
12. National Security Strategy of the United States (NSSUS), March 2006. http://www.whitehouse.gov/nsc/nss/2006/print/index.html (accessed April 2006), p. 27.
13. No author, "Chavez No Friend of Freedom,' *USA Today*, June 22, 2006.
14. Isaiah Berlin, *Two Concepts of Liberty* (London and New York: Oxford University Press, 1958).
15. Israel M. Kirzner, "Human Nature and the Character of Economic Science," *The Harvard Review of Philosophy* VIII (2000): 16.
16. Ibid., p. 19.
17. Sherwin Klein, "The Natural Roots of Capitalism and its Virtues and Values," *Journal of Business Ethics* 45 (2003): 388
18. Adam Smith, *An Inquiry into the Nature and Causes of the Wealth of Nations*, ed. Edwin Cannan (NY: The Modern Library, 1937), p. 423.
19. Robert W. McChesney, introduction to *Profit Over People: Neoliberalism and the Global Order*, by Noam Chomsky (New York: Seven Stories Press, 1999), p. 7.
20. Adam Smith, *An Inquiry into the Nature and Causes of the Wealth of Nations*, ed. Edwin Cannan (NY: The Modern Library, 1937), p. 423.
21. David C. Korten, *When Corporations Rule the World*. (San Francisco, CA: Berrett-Koehler Publishers, 2001), pp. 80-84. Of course, as is well known, there is nothing "free" about "free trade" within the neoliberal paradigm. In other words, the "unfettered market" exalted by neoliberal ideology is largely a myth. As discussed by Robert McChesney, "the same corporations that exult in neoliberal ideology... want and expect governments to funnel tax dollars to them, and to protect their markets for them from competition, but they [also] want to assure that governments will not tax them or work supportively on behalf of non-business interests, especially on behalf of the poor or working class. Governments are bigger than ever, but under neoliberalism they have far less pretense to being concerned with addressing non-corporate interests." See Robert W. McChesney,

introduction to *Profit Over People: Neoliberalism and the Global Order*, p. 13.

22. Franz Hinkelammert, *El Capitalismo al Desnudo*, p. 81.
23. Frederich Hayek, *The Road to Serfdom* (Chicago, University of Chicago Press, 1994). See also John Chamberlain, *The Roots of Capitalism* (Indianapolis: Liberty Press, 1976), p. 10.
24. Milton Friedman and Rose Friedman, *Free To Choose* (New York: Harcourt Brace Jovanovich, 1980), pp. 1-7.
25. Ulrich Beck and Elisabeth Beck-Gernsheim, *Individualization* (Thousand Oaks, CA: Sage, 2002). p. xxi.
26. Gordon Bigelow, "Let There Be Markets," *Harper's Magazine*, 310 (2005), p. 1.
27. Dennis Wrong, *The Modern Condition: Essays at Century's End* (Stanford, CA: Stanford University Press, 1998), p. 21.
28. Alejandro Serrano Caldera, *Los Dilemas de La Democracia* (Managua: Editorial Hispamer, 1995), p. 10.
29. Franz Hinkelammert, *Capitalismo al Desnudo*. p. 81.
30. Alejandro Serrano Caldera, *Los Dilemas de La Democracia*, p. 14.
31. Jung Min Choi and Lawrence Byrne, "Striking back at Empire: a Postmodern Resistance to Neoliberalism and Globalization," in *Globalization with a Human Face*, eds. Jung Min Choi, John W. Murphy, and Manuel J. Caro (Westport, CT: Pareeger, 2004), p. 162.
32. See Max Horkheimer, *The Eclipse of Reason* (New York: Oxford University press, 1947), p. 3. It should be noted that while sociologists, following Weber, often use the term "instrumental rationality" to refer to the unreflective, means-oriented type of thinking that characterized modern societies, Horkheimer and other writers associated with the Frankfurt School often used the term "subjective reason" or "instrumental reason."
33. Horkheimer, *The Eclipse of Reason*.
34. Zbigniew Wendland, "Dialogical rationality as Cultural Foundation for Civil Universal Society," *Dialogue and Universalism*, 15 (2005), p. 117.
35. Herbert Marcuse, *Reason and Revolution: Hegel and the Rise of Social Theory* (New York: Oxford University Press, 1941), p. 155.
36. For a critique and discussion on how contemporary market societies such as the United States are organized around "an obsession with competition and outdoing others", see Alfie Kohn, *No Contest: The Case Against Competition* (New York: Houghton Mifflin Company, 1992).
37. Stephen John Hartnett and Laura Ann Stengrim, "War Rhetorics:

The National Security Strategy of the United States and president Bush's Globalization-Through-Benevolent-Empire," *The South Atlantic Quarterly* 105, no. 1 (2006): 190-194.

38. For a discussion on the various positions of evangelical Christians with respect to neoliberal capitalism/pro-market polices, see Craig M. Gay, *With Liberty and Justice for Whom? The Recent Evangelical Debate Over Capitalism* (Grand Rapids, MI: William E. Eerdmans Publishing, 1991).
39. Luigi Esposito, "The Metaphysics of US Empire in the Post 911 Era and the Challenge to World Democracy," *Cuadernos de ALDEEU* 22 (2006): 33-57.
40. NSSUS 2006, p. 25.
41. Ibid., pp. 7, 32,33, 37.
42. Martha Terrie, "Social Constructions and Cultural Contradictions: A Look at a Christian Perspective of Economics," *Journal of American Culture* 17 (1994): 55-63.
43. Michael Novak, *The Sprit of Democratic Capitalism* (New York: Touchstone, 1982), pp. 84-85.
44. Max Weber, *The Protestant Ethic and the Spirit of Capitalism*, trans. Talcott Parsons (New York: Sribner, 1958).
45. George Ritzer, *Revolutionizing the means of Consumption: Enchanting a Disenchanted World* (Thousand Oaks, CA: Pine Forge Press, 2005), p. 32.
46. Simon Western. "The Social Dynamics of Fundamentalism," available at http://www.ispso.org/Symposia/Boston/Western.htm (accessed June 2006).
47. Daniel T. Griswold, "Seven Moral Arguments for Free Trade," *Cato Policy Report* 23 (2001), p. 14.
48. See, for example, Win Dierckxsens, Del *Neoliberalismo al Postcapitalismo* (San Jose, Costa Rica: DEI, 2000).
49. Jeffery M. Paige, "Finding the Revolutionary in the Revolution: Social Science Concepts and the Future of Revolutions," in *The Future of Revolutions: Rethinking Radical Change in the Age of Globalization*, ed. John Foran (London and New York: Zed Books, 2003), p. 24.
50. These critics include, among others, Antonio Gramsci, as well as writers associated with the Frankfurt School, Liberation Theology, Cultural Studies, and more recently, Inclusive Democracy. Antonio Gramsci, of course, was heavily influenced by Benedetto Croce's anti-positivist stance, as well as Marx's historicism, and insisted that man is nothing but a being of praxis. He writes, . . . "there is no abstract 'human nature,' fixed and

immutable. . . but human nature is the totality of historically determined social relations. . . ." Elsewhere, he states, "human nature is the complex of social relation". See Antonio Gramsci, *Selection from the Prison Notebooks* (London: Lawrence and Wishart, 1998), pp. 133, 355. Among writers associated with the Frankfurt School, the notion of an abstract and fixed human nature is also rejected. Max Horkheimer, for example, states that "human nature is continuously influenced and changed by a manifold of circumstances," and there is "no formula that defines the relationship among individuals, society, and nature for all time". See Max Horkheimer, *Between Philosophy and Social Science*, eds. Frederick Hunter, Matthew S. Kramer, and John Torpey (Cambridge, MA: MIT Press, 1935/1993), pp. 152-153. With respect to Liberation Theology, this perspective, grounded on Christian values, adopts the revolutionary thrust of Marxism to suggest that people's fate is not dictated to by immutable laws of nature. Rather, people are creative beings that "can transform their historical situations in order to create a more just society." Human beings, in other words, are beings of praxis and hence not confined by essential properties that presumably make conditions such as poverty and oppression unavoidable facts of life. Thus, for example, according to Gustavo Gutiérrez "man is seen as assuming conscious responsibility for his own destiny." See Gustavo Gutiérrez, *A Theology of Liberation: History, Politics, and Salvation* (Maryknoll, NY: Orbis Books, 1973), pp. 36-37. Furthermore, it is well known that Neo-Marxists associated with Cultural Studies draw from perspectives such as postmodernism/post-structuralism to break completely from essentialism and hence understand all notions of a fixed human nature as a thoroughly political category that has historically been employed to justify some form of human/social hierarchy. See, for example, Chris Barker, *Cultural Studies: Theory and Practice* (Thousand oaks, CA: Sage, 2003), pp. 221-222. Lastly, Takis Fotopoulos, central proponent of the Inclusive Democracy project, suggests that freedom and democracy cannot be predicated on any preconception about human nature, for this invites a form of determinism that can be easily antithetical to inclusive democracy. See Takis Fotopoulos, *Towards an Inclusive Democracy* (London and New York: Casell, 1997), p. 180.

51. Esposito, "The Metaphysics of US Empire in the Post 911 Era and the Challenge to World Democracy", pp. 56-57.
52. Ibid, p. 57

53. Serrano Caldera, *Los Dilemas de La Democracia*, p. 11.
54. Franz J. Hinkelammert and Henry Mora Jiménez, *Hacia Una Economía De la Vida* (San Jose, Costa Rica: DEI, 2005).
55. Ibid., pp. 36-37.
56. Hinkelammert and Jiménez, *Hacia Una Economía De la Vida*. p. 35.
57. Ibid., 37.
58. David C. Korten, Nicanor Perlas, and Vandana Shiva, "Global Civil Society: The Path Ahead", available at http://www.pcdf.org/civilsociety/default.htm (accessed August 16, 2006).
59. See http://wwoof.org/
60. Korten, Perlas, and Shiva, "Global Civil Society: The Path Ahead," p. 9.
61. See, for example, the various scientific public opinion polls available at http://pipa.org/ and http://worldpublicopinion.org/.
62. Stephen John Hartnett and Laura Ann Stengrim, "War Rhetorics: The National Security Strategy of the United States and president Bush's Globalization-Through-Benevolent-Empire, p. 193.
63. Hinkelammert and Jiménez, *Hacia Una Economía De la Vida*.
64. See, for example, Noam Chomsky, *Hegemony or Survival: America's Quest for Global Dominance* (New York: Metropolitan Books, 2003).

4

A New View of Civil Society from Latin America

John W. Murphy and Manuel J. Caro

INTRODUCTION

Similar to many places around the world, civil society has become an important theme in Latin America. In general, the basic idea is that ordinary citizens should become more directly involved in their governance, or democracy will remain something elusive. Democracy, in other words, is not merely a set of parliamentary practices, but involves the full participation of the citizenry in the planning and operation of a society's institutions. Placed in the hands of a cabal of powerful interests, even if they are elected, the resulting organizations cannot be thought of as democratic. Participation must extend into the processes whereby the overall vision of a society is established, in order for this kind of polity to be achieved.

A recent survey of the rise of civil society in Eastern Europe focused on the clashes between the individual and the state, and the difference between the private and public spheres of social life.[1] In many respects, these conflicts reflect the bifurcation between the particular and the universal that has pervaded the Western intellectual tradition. The result of this dichotomy is that the individual, for example, must struggle for recognition within a state that is considered to be necessary and universal. Additionally, the individual is presumed to be hopelessly biased and idiosyncratic, while the state represents the common good and is all encompassing. And in the end, unless the government is assumed to be an extension of the universal, *anomie* is thought to be inevitable.[2]

Experiences in Latin America, however, have illustrated that equating the government or state with the universal can be disastrous. As discussed by Enrique Dussel, this exalted position has been used regularly to justify the original conquest, in addition to more recent repressive regimes.[3] Those who have wanted to dominate and control persons have been able to link their images of order and progress to the universal, thereby giving these claims almost unquestioned legitimacy. The universal, in this sense, has hardly transcended personal interests to provide a fair and just approach to conceptualizing order. For example, Dussel notes that the "Cartesian ego" became the absolute referent for a new and repressive world in Latin America.[4] In other words, this mechanism provided the alleged neutral vantage point that would be used to judge everyone in the New World.

Various Latin writers argue that trying to establish civil society within this conflict between the particular and universal is not a viable strategy.[5] Civil society must not be simply contrasted to the state, or the universal, but instead should be treated as the source of order. In traditional terminology, civil society should be understood to be a concrete universal that embodies a variety of interests simultaneously that are collectively corroborated. Unless the universal can be transformed in this manner, these Latin critics claim that order must inevitably be equated with domination. In fact, the perspectives and practices that can be most closely associated with the universal will become the norms and ideals of a society.

Much of this change in thinking has been inspired by liberation theology, the widespread creation of base communities, the work of Paulo Freire, and the ethnic diversity in most Latin countries that demands recognition without compromise. As a result of this recent history, many Latin Americans have realized that order does not have to be predicated on abstractions such as nation or state. Indeed, when this strategy has been followed, diversity and freedom have been sacrificed regularly to preserve order. Especially noteworthy is that the assimilation of everyone to specific principles and standards is expected or society will not prevail. In this regard, throughout much of the history of Latin America the nation has been an archetype defined and implemented by outsiders, who have had the power to impose particular social and cultural mores. But even when this construct has had a more local origin, the homogenization of society has been understood as the logical outcome of progress.

Critics such as Alejandro Serrano, however, contend that the only acceptable universal is one that is comprised of diverse viewpoints.[6] Accordingly, he writes that true unity can exist only within diversity. Clearly such a conception is different from the traditional version of the universal. This hybrid universal is not abstract, but exists at the intersection of the numerous perspectives and interests that constitute a society. But contrary to the European approach to civil society, this culturally embedded universal is believed to be significant or substantial enough to provide a reliable basis for social solidarity.

This new rendition of civil society cannot be appreciated fully without grasping a theoretical trend that has emerged recently in Latin America. This manoeuvre relates to the development, for example, of a view of theology, ethics, and globalization that originates "from below" (*desde abajo*).[7] The key point is that all social changes should reflect the desires and traditions of the people who are indigenous to a region. But this shift represents merely the practical side of this issue. Equally important is a philosophical manoeuvre that undermines the ability to establish abstract renditions of the nation or state as universal. Simply stated, this innovation in philosophy has eliminated the space where these universals have been able to reside with impunity.

What these Latin writers are attempting to accomplish is the overthrow of traditional metaphysics, otherwise known as first philosophy. Traditionally the assumption has been made that valid knowledge and order had to be founded on timeless principles that are unaffected by social or cultural contingencies. In this way, normative judgments would be impartial and trustworthy. The result of this belief is that society has been portrayed often in a manner defined as realistic, so that order cannot be legitimately jeopardized. This style of realism, in other words, allows the state or nation to be accorded the status of the universal that transcends existential concerns.

THE PREVALENCE OF REALISM

As Dennis Wrong remarked in his now classic article, most mainstream social analysts have adopted an "oversocialized" image of the person.[8] What he means by this assertion is that in the absence of an overpowering array of institutional forces, the onset of chaos is thought to be inevitable. At every opportunity, persons must be pressured and controlled or society will devolve rapidly into a cacophony of competing claims. Simply put, the unsavory situation envisioned by Hobbes will be realized.

Most important about these institutional constraints is that they must be categorically distinct from the persons who are controlled. In other words, these control mechanisms must occupy a unique ontological plane, that is, they must be considered universal. For, if these institutions have an origin similar to those who must be constrained, any efforts at control will not be very effective. After all, the system of socialization would be replete with contingencies, and thus would not have the authority necessary to deprive persons of their freedom.[9] Institutions would be considered biased and incapable of fostering the common weal because they would not have the appropriate metaphysical pedigree.

In order to have the requisite status, effective social controls must not be linked to any particular political or economic position. Such an association would certainly truncate their legitimacy. A unique philosophical manoeuvre has been invoked, accordingly, to provide institutions with the required universal stature. Predicated on dualism, socialization is thought to emanate from organizations that are divorced from the values, beliefs, and commitments that guide the decisions made by individuals. Institutions are, therefore, touted to occupy an exalted place that allows them to ignore these parochial concerns. Through the machinations of dualism, institutions are stripped of the flaws inherent to persons and transformed into a reliable base of moral order.

As part of this effort, Comte described order to reflect Public Opinion, while Durkheim chose to call this inviolable foundation a "reality *sui generis*". Talcott Parsons is much more modern in this respect and referred to society as a system.[10] In each case, however, the aim is to make the source of morality appear ominous. Only in this way, claims Durkheim, could the longevity of a society be guaranteed. For this reason, Durkheim imagined society to be sacred and the individual profane. And, as the word implies, nothing positive can emerge from the realm of the profane. Merely useless excesses flow from this domain.

Given this context, there should be no confusion about why civil society has not been sought regularly as a source of order. This facet of society, simply stated, originates from the region of the profane and, thus, is not necessarily pristine or rational. As a result of this association with values and desires, civil society cannot be trusted in any way. Furthermore, because civil society is not universal, this side of social existence should not be allowed to rival the state. Such competition would only promote confusion and anarchy. The only reasonable option is that the goals of civil discourse must be expressed through the opportunities supplied by the state. For, according to this dualistic portrayal of social life, the state represents the whole of society.

Nonetheless, this realistic image of the state is not necessarily rational. Most important is that supplying the state with this paramount position has not always benefited everyone equally. Often those who hold privileged positions have been able to justify their misuse of power by identifying themselves closely with this source of authority. Specifically, the norms and ideals that emanate from the state have been treated as synonymous with particular persons or social class. And once this linkage has been thoroughly formalized, through advertisements, textbooks, and other modes of ideology, these groups begin to epitomize the behavioral and cultural standards of an entire society. In the end, these persons are presumed to constitute the universal centre of society. They provide the archetype of normativeness.[11]

Clearly this style of integration from above can be problematic, particularly in a society that claims to be democratic. Diversity of opinions or subcultures, for example, is not an asset but poses a threat to the so-called core of society.[12] Accordingly, civil society can be described easily as comprised of the undisciplined masses that do not comprehend the art of governance. The overall result of this outlook is that entire segments of a society may be marginalized, simply because they have failed to adopt certain values.

In Latin American countries that are so diverse, this sort of realism has come to be viewed with suspicion. As a replacement for this development strategy, various movements are emerging from below and offer a different approach to integration. A type of self-organization is being witnessed that is not predicated on the usual distinction made between particulars and universals. The assumption is that diversity cannot be fostered when one group is able to claim to represent the best that has been created in a society. For example, the Spanish and their criollo offspring tried to support these charges to the detriment of many indigenous persons and entire cultures.[13] Many current social commentators in Latin America are working to avoid a repetition of this tragedy.

MOVEMENTS FROM BELOW

The general thrust of these movements from below is to enable persons to exert some control over their respective destinies.[14] Essential to this process is that they be encouraged to participate fully in the creation and management of important institutions, such as the economy, government, and healthcare. But before this change can occur, the idea must be challenged successfully that institutions are the product of history, and thus are not the result of forces that persons must simply confront and accept. Everyone must engage in the cultural work, in other words, that is necessary for persons to reclaim their institutions. For as long as these organizations remain autonomous, alienation will continue to plague modern societies.

Countries in Latin America are facing the grim reality of globalization, particularly neoliberal policies, that is claimed to be inevitable by planners and financial experts in Europe and the United States.[15] But in order to alter this course of history, as Marx suggests, persons must not merely interpret or respond to these conditions, but must be in a position to propose alternatives. The redirection of history, simply put, must be seen as a real possibility.

But in order for this new culture to come to fruition, the traditional relationship of persons to history must be seriously rethought. Especially noteworthy is that the autonomy of the resulting implacable institutions must be undermined. The movements from below have adopted various means, borrowed from Marxism and other philosophies, to reveal the untenability of the dualism that sustains this perspective on history. These militants argue that because all knowledge is mediated by praxis—in the forms of language, labour, faith, or commitment—the power of realism has been irretrievably compromised. They point out that realism is predicated on existential abridgement that can never be achieved, and therefore the basic conditions of realism cannot be met.[16]

Basically, their claim is that realism has been an illusion, and thus describes reality in a thoroughly contradictory manner. Institutions are assumed to be autonomous, although they are thoroughly meshed with personal and collective experiences. Supporters of movements from below no longer give any credence to this sort of legerdemain. Their argument is that nothing is inherently autonomous, neither history nor institutions. Subsequent to the collapse of dualism, realism loses its *raison d'etre*. And in the absence of dualism, all forms of knowledge must compete for recognition and acceptance.

As part of this rejection of dualism, the usual justification is lost for the differentiation that is made between particulars and universals. Now all that exists are modes of experience that can be treated as if they are either particular or universal. When these identities are sustained by experience, they cannot be accorded the status associated with fundamental ontological states. Their final designation is uncertain and depends on how *praxis* is enacted and institutionalized. With a shift in interest, for example, a former universal may become inconsequential and viewed as a fleeting appearance.

Universals are now thought to be historical and subject to the vagueness of this process. As Walter Benjamin says, every day is now Judgment Day, and progress is simply debris piled skyward.[17] Consequently, there is no universal destiny and institutions can be remade to fulfill the desires of the populace. In this regard, the role of citizens in social life can consist in far more than validating the institutions that are delivered by history and assumed to be crucial to the survival of society. The prospect exists, for example, of embarking on an entirely novel future.

A NEW VERSION OF CIVIL SOCIETY

With the particular and the universal intimately connected in a single movement that is mediated completely by human action, civil society is thrust into a new role in the development of a society. Civil society, in short, does not represent a minor component in an overriding system. Likewise, corroboration by the state is not necessary for the proposals made by civil society to have validity. Civil society is now in a position to give a society an entirely new identity and direction.[18]

This change in orientation has been manifested in Latin America in several ways:

1. The focus has shifted appreciably to grass roots organizing. In general, the idea is that all politics begins with the people. The aim is to move away from the verticalism and "caciquismo" that has characterized traditionally politics in Latin America. Organizations are thus arising regularly that are devoted to supplying common persons with the skills required for them to participate fully and make significant contributions to every sphere of social life. Consistent with the widespread dissemination of education and opportunities, the assumption is that the wholesale marginalization of entire sectors of Latin societies can be ended.

2. Along with the elevation in importance of the popular classes, persons have been encouraged to rethink the nature and scope of politics.[19] This juncture is where the issue of power is addressed. Activists now recognize that participation is insufficient unless the traditional centres of advantage and corruption are eliminated. Movements are underway, for example, that are calling for the total transparency of government through the widespread dissemination of information and public debates on crucial issues. Perhaps most important is the pervasiveness of a new attitude that hierarchy and centralization are impediments to democracy, and that persons from all classes of society have the ability to govern themselves. Common persons are clamoring for involvement and appear to be unwilling to accept the old excuses for elitism.
3. There has been a marked increase in the presence of "mass organizations".[20] These are grass roots groups that have been developed to address a new range of needs, as well as to serve as a countervailing force to traditional political parties. Women, farmers, and neighbours, for example, have formed interests groups that have become sufficiently powerful to provide the political process with a new agenda. These groups are large and influential enough to outline a renewed vision of society, and have the power and enthusiasm to implement such a project. These organizations, in other words, have come to be perceived as instrumental to the political process, rather than as an adjunct to this activity.
4. In general, various academics and lay persons are calling for the development of a new social contract, a type of New Deal for Latin American societies.[21] The idea is that entirely different social arrangements can be implemented through the broad participation of the masses in forming new rules of engagement. Here, again, the issue of power is addressed. The assumption at this juncture, as opposed to J.S. Mill or, possibly, John Locke, is that a contract is valid only among equals.

Accordingly, persons can come together as full members of society and begin to negotiate a social agenda that reflects the outlooks of all of the parties involved. Clearly the point is to end the exploitation that has been enforced as normal for years in Latin America.

5. The recent rise in interest in civil society is predicated on the principle that peace cannot last without justice. In the past, so-called peace accords have been reached that have resulted momentarily in tranquility. The key difference between peace and tranquility is that the former requires that the system of repression be totally dismantled, and that reconciliation meetings be convened to discuss and redress past injuries. The evil deeds of the past cannot simply be swept under the carpet, nor can wanton revenge be encouraged. What is required is the honest assessment of all past misdeeds and their open and fair adjudication.

What is fundamental to this interest in civil society is that the legitimacy of government is no longer presumed to be derived solely from sovereignty. Authority, stated differently, is not sufficient to guarantee that institutions will not be divisive and disruptive. Claims of universality are not significant enough to insure that these organizations are not exclusionary.

Not everyone, however, has embraced these principles. These popular organizations are a threat to many sectors of Latin societies, and these privileged classes have tried continually to thwart the efforts of those who want to build a new, and more inclusive, society from below. Nonetheless, these themes have become entrenched and are difficult to remove. As a result, the pursuit of total democratization continues, although with periodic setbacks.

Even in view of this resistance, many Latin critics are pressing the issue that governmental legitimacy comes from true participation and the consent of those who are governed.[22] Most important in the light of current discussions, however, is that these traits are not necessarily a part of the neoliberal economic and cultural programme. Although there is a lot of talk about participation and competition at the marketplace, little attention is paid to the obstacles related to the economy, gender, or class that may disenfranchise many persons. In this sense, neoliberals have failed to address as issue that is central to those who support the rise of civil society in Latin America. That is, fairness cannot reasonably be expected unless the social and cultural conditions are created that foster this outcome. The development of civil society, accordingly, represents the onset of a very different political culture from that championed by liberals or neo-liberals.

CONCLUSION: HYBRID INSTITUTIONS

In Latin America nowadays, civil society is neither contrasted to the state nor viewed as a niche where non-governmental affairs can be conducted. This facet of society, instead, is understood *to be* the government. Civil society is the source of the ideas, motives, and desires that provide the foundation of a responsible order, that is, an order that embodies the will of the people. As a result, institutions are neither monolithic nor estranged from the citizenry.

Because there is no possibility of transcendence entering into this version of order, institutions can only be referred to as hybrid.[23] Rather than being based on a reality *sui generis*, order exists at the nexus of various modes of existence. Accordingly, institutions are nothing more than a composite of the different existents that were formerly called particulars. These organizations are thus not pure but fuzzy, uncertain, and ambiguous. They represent numerous participants and the contract that they will forge among themselves.

There are no longer any universals or particulars, simply modes of existence that are juxtaposed. To borrow from Theodor Adorno, social order is simply a "constellation" of these factors.[24] The key to this style of social imagery is that there is no inherent centre or margin; likewise, there is no fundamental identity and difference. Instead, there are merely different arrangements of how reality should be portrayed that can be reordered without any metaphysical justification. How these outlooks are prioritized depends on the nature of the contract that is enacted.

As should be noted, institutions are not immune to the dynamics that plague every aspect of social existence, despite claims to the contrary made by realists. In a manner of speaking, these organizations are little more than habitual ways of constructing social life that can be rethought and altered. Institutions simply chart the decisions that have been made about how a society should operate, although not all persons have always participated equally in this process. In fact, large segments of Latin societies have been held accountable regularly to contracts that they did not formulate or view as valid.

Institutions are thus nothing more than elaborate concoctions. And because they are not transcendent, these organizations do not provide a safe haven from competing attempts to (re)define the course of history. Even the most strident dictator is grounded on a fragile but illegitimate contract, although the practical underside of every style of government is often concealed from the public. In fact, many powerful but illegitimate forces benefit from what Plato referred to as the grand lie—that is, that governments represent some transcendent scheme.[25] Obviously a host of writers in Latin America are trying to destroy this illusion, as a result of placing civil society at the heart of order. For when government and the accompanying institutions are equated with civil society, everyone is suddenly on an equal footing with regard to setting the social agenda.

NOTES

1. Krishan Kumar, "Civil Society: An Inquiry into the Usefulness of a Historical Term", *The British Journal of Sociology* 44, no. 3 (1993): 375-395.
2. Emile Durkheim, *Sociology and Pragmatism* (Cambridge: Cambridge University Press, 1983), pp. 82-85.
3. Enrique Dussel, *1492: El Encubrimiento del Otro* (Bogotá: Ediciones Antropos, 1992), pp. 55-75.
4. Ibid., p. 67.
5. Karlos Navarro and Birgit Gernstemberg, *Introducción a la Historia del Pensamiento Latinoamericano* (Managua: Fondo Editorial CIRA, 2002), pp. 151-164; See also, Leonardo Boff, *El Cuidado Esencial* (Madrid: Editorial Trotta, 2002), pp. 17-28.

6. Alejandro Serrano Caldera, *Las Dilemas de la Democracia* (Managua: Editorial Hispamer, 1995), pp. 58-59; p. 81.
7. Francois Houtart and Francois **Polet**, *El Otro Davos* (México, DF: Plaza y Valdés Editores, 2000), pp. 63-84.
8. Dennis Wrong, "The Oversocialized Conception of Man in Modern Society," *American Sociological Review* 6, (1961): 183-193.
9. Jean-Paul Sartre, *Anti-Semite and Jew* (New York: Schocken Books, 1969), pp. 133ff.
10. John Murphy, *Postmodern Social Analysis and Criticism* (Westport, CT: Greenwood, 1989), pp. 10-13.
11. Alejandro Serrano Caldera, *El Doble Rostro de la Postmodernidad* (San José, Costa Rica: Editorial El Amanecer, 1994), p. 196.
12. Arthur Schlesinger, *The Disuniting of America* (New York: W.W. Norton, 1993).
13. Carlos Fuentes, *El Espejo Enterrado* (México: Taurus, 2001), pp. 181-184.
14. Orlando Núñez Soto, *El Manifiesto Asociativo y Autogestionario* (Managua: CIPRES, 1998), pp. 109-128.
15. Franz Hinkelammert, "La Economía en el proceso actual de globalización y los derechos humanos." *El Huracán de la Globalización*, compilado por Franz Hinkelammert. (San José, Costa Rica:DEI, 1999), pp. 239-249.
16. Gregorio Morales, *El Cadáver de Balzac* (Alicante: Ediciones Epigono, 1998), pp. 2-23.
17. Walter Benjamin, "Theses on the Philosophy of History," in *Illuminations* (NY: Schocken, 1969), pp. 253-264.
18. Serrano Caldera, *Los Dilemas de la Democracia*, p. 57; p. 108.
19. Juan Bautista Arríen y Miguel De Castilla Urbina, "La Experiencia Nicaragüense el la Construcción Democrática desde la Educación," *La Democracia y sus Desafíos en Nicaragua*, compilado por Alejandro Serrano Caldera (Managua: Fundación Friedrich Ebert, 2001), pp. 211-245.
20. Gary Ruchwarger, *People in Power* (South Hadley, MA: Bergin and Garvey, 1987), pp. 36-64.
21. Alejandro Serrano Caldera, *Hacia un proyecto de Nación* (Managua: Fondo Editorial CIRA, 2001), pp. 149-155.
22. Mónica Baltodano Marenaro, *Democratizar la Democracia* (Managua: Ediciones Graphic Print, 2002), pp. 39-58.
23. Nestor Garcia Canclini, *Hybrid Cultures: Strategies for Entering and Leaving Modernity* (Minneapolis: University of Minnesota Press, 1995).
24. Theodor Adorno, *Kierkegaard: Construction of the Aesthetic*

(Minneapolis: University of Minnesota Press, 1989), pp. 91-92.

25. Karlos Navarro, *Entre el Poder y la Historia* (Managua: Centro Nicaragüense de Escritores.2000), pp. 21-32.

5

Can Quantum Mechanics Facilitate the Humanities and the Discourse on National Identity?

Carlos Largacha-Martínez

INTRODUCTION

There is a seductive argument that humanity is very inclusive, but in the end represents a particular version of humanism that is often mistaken for diversity. Education and/or development, for example, is supposed to bring persons in touch with a "new humanity". However, this version of humanism is reductionistic and, in the end, ironically, not very humanistic.

Discussions about humanity have a lot in common with those related to national identity. National identities are supposed to be inclusive, but contemporary debates reveal the shortcoming of this thesis. In an idyllic fashion, the term "humanity" has been used to proposed an ideal version of the world, along with the goals that should be followed. Some have called this vision the "global village". Humanity thus falls into the trap of equating unity with homogeneity. What is needed, instead, is unity within diversity. This alternative is complex, and this paper wants to shed some light on this complexity. In the end, the point is to provide a new image of humanity that is consistent with the revolutionary philosophy of quantum mechanics. And once this perspective is understood, new approaches to social development might be possible that are not reductionistic.

THE EXCLUSIVE NATURE OF (TRADITIONAL) HUMANISM

The work done by Philippe Chanial in reviewing several texts by John Dewey— *democratic humanism*—is salient to the approach that is used in this research project about human nature and/or human purpose.[1] He argues:

Nature may not be worshipped as divine even in the sense of the intellectual love of Spinoza. But nature, including humanity, with all his defects and imperfections, may evoke heartfelt piety as the source of ideals, of possibilities, of aspiration in their behalf, and as the eventual abode of all attained goods and excellences.[2]

Regardless of all the debates and critiques that can be directed at John Dewey's radical liberalism and/or democratic humanism,[3] his work provides a good starting point to a discussion about human nature. In order to "arrive" at—who is the other?—it is important to delineate who or what is a human being. Because the point is to approach this topic in a unique way, from a quantum perspective, Philippe Chanial's readings of John Dewey are helpful. As stated before, the emergence of human potentialities is one of the aims of this research, and thus Dewey's words are relevant:

> Find out how all the constituents of our existing culture are operating and then see to it that whenever and wherever needed they be modified in order that their workings may release and fulfill the possibilities of human nature.[4]

The phrase "find out" refers to the emergence of the actualized being, which has cultural understanding as a relevant goal. Later, Chanial highlights important facets of Dewey's focus on human potentialities and the malleability of human nature.[5] The approach taken by Dewey and Chanial's interpretation correlates with O'Murchu's *Quantum Theology*,[6] where God is seen more as a holistic force than an anthropocentric figure, and with Danah Zohar's vision of an "immanent God" that does not preclude the transcendental God of the Judeo-Christian tradition, or the emergence of God from human discourse.[7]

The "basic question" is similar to the one stated before; that is, the emergence of human nature is not something fixed. In this sense, human nature is "denaturalized". Once this has occurred, Dewey and Chanial are in agreement with RQM—relational quantum mechanics—when they state that nothing exists absolutely; everything is relative to interaction with other elements.[8] As quantum mechanics reveals about the subatomic world, nature is something complex and highly creative, where humans co-create reality.

In order to show the exclusive nature of (traditional) humanism, it is worthwhile to mention Stevenson´s anthology, *The Study of Human Nature*.[9] What is striking about this anthology is that the majority of authors have a "half-empty" vision of the human being, and there are scant connections and/or correlations with Modernity's foundations—which explains the relevance of this project's second chapter—and how the related socialization produces the competitive, comparative, egocentric, individualistic being that is the centrepiece of the modern world. In this regard, the *telos* of Modernity is manifested in competition and individualism. As an aside, that is why Adam Smith's seminal work is *The Wealth of Nations*—where the invisible hand is only mentioned once!—and not *The Theory of Moral Sentiments*.

The main problem with these approaches is that they became a self-fulfilling prophecy. Freud's ideas of the id, ego, and super ego are the psychoanalytic counterpart to Hume and Hobbes' depressive picture about human nature. For Freud, "the instincts in the id press for immediate satisfaction at all costs", but then comes the ego, which "undertakes the steering" of id's driving force.[10] Immediate satisfaction or the pleasure principle is changed by the ego into the "reality principle", not to alter the external world but "to establish in it intentionally the conditions which make satisfaction possible ... [and] such decisions make up the whole essence of worldly wisdom."[11] Social comparison and competition are at the basis of guiding the world in this direction.

With this dehumanized imagery of the human being comes

another depressing fact: the method that is used to support this end. Since Descartes' dualism, the mind was separated from the body, while the latter was objectified and made the focus of the study of human nature. The result is that human nature has a *bodily* nature. When psychology, sociology, and anthropology arrived, nothing changed; they wanted merely to apply the natural sciences to the project of identifying the essential and destructive human features.[12] At this juncture, in 2008, there have been several changes, but the power elite continues to manipulate this image of the human being. For example, take Joseph Stiglitz's book about globalization, wherein he talks about the economists from the World Bank and the IMF, and how their attitudes, behaviours, and beliefs are mainly pragmatic, dogmatic, and ignore what their numbers reveal.[13] These organizations, simply put, are extremely disconnected from human beings, their cultures, and the situations in their respective countries.

What is needed are complex solutions to this complexity, not reductionistic ones. However, this change is not easy, as stated before. Modernity has left a big imprint on the world. Konrad Lorenz puts it well when he states that modern man "is not good *enough* for the requirements set by the enormously expanded, anonymous society of later cultural epochs, which demand that he should behave towards any completely unacquainted fellow human being as if he were a personal friend".[14] In the end, alienation and hypocritical role taking merge together to produce the *citizen*.

In this way, this project wants to dwell on alterity, or otherness, or the Other as *truly* Other. The hypothesis is that it is useless to speak about human nature without speaking about the Other. There is nothing like human nature in abstract, neutral, or objective terms. Everything is relational! That human nature is *social* is one of the main contentions of this project, and is a foundational principle of a humane society. Accordingly, *the human purpose is to know the Other*. Instead of asking about the human being or human nature, the question that anchors this work is: Who is the Other?

The Other is also identified as the constitute other,[15] which "refers to that which a person considers to be entirely unrelated to their own concept of their self-identity". Accordingly, the Other is not the sole focus of attention. The other is part of my self-identity, which is part of the human purpose. For example, definitions that exclude or isolate the Other are transcended by Enrique Dussel, and other authors who defy the logic of Modernity.

The question *"Who is the Other?"* is not written in stone, in an absolute way. Some person has to ask this question, and by asking recognizes the existence of someone else. This other is not foreign, but a part of the I. Thus, the Thou exists conterminously with the other, either intuitively, imaginatively, or corporeally. I and Thou exist simultaneously when *"Who is the Other?"* is asked; it is impossible—from a quantum perspective—to comprehend them fully as an amalgamated-single-unit or independently. That is why who the human being is or what human nature is are inappropriate questions, except within the confines of Modernity.

This exercise does not negate me, or the I, by obscuring identity or personality. On the contrary, what alterity does is to expand and broaden the human being. The hypothesis here, as stated before, is that one of the key foundations of being human is social embeddedness. And starting from the Other, what actually happens is that the social agenda is expanded. There is no contradiction here, as the indeterminacy and complementarity principles indicate. This is not to say that persons behave as electrons, but that there is no contradiction between the Other, personal freedom, and social reality. In words of the Nobel laureate and co-discoverer of quantum mechanics, Werner Heisenberg:

> One could speak of the position and of the velocity of an electron as in Newtonian mechanics and one could observe and measure these quantities. But one could not fix both quantities simultaneously with an arbitrary high accuracy. ... They are usually called relations of uncertainty or principle of indeterminacy. ... The other way of approach was Bohr's concept of complementarity. ... Bohr considered the two pictures—particle picture and wave picture—as two complementary descriptions

> of the same reality. ... If one takes into account those limitations which can be expressed by the uncertainty relations, the contradictions disappear.[16]

How was identity socially constructed from Modernity? Although there is no clear-cut definition of Identity, it is generally understood as the individual, independent characteristics of each human being. Modernity obviously shaped that definition. But now, alterity provides a different focus. Specifically, the difference is the hypothesis that, in principle, social relations will be more nonviolent and tolerant of the Other, and social relations will construct a field where human potentialities are more likely to be actualized.

Alterity considers the I and the Thou *as two complementary descriptions of the same reality.* Indeed, this association is indeterminate, uncertain, and non-contradictory. Furthermore, it is worthless to try to find the ultimate end of the I. The purpose of the I is established simultaneously with the Other in an ambivalent manner. Even if persons understand one another, they can interact with a third party that changes the identities of each one. Hence, a "new" identity emerges. This eruption or change exposes what Gadamer and Dussel call *horizons*, which are endless and expand during any deep social interaction.

Co-identity-emergence and horizons are akin to what Jung calls *inflation*,[17] where there is an "extension of consciousness" that "produces an enlargement of the personality leading to the state of inflation ... [having] impersonal characteristics of humanity". In a sense, alterity leads toward humanity, the sense of belonging to the whole, or what is called "brotherhood" by Christians. Carl Jung understood this inflation or emergence in the I and Thou interaction to "be a kind of supra-individual psychic activity, a *collective unconscious*, as I have called it, as distinct from a superficial, relative, or personal unconscious".[18] Some postmodernists, like Schutz, have called it intersubjectivity.

Once the difference between the Other and human nature is scrutinized, and knowing that the starting foundation of humanity is that the human purpose is to know Who is the Other, delving into how the Other is discovered becomes important. And once the Other is understood as a truly Other, then virtues can be formulated and operationalized, and a humane society can emerge, or is more likely to be actualized.

Argentinean philosopher and intellectual Enrique Dussel is a key figure in terms of alterian social philosophy. He is the author of the seminal work, *Introducción a la filosofía de la liberación*—Introduction to the Philosophy of Liberation—which he wrote while in exile during the 1970s. Since then he has been a mainstream figure, having public debates with Karl Otto Apel, Levinas and others, and is given a status close to Heidegger and Hegel. Dussel's key point is that philosophy must always begin and end in the world, which is created through concrete dialogue with others. In this regard, Dussel inextricably invites the I and the Others as a basis for humanity.

HUMANITY, THE NATION, AND THE POLY-NATION

Nonetheless, traditional humanism overlooks rich diversity and the need to protect this trait. This juncture is where diversity has to be reviewed in order to reveal the profound need for a different theoretical approach to humanism, where quantum mechanics appears as a possibility, including the moral position that emerges from complementarity (from the Copenhagen Interpretation).

In general, the world is desperately searching for an answer to integration with tolerance, diversity, and heterogeneity. As Kymlicka argues, "Identifying the bases of social unity in multinational states is, I believe, one of the most pressing tasks facing liberals today".[19] This work has made the point that diversity cannot be understood within Modernity. Similarly, the nation-state actually represents a diversity that is essentially contradictory. Additionally, mainstream logic cannot handle the non-violent coexistence of several cosmo visions. This is why a holistic approach to alterity is relevant today. As Gerald Kernerman states about the multicultural reality, "Few topics have generated more debate in Canadian politics than the relationship between unity and diversity".[20]

The deconstruction done thus far, added to the theoretical framework of quantum humanism, provides the platform for structuring an examination of Colombia—the focus of the Conclusion.[21] In fact, the last sections of this work are linked to the multicultural debate. Without this final discussion, the analysis of Colombia—or any other country—would be curtailed. Additionally, in the multicultural debate is where the polynation and quantum humanism acquire all their fullness and strength.

The aim of the polynation is to illustrate that integration within diversity can be achieved without reductionism and "high-level" abstraction. In this regard, quantum humanism allows for the emergence of a non-exclusive diversity, since face-to-face interaction defines the *type* of diversity, and how much that diversity can be extended—what Gadamer, Dussel, and Kymlicka call the expansion of horizons. Thus, people interacting do not simply transform the nation; rather, the nation is an outcome of this process of constructing diversity.

What has been happening in the debate about the nation is that people traditionally construct identities without interaction with the Other, or through an individualistic process. Quantum humanism, and its sociopolitical counterpart, the polynation, reveals that identities cannot be created without full integration with the Other. Hence the identity problem is solved. Since every identity is constructed through interaction with the Other (alterity), particulars and universals disappear within the polynation. In this sense, the nation is constructed from alterity and the interaction with the other. Hence national identity should start from the ground, or face-to-face interaction. In that situation, there is no nation, since *we (I+Thou) are the nation*, the interaction with the Other as a true other.

An important academic and philosopher dealing with these themes is Will Kymlicka, who has been addressing the issue of diversity in his own country, Canada. In that country, Québécois, English descendants, and aborigines are trying to develop unity within diversity. Kymlicka situates the topic within the construct of "cultural pluralism", and from this platform analyses diversity. From a liberal sociopolitical standpoint, his argument focuses on the existence of two different, albeit interconnected, issues: "multinational states and polyethnic states".[22] He claims that cultural pluralism or multicultural citizenship can be handled using these two political constructs. In point of fact, his book *Multicultural Citizenship* is devoted to this endeavour.

For him, multinational states help to *administer* diversity to national minorities (ancestral people), and polyethnic states are useful for ethnic groups—mainly immigrants. Both coexist in countries such as Canada and the United States.[23] Nonetheless, Kymlicka acknowledges the difficulties and different interpretations of the term "multiculturalism".[24] Multiculturalism, for him, "arises from national and ethnic differences", where culture is "synonymous with 'a nation' or 'a people'—that is, as an intergenerational community, more or less institutionally complete, occupying a given territory or homeland, sharing a distinct language and history".[25] In a way, a national identity is synonymous with culture. With this definition, he is departing from the traditional usage of the term in the United States, where excluded groups must also be considered. What these groups want is a dignified recognition coming from the whole society, but the complexity starts when some of these groups have a self-identity similar to a minority, for example, peasants. By the way, there is a debate nowadays between two different peasant organizations in Colombia about how they should be recognized by the Constitution: as a minority or as a social movement.

For Kymlicka, the concern lies with the concept and definition of "culture", and how to handle manycultures, or multiculturalism.[26] For him, non-ethnic groups cannot be regarded as part of the multiculturalist debate, because if "customs" are included, then everybody should be included, even "voluntary associations", and in the end the whole of civil society. Still, Kymlicka asserts that "an adequate theory of the rights of cultural minorities must therefore be compatible with the just demands of disadvantaged social groups".[27] His theory includes three forms of Group-Differentiated Rights—using Iris Young's concept of 'differentiated citizenship': self-government rights, polyethnic rights, and special representation rights. But if alterity, complexity, and critical ethics (social justice) are part of the picture, then quantum humanism can complement his theory, and produce a more robust image of society, that is, the polynation.

Daniel Bonilla acknowledges that "unfortunately in Colombia [multiculturalism] has not been studied in depth, from the political philosophy and the law, the challenges and opportunities that imposes the fact that this is a country culturally diverse".[28] Not even in Latin America is there a philosophical model that can serve as the framework for this endeavour. This work wants to fill, in part, this theoretical vacuum. Bonilla uses Charles Taylor's "politics of recognition" and Will Kymlicka's version of "multicultural citizenship" in order to review the Constitutional Court's decisions of how to solve the tension between a liberal unitary Republic and the fact stipulated in the 1991 Constitution that proclaims Colombia as a polyethnic and polycultural nation-state.

That is, how has multiculturalism been *operationalized* through the legal framework and constitutional theories? What Bonilla is looking for is a legal and philosophical approach to handle "cultural hybridism and the coexistence of multiple cultural visions in the same geographical-political space",[29] which presupposes four problems to be solved: 1. resources redistribution within diverse cosmovisions; 2. the role of the state in weighing that diversity; 3. identifying the interests coming from different cultures that are fair and should be politically recognized; and 4. determining how to reconcile the unity with diversity, or how to coexist recognizing and accepting the differences of others.

Yet there is a problem with these positions once minorities that are neither "historical" nor "ancestral" enter into the debate. For example, Kymlicka defines the nation as a "historical community, more or less institutionally complete, occupying a given territory or homeland, sharing a distinct language and culture".[30] Additionally, "a country which contains more than one nation is, therefore, not a nation-state but a multinational state".[31] Clearly, Kymlicka's multinational state is discriminatory, for his version of the polynation does not include a wide range of persons.

Similarly, Daniel Bonilla argues that the polycultural and polyethnic dispositions of the Colombian Constitution pertain only to ethnic minorities, mainly aborigines and African-descendent groups, and excludes, for example, peasants. For Bonilla, "to exercise control over a territory is a necessary condition for self-government".[32] Accordingly, polyculturalism cannot be understood within *cultural spaces*,[33] because subcultures within that territory would not necessarily deserve recognition. The problem for Bonilla and the Colombian Constitutional Court is that cultures are understood as "ancestral",[34] thereby discriminating against contemporary cultures and self-identities, such as the ones analyzed by Jesus Martín-Barbero. In Bonilla's writings, the words "ancestral lands" appear several times as a legitimate source of power for minorities in order to be understood by the nation-state. Indeed, the Supreme Court makes this gambit[35] as a part of Colombia's legally proclaimed multicultural state.[36]

In a similar way, Catalina Botero writes about multiculturalism and indigenous people, explaining that the Constitution gives legal recognition only to "national minorities or ethnic groups".[37] Botero thinks that the National Court uses Kymlicka's definition of a *multicultural state*, where the majority lives together with national minorities, understood as "communities that are ancestrally embedded in a political, social, economic, and cultural organization, which is different from the hegemonic society or majority".[38] Both Kymlicka and the Colombian court discriminate against those cultures that are not ancestral or do not have a territory. This type of multicultural vision is transcended in this work. Nonetheless, Kymlicka argues that ethnic groups do not want self-government,[39] but to integrate themselves into the majority if cultural traditions are provided.[40] It seems that with this definition the problem is solved. However, not all cultures want to be integrated into the majority, and more important, the definition of integration comes from a liberal democratic approach. But what about immigrants or ancestral people without a territory, such as Colombian gypsies?

Another downside is the researchers' inability to develop a

horizontal vision, that is, a non-hierarchical version of coexistence. As presented earlier, horizontal does not mean exclusively a cooperative type of organization, or a setting where everybody has to participate in all decisions; instead, horizontal means a hybrid or rhizomic reality, where, having a "super-set" of axioms that define the cultural or national field (Bourdieu), or the horizon (Dussel), is impossible. For example, the so-called Canadian school of ethnic studies does not transcend the whole/part dichotomy, while arguing that "multicultural nationalism is an ambiguous zone ... [that] the competing nationalisms are concerned in one way or another with the Canadian political community as a whole, and with defining its parts". This outlook produces an ambiguous outcome where "Canadians cannot get 'beyond' these oppositions to achieve unity, however, despite their desire to do so".[41] Quantum theory, as presented, does not *exist* in an ambiguous but an ambivalent zone. In fact, Latin Americans *exist* in a region of contrasts; contrasts that coexist simultaneously, *ambivalently*. The whole and parts coexist concurrently, holographically. Yet, they are the *same*, since the part can be found in the whole and vice versa.

This logic of the democratic liberal tradition, as argued before, cannot handle ambivalence. This ambivalent liberalism is what Bonilla refers to as "illiberal".[42] In this regard, Canadians need to transcend oppositions and dichotomies, not only because they "hinder us from pursuing more promising political paths", as Kernerman argues,[43] but also because they provide a platform that, *in principle*, cannot handle diversity. True multiculturalism must transcend dualism and dichotomies, but this change is impossible within the traditional Western mindset. That is, Modernity and true multiculturalism are theoretically opposed, with minimal intersections. No wonder there has not been a real solution to the problem of diversity in Canada.

Kernerman, Taylor, Kymlicka are approaching the solution—deep diversity, differentiated citizenship—but have not yet arrived at this point. Quantum humanism is a theoretical framework compatible with radical multiculturalism that can lead to the development of an inclusive society—with an emphasis on the integration of contrasting but complementary elements. Although the "intertwined" visions present in the "new Canada" have made impressive improvements, the effects of modernity are still present. In this sense, Kernerman argues:

> These nationalisms [Québécois, pan-Canadian, Aboriginal, or other "nations"] have some conception of the parts and the whole, and so they operate according to a logic of identity [of Modernity]. Here, diversity is conceived of as an assortment of different identities, and difference is understood superficially to mean difference among the various identity categories. An identity is, in effect, a unit of difference. The logic of identity is grounded in a refusal of alterity, a denial of complexity, in favor of reified and simplified identity categories.[44]

Kernerman has clearly delineated the problem: *The logic of identity is grounded in a refusal of alterity, a denial of complexity.*[45] Alterity and complexity, it should be noted, are central to quantum humanism. Nonetheless, Kernerman contends that the *embrace of diversity* in the Canadian conversation is inevitably troubled, "since the challenge of diversity is premised on a threatening other, no matter how this other is embraced and celebrated".[46] In short, the other is not seen as a truly Other. How can real multiculturalism emerge from these bases? The imperative of unity, or "the quest for identity in nonidentity", as Kernerman puts it, "cultivates even greater anxiety over the basis for national cohesion".[47] Without the quantum theory, or a similar framework, this anxiety cannot be solved since it mirrors the need "to determine how the various parts relate to one another, and to the whole, and especially how these parts will be kept together in the form of a whole".[48] The holistic *nature* of quantum theory—RQM, relational quantum mechanics—can solve this conundrum, due to the uncertainty and complementarity principles where the part and the whole are entangled and undifferentiated, albeit without losing their single-interdependent "existence".

The other side of this story is that diversity is seen by modernists as undermining a national identity; thus, the nation-state cannot "develop" due to the *immanent* barriers linked to diversity. This unfortunate version of multiculturalism explains why Colombia's situation is seen as "under-developed" and why Colombians deserve their present chaotic condition. Clearly there is a need for the polynation. The 1995 Quebec referendum is important to this discussion. The proposals or "reversals through differentiation" get more support in Canada—and Colombia—with ideas like "differentiated citizenship, asymmetrical federalism, a distinct society clause, Aboriginal self-government, affirmative action, group-based representation, and so on".[49] One of these proposals is Kymlicka's multicultural citizenship or differentiated citizenship.

In a way, Kymlicka recognizes the problem when he states that multinational states are only for national minorities and polyethnic states are for ethnic groups. Accordingly, he is not working with other *groups* such as women, unions, etc. As stated before, this author thinks that his theory passes the test for *other* non-ethnic groups. When dealing with how to accommodate "national and ethnic differences", Kymlicka proposes "three forms of group-specific rights": self-government, polyethnic, and special representation.[50] None, however, seems capable of incorporating a wide range of diversity without conflict.

QUANTUM MECHANICS AND THE ELEMENTS OF THE HOLISTIC OPTION: A NEW FORM OF INTEGRATION THAT DOES NOT PRIVILEGE THE 'WHOLE'.

Using quantum mechanics for understanding/defining human nature is a risky project, since, as Werner Heisenberg states: "the most difficult problem, however, concerning the use of the language arises in quantum theory.[51] Here we have at first no simple guide for correlating the mathematical symbols with concepts of ordinary language". Bohm uses the *rheomode* as an example of how language adopted from Modernity is reductionistic—fragmentation of thought as its outcome—and does not incorporate the fullness of quantum reality, or human potentialities.[52] This could explain why, for some people, Danah Zohar's ideas about human nature and consciousness defined by the new physics sound "arcane", as when she raises the question,

"Are electrons conscious?"[53] Heisenberg summarizes all these arguments when he claims that "it may be easier to adapt oneself to the quantum-theoretical concept of reality when one has not gone through the naïve materialistic way of thinking that still prevailed in Europe in the first decades of this [20th] century."[54] Note that Heisenberg wrote this almost half a century ago!

Some scholars argue that the change from a God-centred to the science-centred universe promoted by Modernity did not change the centredness of the endeavour. That is to say, God was replaced by a *quasi-divine* structure: science and reason. Accordingly, the social sciences born in the 19th century adhered to the natural science model and started to idolize measurement, quantitative analysis, data, and facts. In short, they were committed to the isomorphism effect. How is this project going to avoid falling into the same cul-de-sac? Basic to this project is the assumption that the use of quantum mechanics can assist the social sciences, including the planning process, to become more humanistic.

However, if knowledge is socially constructed, then is it impossible to evade any type of isomorphism? Is knowledge going to be constructed from society and social acts? Thus, these questions should be changed and some corollaries introduced. For example, what steps must be taken into account in order to ameliorate the reductionism produced by the quantitative social sciences? In general, holism appears to be the solution.

But who says that humans behave like nature? What is the advantage of drawing a parallel between the explanation that quantum mechanics provides of the laser beam and multiculturalism or radical pluralism? Or, can the chaos theory be useful in understanding juvenile delinquency, in addition to coherence and resonances? What if some human potentialities can be understood with the use of quantum mechanics or complexity theories? Still, the question is: are these comparisons being extended too far?

Since knowledge is as infinite as human potentialities, and actualizations exist within a finite but expanding framework, there will always exist a subtle type of reductionism. However, this possibility can be reflected upon, so that the proper categories of analysis are adopted. Nonetheless, quantum humanism does not represent a subtle change. The hypothesis here is that if this new model is implemented, several human problems— at least *in principle*—would disappear, and newer ones would be tackled in a more humane, balanced, and harmonized manner.

As Zukav puts it, "Everything, from the beginning of time, has been predetermined, including our illusion of having a free will. ... According to quantum mechanics, however, it is not possible, even in principle, to know enough about the present to make a complete prediction about the future."[55] Using the double-slit experiment, Zukav reminds the reader that no one can calculate where a single photon will strike, like where the billiard ball will hit one of the sides of the table, but only the probability or tendency to happen. The question is, therefore, "what determines where the photon [billiard ball] will land [hit]?" In response to this question, Zukav provides the response given by quantum theory: "pure chance".[56]

Pure chance! This is where Einstein talked about God playing dice as something absurd. The analogy for lay people is perfect, but Einstein was talking with Max Born, and so Einstein, I expect, must have known that if persons had *perfect* information about the size of the dice, the force with which they are thrown, the friction of the air, fabric, etc., they would be able to know *exactly* what numbers the dice will show, every time, as post-modernist Jean-Francois Lyotard argues.[57] Therefore, probability is the absence of perfect information, not the impossibility of human beings knowing something in an infinite time frame, or stated differently, *in principle*. Werner Heisenberg argues that "probability in mathematics or in statistical mechanics means a statement about our degree of knowledge of the actual situation".[58] Similarly, Lyotard argues that "on the level of microphysics, 'better' information—in other words, information with a higher performance capability—cannot be obtained".[59] The difference between probability and chance is colossal. With probability there is the *illusion* of free will, because of the impossibility of knowing the future. Thus the infinite time frame ends up being just the present. With pure chance, or just chance, free will *truly* exists, regardless of the amount of the information available about potentialities/capabilities.

In the first pages of his book *The Tao of Physics*, Capra shows the difference between the two epistemologies, the Newtonian and the Holistic. He acknowledged that this "progression" toward a more holistic view of reality is the outgrowth of having put too much emphasis on self-centredness, analysis, rationality, science, competence, and expansion.[60] Now, new emergent realities are based, conversely, on integration, synthesis, intuitive wisdom, religion, cooperation, and conservation respectively. Mechanistic and causal approaches like the ones emphasized in the scientific method supported non-ambiguous connections, where ambivalent realities were considered irrational.[61] Quantum mechanics redefined and deconstructed rationality. And thus the traditional laws of physics are being transcended. More dimensions are discovered, the vacuum now has emergent properties, and non-sensorial perception is possible.[62] Everything is interconnected. Holism is not that the whole is greater than the sum of its part; holism, instead, is a hologram.[63] In this sense, the parts and the whole are the same.

In his book *La trama de la vida*, Capra continues to show the need for a change in paradigm—or epistemology—that, for him, is already happening. Capra makes a quick review of this "paradigm change", which extends from "the mechanistic perspective of Descartes and Newton toward an ecologic and holistic vision".[64] In this example, ecology refers not *just* to the environment, but is a systemic—open—vision of how things work. For Capra, "the change of paradigm requires an expansion, not only of our perceptions and ways of thinking, but also of our values".[65] Accordingly, he created a list of the constituencies of the two paradigms,[66] which he named *assertive* and *integrative*—or *modernitous* and *quantic*.[67]

Thinking/Knowledge		*Values*	
Assertive	*Integrative*	*Assertive*	*Integrative*
Rational	Intuitive	Expansion	Conservation
Analytic	Synthesizer	Competition	Cooperation
Reductionistic	Holistic	Quantity	Quality
Linear	Non-linear	Domination	Association

Source: *La trama de la vida*, Fritjof Capra (2001:31).

Most important is that, combined with alterity, the quantum theory provides a novel vision of the epistemological change depicted by quantum humanism. The implications are enormous, and some scholars have tried to apply this approach to various arenas. The point, however, is the importance of quantum mechanics for the social sciences. As Gregorio Morales argues, "We are at the beginning of a period where the humanities and sciences are converging thanks to the increasingly general recognition that both are valid ways of knowing the world".[68]

Ir-reducibility, *non*-locality, *time*-reversibility, *in*-determinism. All of these are words or concepts that counter Modernity. They all negate what Modernity states is the true version of knowledge. All of these concepts are constitutive elements of holism, or a holistic vision of society and nature. Humans, therefore, in the best sense, are *ir*reducible, *non*local, *time*-reversible, and *in*deterministic. As Henry Miller, the writer, argued, "I obey only my own instincts and intuition. I know nothing in advance".[69] Intuition, as argued before, is clearly *ir*reducible, *non*local, *time*-reversible, and *in*deterministic. Everything said so far is appealing. However, it was Bell's theorem that actually gave the coup d'etat to Einstein, Newton, and all *deterministic* writers.

Some academics consider John S. Bell's theorem to be one of the most challenging discoveries, compared with Galileo's and Einstein's. In their Preface, McMullin and Cushing claim, "It was only with John Bell's formulation of his now celebrated theorem in 1964 that the full measure of the challenge came to be appreciated".[70] Non-locality, or action-at-a-distance, or superluminal interaction is the challenging discovery. This is the butterfly effect but instantaneous, disregarding—or redefining—time and space! In a extremely brief description, Bell's theorem states that two electrons that interact will be connected, or entangled, *forever*. In a word, holism has been mathematically demonstrated.

Technically, this theorem is known as Bell's inequalities—or the hidden-variable thesis—and appears in a paper he presented in 1965, written to refute the correlation that supported the Einstein-Podolsky-Rosen (EPR) paradox—or stalemate, as Nick Herbert calls it.[71] Bell's theorem, or Bell's inequalities, reveals not only the *collapse of the wave-Modernity*, but actually demonstrated that a key figure such as Albert Einstein was wrong. Einstein, who discovered the *quantas* of light, and identified the observed-contextualized reality in the space-time fourth dimension, was not able to expand further his discoveries to the quantum *reality*. Therefore, Bell's nonlocality represents the collapse of Modernity and of Newton/Einstein! When non-locality is part of the big picture, nobody can relax. As Feynman stated, nobody can say that he or she truly understands quantum mechanics. But what Bell's theorem and Heisenberg's principle are saying—besides other things—is the impossibility of knowing all, *in principle*.

Yet, what is Bell's theorem? Michael Esfeld argues that "the famous theorem of Bell (1964), to put it in a nutshell, [is] that the emission of these two systems from the source cannot be a common cause that screens the one measurement outcome off from the other measurement outcome".[72] Nick Herbert succinctly states that "the gist of Bell's theorem is this: *no local model of reality can explain the results of a particular experiment*. In short: reality is non-local".[73] Sometimes this idea is called the *entanglement* principle, since once two photons have interacted, they will be entangled forever—or at least as long as they exist—regardless of how far they are apart ("action-at-a-distance" or "faster-than-light interaction"), or how their behaviour is diachronically linked ("time-gap interaction").

What is being described *is* the *instantaneous* butterfly effect, or in a word, holism. Werner Heisenberg argues similarly that the Cartesian partition—or dualism—"has penetrated deeply into the human mind during the three centuries following Descartes and it will take a long time for it to be replaced by a really different attitude toward the problem of reality."[74] This is what quantum humanism is all about. In short, cognitive perception represents more than what is "out there," while social interaction is not a present-state but a timelessness feeling of "being there" that really is "becoming there". Hence, past, present, and future have to be deconstructed in order to become more attuned to potentialities and possible-actualities of human beings. In the end, time is thus not autonomous.

At this juncture it is important to spend some time with Gödel's theorem, since if looked at carefully, this idea is a *pseudo-*mathematical *demonstration* of quantum holism and fits perfectly with Jung's collective unconscious. As Penrose writes, "The hopes of Hilbert and his followers were dashed when, in 1931, the brilliant 25-year-old Austrian mathematical logician Kurt Gödel produced a startling theorem which effectively destroyed the Hilbert programme".[75] In this respect, Gödel is the Galileo of our times. Simply put, he *demonstrated* mathematically what qualitative scholars have been arguing for a long time, i.e., knowledge is not autonomous.[76] Gödel's theorem showed that

> Any such precise ('formal') mathematical system of axioms and rules of procedure whatever, provided that it is broad enough to contain descriptions of simple arithmetical propositions ... and provided that it is free from contradiction, must contain some statements which are neither provable nor disprovable by the means allowed within the system. The truth of such statements is thus 'undecidable' by the approved procedures.[77]

In many respects Gödel announced the impossibility of discovering an autonomous, absolute foundation of knowledge. As he illustrated, the initial steps in any algorithm are not provable—they are based on certain decisions that are made and accepted as valid. This *undecidability* is similar to uncertainty and complementarity principles "mingled" together, but coming from mathematics. What Gödel's theorem reveals is that, *ad infinitum*, there will *always* be a set of meta-axioms—meta-narratives as Lyotard would call them—that could not be explained by the Grand-set, or that, simply stated, are not contained in the Grand Theory. Consistent with quantum theory, the basis premise of Gödel is that reality, even mathematical forms, are connected to a human presence that cannot be transcended by any set, Grand or otherwise.

The relationship between quantum mechanics and the social sciences can be a fruitful one, if, among other things, this association supports a vision of the earth that is more humane and holistic, as expressed by Bohm. This holistic approach, Wilber argues in his *Holographic Paradigm*, "cannot be discovered by a science that attempts to break the world into its parts".[78] This mandate has a huge problem, nonetheless, since science has been based traditionally on determinism, causality, reductionism, and replicability, which are inconsistent with quantum holism.[79] Furthermore, the difficulty with establishing the polynation is that many critics cannot move beyond the parts, or the parts connected by some super-set, or society. Such a solution to diversity will be, similar to its application to the natural world, reductionistic and counter-productive. What is needed, instead, is a way of conceptualizaing a new, less hierarchical relationship between the parts and the whole.

CONCLUSION

In today's world, the polynation is a very important concept. Many countries, including Colombia, are very diverse and comprised of many cultures. Within this context of the proliferation of cultural diversity, the key issue is how to construct some sense of social solidarity. The old method of simply arguing that everyone should assimilate to one cultural ideal is neither acceptable philosophically nor practically. In other words, no longer are persons prepared to accept the sacrifice of their cultural ideals, in order to produce a nation that does not recognize their presence.

In Canada, for example, the process of establishing a national project ran into a serious roadblock. Specifically, the members of the so-called "Canadian School" of ethnic studies—such as Kymlicka and Charles Taylor—could not overcome the traditional realist alternative. That is, a universal reality had to be established in order to join the competing parties. This reality sui generis, accordingly, would represent the so-called Canadian reality and unite all persons into a functional nation.

The problem that emerged immediately related to the status of this ultimate reality. That is, which culture would be treated as universal, while all others faded into the background? Due to the strong English heritage present in Canada, the case was made that this culture should be dominant. The French, as might be expected, objected to this maneuvre. And the result of this logjam was ongoing conflict over the fundamental character of Canadian society.

In view of the quantum theory, however, this realist position is no longer a viable alternative. Such realism rests on dualism and the possibility of establishing a neutral base of norms that, in the end, can be treated as existing sui generis, something akin to a Platonic ideal. In more social terms, the universal norms and values presupposed by Talcott Parsons, which bind society together, are similarly abstract. Nonetheless, subsequent to the demise of dualism, the justification of such abstractions is no longer possible. All norms, even those touted to be universal, must emerge from "someplace" and reflect a particular perspective.

Given this predicament, how can society be united? The quantum theory has an answer to this dilemma. Most important to remember is that dualism is jettisoned in every aspect of this philosophy. In this regard, knowledge does not exist divorced from a perspective that is tied intimately to human consciousness. Likewise, the general organization of elements does not conform to the shortcomings imposed by dualism.

Traditionally, elements have been viewed in an atomistic manner. Consistent with this version of dualism, elements are categorically distinct; consistent with the logic of Artistotle, each element is self-contained and has exact boundaries, i.e., parameters, that separate it from all others. Additionally, space serves as a mechanism that keeps these factors apart. But without dualism, this entire edifice collapses. In the absence of dualism, in other words, elements can cross paths, and thereby lose the sense of exactness produced by dualism. In current parlance, the result is that identities can become fuzzy.

This fuzziness, however, is a strength rather than a weakness in quantum theory. Quantum theorists recognize that elements can be organized on the basis of ambivalence, and thus freedom and spontaneity is preserved in the world. Elements, stated differently, can be organized without defining their parameters in a manner that would imply that the universe is static.

In order to avoid such a silly conclusion, quantum theorists recognize that order can be predicated on the recognition of diverse elements. Such an outcome is made possible through the "complementarity thesis". What this thesis proposes, stated simply, is that in the absence of dualism, identities are not isolated. In fact, the identity of one element is not recognizable without the contrasts or perspectives provided by others. Accordingly, each element is implicated in the identity of a range of others, and the composite of these factors gives a holistic view of the universe.

With regard to social life, however, an equally profound message is conveyed. Specifically, the possible unification of different elements does not require the intervention of some a-perspectival position (i.e. Grand Set) that can transcend the limitations of each perspective and forge them into a unified whole. Rather, through the juxtaposition of different elements, mutual adjustments can be made. In other words, elements can be directly related—as they cross each other's path—so that a mosaic is created. In fact, each element is thus valuable and contributes to the overall picture that is created.

With regard to the creation of a nation, a similar image is suggested that is at the root of the poly-nation. That is, a nation can be organized around diversity, without imposing a repressive culture that must be recognized as universal, even if this perspective is understood by many persons to be irrelevant or, possibly, harmful. Without these universals, persons can organize themselves in a way that preserves the uniqueness of each group. Through the direct recognition of others a sense of stability and longevity can be established between persons, as they adjust to each other's position and integrate these various perspectives into coherent order.

In more political terms, the resulting order represents a loose federation of communities. These groupings, accordingly, can negotiate how their mutual contact and commitments will be preserved. As opposed to the Canadian model, no one has a legitimate claim to control the outcome of this process, so that the domination of a particular community is guaranteed. Therefore, the outcome is truly negotiated and reflects the diverse claims that might be made. But because of the equality of these claims—none has ontological priority—no particular one can infringe on any other.

A condition of reciprocity is thus established from the ground up. The end result can be referred to as Colombia, or by any other name. But the general idea is that a nation does not have to be homogenous to survive. As is revealed by the thesis of complementarity, order can be sustained through the juxtaposition of opposites and their continuous interaction. A polynation, accordingly, is compatible with this foundation of regularity that does not demand the submission of every community to some abstract whole. The whole is now found in the parts, rather than an abstract principle.

At first this proposition might sound wildly utopian. But what is established is really something very pragmatic, that is, a context for the true and fair negotiation of how various communities will interact, politically and economically, to form a nation without marginalizing certain groups. The foundation of the quantum theory specifies that no element can claim legitimately the status necessary to inferiorize others. Finally, the nation can reflect the diversity that is present in societies such as Colombia and most other countries in Latin America, without the fear that chaos will automatically erupt. Certainly this social imagery represents an improvement on the traditional position that required the assimilation of everyone to a similar cultural ideal in order for a nation to be identified and survive.

NOTES

1. Philippe Chanial, "Is the Democratic Ideal Conceivable without the Notion of Human Nature? On John Dewey's Democratic Humanism," *Diogenes* 49, no. 3 (2002): 71-77.
2. Ibid, p. 75.
3. Or religious humanism, or naturalistic humanism for Chanial.
4. Chanial, "Is the Democratic Ideal Conceivable without the Notion of Human Nature? On John Dewey's Democratic Humanism," p. 75.
5. Ibid.
6. Diarmuid O'Murchu, *Quantum Theology* (London: Crossroad Classic, 2003).
7. Danah Zohar, *The Quantum Self* (New York: Quill / William

Morrow, 1990), p. 226.

8. Federico Laudisa and Carlo Roveli, "Relational Quantum Mechanics," in *Stanford Encyclopedia of Philosophy* (2002), http://plato.standford.edu/entries/qm-relational.
9. Leslie Stevenson, *The Study of Human Nature* (NY: Oxford University Press, 1981).
10. Ibid, p. 171.
11. Ibid, p. 172.
12. Immanuel Wallerstein, *The Essential Wallerstein* (New York : W.W. Norton, 2000); Arturo Escobar, *Encountering Development: The Making and Unmaking of the Third World* (Princeton, NJ: Princeton University Press, 1995).
13. Joseph E. Stiglitz, *El malestar en la globalización* (Bogotá: Taurus, 2002).
14. Stevenson, *The Study of Human Nature*, p. 232.
15. Nishida Kitarô argues, "The centre of the self is not limited to the interior of the individual; the self of a mother is to be found in her child."
16. Werner Heisenberg, *Physics and Philosophy: The Revolution in Modern Science* (NY: Prometheus Books, 1999), pp. 42-43.
17. Carl Jung, *Portable Jung* (Middlesex: Penguin, 1976), p. 104.
18. Ibid, p. 34.
19. Will Kymlicka, *Multicultural Citizenship* (Oxford: Oxford University Press, 2004), p. 9.
20. Gerald Kernerman, *Multicultural Nationalism* (Vancouver: UBC Press, 2005), p. 3.
21. Carlos Largacha-Martínez, *Theorem for a Holistic-Humanistic Model of Development* (University of Miami Dissertation, 2006).
22. Kymlicka, *Multicultural Citizenship*, p. 11.
23. Ibid, pp. 17, 22.
24. Ibid, p. 17ff.
25. Ibid, p. 18.
26. Ibid.
27. Ibid.
28. Daniel E. Bonilla Maldonado, *La ciudadanía multicultural y la política del reconocimiento* (Bogotá: Uniandes, Fac. de Derecho, 1999), p. 12.
29. Ibid, p. 9.
30. Kymlicka, *Multicultural Citizenship*, p. 11.
31. Ibid.
32. Bonilla, *La ciudadanía multicultural y la politica del reconocimiento*, p. 3.

33. What Fredrik Barth (1998: 15) calls social boundaries, although they can have a territorial constituency.
34. Bonilla, *La ciudad multicultural y la politica del reconocimiento*, 3.
35. In Bonill's perspective.
36. Article 7 of the National Constitution.
37. Catalina Botero, *Multiculturalismo y derechos de los pueblos indígenas en la jurisprudencia de la corte constitucion* (Unpublished manuscript FLACSO, 2004), pp. 6, 9.
38. Ibid.
39. Kymlicka, *Multicultural Citizenship*.
40. Botero, *Multiculturalismo y derechos de los pueblos indígenas en la jurisprudencia de la corte constitucion*, p. 10.
41. Kernerman, *Mulcultural Nationalism*, pp. 5, 4.
42. Bonilla, *La ciudadanía multicultural y la politica del reconocimiento*.
43. Kernerman, *Mulcultural Nationalism*, p. 4.
44. Ibid, p. 6.
45. Ibid.
46. Ibid, p. 17.
47. Ibid, p. 18.
48. Ibid.
49. Ibid, p. 23.
50. Kymlicka, *Multicultural Citizenship*, p. 27.
51. Heisenberg, *Physics and Philosophy: The Revolution in Modern Science*, p. 177.
52. David Bohm, *Wholeness and the Implicate Order* (London: Routledge, 2002), p. 34.
53. Zohar, *The Quantum Self*, p. 50.
54. Heisenberg, *Physics and Philosophy: The Revolution in Modern Science*, p. 202.
55. Gary Zukav, The Dancing Wu Li Masters: An Overview of the New Physics (London: Bantham, 1979), p. 26.
56. Ibid., p. 68.
57. Jean-Francois Lyotard, *The Postmodern Condition* (Minneapolis: University of Minnesota Press, 1984), p. 57.
58. Heisenberg, *Physics and Philosophy: The Revolution in Modern Science*, p. 40.
59. Lyotard, *The Postmodern Condition*, p. 57.
60. Fritjof Capra, *El tao de la física: Una exploración de los paralelismos entre la física moderna y el misticismo oriental* (Málaga: Editorial Sirio, 2001).
61. Ibid, p. 45.
62. Ibid.

63. Ken Wilber, "A New Perspective on Reality" in *The Holographic Paradigm and Other Paradoxes* (Boston: New Science Library, 1982), pp. 5-14.
64. Fritjof Capra, *La trama de la vida. Una nueva perspectiva de los sistemas vivos* (Barcelona: Anagrama, 2000), p. 27.
65. Ibid, p. 31.
66. This list is taken from his Spanish version *La trama de la vida*. The translation is mine.
67. Quantic refers to quantum. *Modernitous* does not exist but is used in orer to distinguish it from 'modern' which has a different interpretation. *Modernitous* would mean, in a similar way to quantic, Modernity. Modern is something advanced or tehnological embedded.
68. Gregorio Morales, *El cadáver de Balzac* (Alicante: Ediciones Epígono, 1998), p. 9.
69. As cited in Gary Zukav (1979: 119).
70. Ernan McMullin and James T. Cushing, *Philosophical Consequences of Quantum Theory: Reflections on Bell's Theory* (Notre Dame: University of Notre Dame Press, 1989), p. xi.
71. Nick Herbert, Quantum Reality, Beyond the New Physics: An Excursion into Metaphysics and the Meaning of Reality (New York: Anchor Books, 1987), p. 210.
72. Michael Esfeld, "Quantum Holism And The Philosophy Of Mind," *Journal of Consciousness Studies* 6, no. 1 (1999): 24
73. Herbert, *Quantum Reality, Beyond the new physics. An excursion into metaphysics and the meaning of reality*, p. 199.
74. Heisenberg, *Physics and Philosophy: The Revolution in Modern Science*, p. 81.
75. Roger Penrose, *The Emperor's New Mind* (Oxford: Oxford University Press, 1999).
76. Russell's paradox. See Penrose, 1999:131, "R is the set of all sets which are not members of themselves."
77. Ibid, p. 133.
78. Ibid.
79. Wilber, *The Holographic Paradigm and Other Paradoxes*; Rupert Sheldrake, "Mind, Memory, and Archetype Morphic Resonance and the Collective Unconscious - Part I," *Psychological Perspectives* 18, no. 1 (1987): 9-25; Herbert, *Quantum Reality, Beyond the New Physics: An Excursion into Metaphysics and the Meaning of Reality.*

6

Is there any Hope Left for Colombia?

Dana Rasch

INTRODUCTION

Colombia has one of the worst human rights records in the world.[1] This fact is particularly evident if you are fighting for labour rights, as estimates have shown that over 400 trade unionists have been murdered and 1,300 have received death threats during the current presidential term of Álvaro Uribe.[2] Furthermore, although the Uribe Administration will brag about the economic progress of Colombia during the last six years,[3] almost 70% of Colombians still live below the poverty line.[4]

The high level of poverty in Colombia, accompanied by the danger that seemingly lurks everywhere, has created a divide between the rich and the poor in Colombia that represents two separate worlds. One is filled with privilege, the other with abject poverty. But perhaps even more alarming than the class situation is that recent research in Bogotá has revealed that the elites[5] believe social class is organized as a reality *sui generis*.[6] In other words, the elites want people to feel that there is no possible way to alter or change the existing class arrangement, and the only option is to fit into the existing social order.

In this paper, I argue that this elitist ideology is an attempt to enforce neoliberal economic policies, such as free trade, in an effort to continue (and further) the current exploitation on the part of the elite. Although this agenda appears to be working well, recent mass protests in Colombia against the privatization of public education have revealed that many do not want these neoliberal policies to be implemented. Unfortunately, however, the neoliberal agenda is being legitimized by civil society. In this regard, civil society in Colombia, which is often believed to be the only way to create social change in today's world, encompasses primarily Non-Governmental Organizations (NGO).[7] And although "leftist" NGOs would seem to be ideologically distinct from neoliberals, they do share an important similarity: a desire for a non-interventionist state. In turn, NGOs that represent civil society have only furthered the neoliberal agenda.

To add to this dilemma, the only available counter-ideology to neoliberalism is offered by revolutionary groups, such as the Armed Forces of the Colombian Revolution (FARC) based on Marxism, which are no longer seen as offering a viable alternative to the status quo for many of the youth living in urban areas such as Bogotá. The diminishing influence of the revolutionaries, however, is not necessarily because their ideas are outdated, but due to the war that has been carried out against them by the state, elites, and paramilitaries backed by the U.S.[8] This brings up the question, "Is there any hope left for Colombia?" I argue that such hope rests on a new vision of civil society. Only if a new social imagery is developed for civil society that is based on a community building and empowerment instead of NGOs acting as intermediaries to organize and represent the people in a hierarchical relationship between the state and individuals, can a counter-ideology be developed that is antagonistic to the state, and is democratic as well as inclusive.

CONTROL AND MANIPULATION BY THE ELITE

Similar to many Latin American countries, Colombia was brutally colonized by Spain, beginning with the first Spanish settlement in 1509.[9] In the quest for riches, particularly gold, the indigenous population was tortured, killed, and pressed into submission by the Spanish conquistadors. Ever since the Spanish arrived in Colombia, the exploitation of the Colombian people has become the norm, and, in turn, violence has also become quite common in order to maintain (and protest against) the prevailing order. Although Spain relinquished "official" control of Colombia after the successful liberation efforts led by Simon Bolivar in the 19th century, an oligarchy of elites have dominated Colombia to this day and have used force to perpetuate their power.

Perhaps the most violent political episode in Colombian political history began on April 9, 1948, when a popular leftist leader Jorge Eliécer Gaitán, who promised land reform and an end to the tyrannical two-party system, was assassinated in the capital of Bogotá. Immediately after his assassination, riots broke out throughout the country. Over the next ten years, more than 200,000 Colombians were killed and billions in property damage was reported. This period has become known in Colombian history as "La Violencia".[10]

In 1953, General Gustavo Rojas Pinillas seized the presidency through a military coup supported by liberals and conservatives.[11] However, the elites that ran these parties, particularly conservatives, learned quickly that the populist leader's plans did not fit neatly into their agenda. But Pinillas' popularity grew with the people as he pushed for land reform and other means that undermined the oligarchy in Colombia.[12] By 1956, the leaders who sat atop the liberal and conservative parties realized that "La Violencia" and President Pinillas were not only doing little to advance their hegemony (and of course their riches) but were actually challenging their power. In turn, the parties aligned and signed a truce called "Frente Nacional" (National Front). Through this pact, both parties agreed to share political power, and the coalition officially began in 1958 when a military junta removed Pinillas from power.[13] The National Front lasted until 1974 but the political scene has not changed. As Ingrid Betancourt has pointed out, the political system is as corrupt as ever and manipulated by the elite.[14]

La Violencia and the National Front coalition are historic moments in Colombian history. The National Front, in particular, proved that the elites were willing to put aside the welfare of the people in order to gain seigneurial status in Colombia. In fact, Colombian history reveals this willingness as a trend, not an aberration. Kline points out astutely, that the liberals and conservatives on "twelve occasions between 1854 and 1949...entered into a coalition with all or part of the other political party".[15] In this sense, although these two parties supposedly do not share the same ideology, they do experience the same privilege. And in the end, they want to maintain that privilege by any means necessary. Clearly, the state has never invited the overall population of Colombia into their democracy. And in turn, the political manipulation of the elites has done little to relieve the pain and suffering of Colombians, who, as mentioned earlier, live mostly in dire poverty.

THE RISE OF THE REVOLUTIONARIES

The inability of the state (and elites) to create a democratically inclusive society certainly became clear to many Colombians in the early 1950s, when peasant defence groups formed to protect their land from thieves (the state and elites) during La Violencia.[16] These armed defence groups were highly successful even after the National Front was in place in 1958. Richani argues that the government and the elites, backed by the U.S., were attempting to put an end to the "independent republics" of peasants who were trying to defend their land and, eventually, launched an aggressive military campaign against the campesinos in 1964.[17] But the peasants managed to hold their ground and maintain control of their land. In 1966, the peasant groups formed the Armed Forces of the Colombian Revolution (FARC) with close connections to the Communist party.[18]

Over the years, a number of other revolutionary groups were formed, including the now defunct M-19 (Movimiento 19 de Abril) and EPL (Ejército Popular de Liberación). However, although the FARC is the most well-known revolutionary group, The Army of National Liberation (ELN) was actually the first to emerge officially, ironically, on July 4, 1964.[19] The ELN is still active today, and, unlike the FARC, originated in the urban middle-class. Indeed, ELN has an estimated current membership of as many as 5,000 members.[20]

These revolutionary groups appeared in Colombia because

they wanted to create a new and just world, and, in turn, present a counter-ideology to the corrupt and elitist dominated state. For a number of decades, these revolutionary movements were quite popular; however, in the last twenty years their popularity among the general people has declined. In particular, Kline argues that during the 1990s popular support for the FARC diminished greatly for a number of reasons, such as the war waged by the United States, paramilitary pressures (United Self Defense Forces of Colombia - AUC), and the harming of civilians by the FARC.[21] Moreover, due to the FARC's peasant legacy coupled with their inability to penetrate the urban areas due to political and paramilitary violence, the urban youth often do not see this movement as a viable alternative.[22]

But without a viable counter-ideology, the elites are able to push their neoliberal agenda with seemingly little resistance by painting a picture of society that can be characterized as ontological realism.[23] This dilemma has left the people of Colombia searching for answers and alternatives. In the following sections, I shall discuss these current alternatives and end by offering a new vision.

SOCIETY CANNOT BE CHANGED

I arrived in Colombia in May 2006, to carry out research at Colegio Nueva Granada (CNG),[24] an elite private school located in Bogotá. My plan was to evaluate (via a questionnaire) an educational programme at this school for my doctoral dissertation at the University of Miami. A few days before my arrival, I sent a copy of the questionnaire to one of the administrators at CNG, whose husband was planning to pick me up at the airport (they are both members of the elite in Colombia). The day I arrived, not even five minutes after picking me up, I was interrogated relentlessly about the questionnaire and how it could not be used, because the results would surely reveal that the programme was having little impact on the attitudes and behaviour of the students toward the poor in Colombia. I was even told that the questions were a waste of time, because everyone in Colombia knows the answers. At the outset, this incident was simply seen as a knee-jerk reaction to challenging the social, cultural, and political status quo in Colombia. However, the research at this elite institution revealed a disturbing pattern that is much bigger than one person.

A dominant theme that prevailed throughout the research is that everyone must be realistic, and, in turn, understand that there is no hope for significant change in Colombia. In this regard, the elites feel firmly that social change is impossible. In particular, the manner in which the social class is organized will never be altered. This prevailing realist mindset is bleak, but clearly benefits those who tout these prophecies. In the interviews, students continually repeated this ideology. For instance, one student was asked about the possibility of having a friendship with a person located at the lower end of the social spectrum in Colombia:

Interviewer: If you had a friend who was in the "low class", would people make fun of you?

Senior: Probably. They would look at you differently, and you would look at them differently. It's just the way it is, it is never going to be solved. Unless they get better pay and there's more of a middle class than a lower class.

Interviewer: So the divide between rich and poor is really strong here?

Student: Really, really strong.

Interviewer: And it's going to be almost impossible to change, unless...?

Student: Unless a miracle happens. Pretty much, yeah.

Another student who was asked about the possibility of changing the social makeup of Colombia added:

Interviewer: Do you think that the class divide, like the class structure, the division between classes in Colombia could ever really be changed?

Student: No, I don't think it will ever be changed because poor people don't have opportunities, and poor people don't have opportunities and that is what makes people succeed. You can be like really hard worker or there are some people who actually succeed because of hard work but that's not the case here. It's the sad reality.

Interviewer: Even if you are poor and you work hard, most of the time you are not going to make it?

Student: Uh huh, that's right. So they are never gonna go because maybe like they win the lottery or something they are never going to go up.

And lastly, another student added the following about how society is supposed to operate:

> I know it would be a lot better if it was equal, but that's practically utopian, it's practically impossible, because there is always going to be, for me to be rich, there has to be someone poor or for someone to be poor, there has to be someone rich.

Certainly, I could go on with many similar quotes but the point is clear. Although many of the students believed that the way Colombia existed was unjust, there was simply nothing they or anyone else could do about the situation. In this regard, the elites are attempting to defend and further their privilege by advancing the idea that a class division is necessary and can never be altered. Therefore, society exists as a reality sui generis. This concept - reality sui generis - is attributed to the work of Emile Durkheim, who believed that the purpose of sociology is to unearth social facts that existed sui generis.[25] As Durkheim wrote, a sui generis fact has "its own unity, individuality, and consequently its own nature - a nature, furthermore, dominantly social".[26] In other words, social facts exist outside of both the individual and society. Accordingly, these social facts are overpowering and individuals have little opportunity or chance to alter these truths.

With Colombian elites pushing the idea that social class exists sui generis, their message to everyone is: there is nothing a person can do! Clearly, the implications for this type of realist-based social imagery are disastrous for the two-third of the Colombians who live in poverty. Obviously, fatalism is at the core of this realist message. But even more damaging is the idea that one must simply fit into the existing reality and promoting an alternative vision is a waste of time and energy. How beneficial this imagery is to the elites!

Certainly, the option of simply finding a niche in the existing social order is not much of an option for the majority of people in Colombia, and, not surprising, many have attempted to resist this type of social imagery. In fact, during a trip to Colombia in the summer of 2007, I witnessed firsthand two mass protests on consecutive days. Both were against the neoliberal policy of privatization in the field of education. The first was a student-led takeover of La Universidad Pedagógica in Bogotá. The second was a street march that consisted of approximately 10,000 participants and stretched for miles along Avenida Séptima.

However, although a number of Colombians are attempting to resist this ideology, the vast majority of citizens has adopted the ideology of the elites and believes they cannot change their world. After years of exploitation and corruption, Colombians realize the government is not there to help them, and many understand that the new neoliberal economic policies will only destroy the country further and make the rich even richer.[27] But with the decreasing popularity of the revolutionaries, thus resulting in an absence of a viable counter-ideology to realism, what alternatives are left to the people living in poverty in Colombia?

The question now is: what can be done to change the situation in Colombia? In the following sections, I argue that the answer lies with civil society. Many scholars will make the same argument, that civil society is the best possible alternative for creating social change. Hence, around the globe, the development of civil society has become the focus for many who desire social change.[28] However, the current conceptualization of civil society in Colombia is extremely beneficial to the elites, and, thus, I offer a new vision for the people.

THE SOLUTION: CIVIL SOCIETY?

For many, the development of civil society is seen as the only hope for building a true democracy.[29] But what does the term "civil society" actually mean? Baker reveals that philosophers first introduced the concept of civil society during 18th-century Scottish enlightenment.[30] During this period, philosophers were concerned with the growing power of the state, along with the market, and argued that people lacked a certain "public spirit". In turn, these philosophers argued that a "universal" civil society was necessary in order to "check the power" of the state and restore civic responsibility in people. However, as Baker argues, the Scottish philosophers' conceptualization of civil society was not "yet fully modern".[31]

In the 19th century, G.W.F. Hegel revived the concept and is credited for being the first to introduce civil society as a separate sphere from the state.[32] However, for Hegel the state must "rule and guide" civil society, and therefore, Karl Marx proceeded to criticize heavily and dismiss civil society as simply a "bourgeois" ideal. Not surprisingly, with the disapproval of Marx, the concept was a dead issue for quite a while in academia.

But in the 20th century, civil society was once again re-conceptualized (and revitalized) by the Italian Marxist Antonio Gramsci, and has since emerged as a possible source for real democracy. Gramsci characterized civil society as a non-economic and non-state sphere that may or may not legitimize state rule.[33] And in this sense, Gramsci gave civil society an autonomous nature for the first time. As Baker states, "He [Gramsci] was therefore the first to articulate the idea that civil society, in a moment of counter-hegemony, could actually be resistant to state power as, in his well-known phrase, so many 'earthworks and buttresses'".[34] In other words, civil society may exist independently of the state and the market and can define the role and direction of these two spheres.

In this regard, there are two elements to civil society that are pivotal in discussing the role civil society plays in Colombia: autonomy and counter-ideology. First, civil society, as Gramsci proposed and contrary to Hegel, is supposed to be separate from other spheres, such as the state and market. In other words, civil society must be autonomous and operate independently of these realms. However, the way that civil society has often been characterized is as an intermediary or a "go-between" for the state, market, and individuals.[35] But this image regularly becomes problematic, because a hierarchical image of society is often the result. In this sense, the state, along with the market, exists at the top with the people toiling at the bottom, and civil society acts as an intermediary between the two. As the early Scottish philosophers proposed, civil society would essentially defend and represent the people in this position. However, this has not been the case in Colombia. Instead, civil society appears to be falling into the Hegelian trap where the state, and the market, are ruling and guiding civil society.

In this sense, James Petras points out that the developments over the past three decades have made NGOs the primary element that comprises civil society in Latin America.[36] This is certainly true in Colombia. In theory, an NGO is a non-profit organization that exists outside of the realm of state control and aims to bring democracy "from below" and promote social equality.[37] However, the autonomy of these organizations has been brought into question in the last decade.

In particular, Petras argues that the World Bank, the organization most well known for imposing neoliberal reform in the 1980s in a number of Latin American countries, increased its funding to NGOs in the 1980s.[38] And this relationship seems plausible because NGOs and neoliberals have "shared interests, purposes, and values", with respect to opposing state control. In this regard, Petras argues, "There is a direct relation between the growth of social movements challenging the neoliberal model and the effort to subvert them by creating alternative forms of social action through NGOs".[39] And although NGOs will maintain they are opposed to a neoliberal agenda, their growth and power appears to be related directly to the advancement of these economic policies. As Petras points out, while neoliberals were destroying Latin America economically through their laissez-faire governmental trade policies, the NGOs were receiving increased funds from neoliberal agencies such as the World Bank to develop short-term projects to alleviate the pain and suffering brought on by governmental polices that benefit only a select few.[40] Clearly, the state and the market have a tremendous influence on NGOs, and, in turn, civil society is not autonomous in Colombia. In this sense, to paraphrase Carmody, whose interests are being advanced by civil society?[41] Clearly, in this instance, the interests of the people are not represented. Again, this failure seems likely because civil society is conceptualized as an intermediary and accepts a hierarchical image of society with power coming from the top.

The second important element is that civil society is instrumental in legitimizing the state. In this regard, Gramsci argued that civil society must be antagonistic, or this realm becomes simply another surrogate for the dominant classes. As Gramsci proposed, civil society should be an ideological counter to those in power. However, this has not happened in Colombia, as the state and the "total market" are in complete control of this domain.[42]

Once again, conceptualizing civil society within a social hierarchy in Latin America as an intermediary allows much of this to happen. If civil society is simply an intermediary between the state, the market, and individuals, the ideology that develops is not likely to challenge state action. As Carmody argues, when this situation occurs, "the power of the state is bolstered and structured through the workings of civil society".[43] Clearly, with NGOs acting as the prime element of civil society, this trend is visible in Colombia.

Overall, civil society in Colombia has not developed as Gramsci intended. The NGOs, who simply coordinate the state, market, and the people, have been co-opted from above and lack any critical spirit. Thus, an alternative ideology has not developed and the people of Colombia do not seem to have any viable alternatives. In fact, civil society appears to simply legitimize the state and neoliberalism, thus reinforcing the realist ideology of the elite that social change is not possible. But if this situation is to be reversed, a new image of civil society needs to be developed.

A NEW CIVIL SOCIETY

In the summer of 2006, several colleagues and I traveled with a group of students from La Universidad de Santo Tomas (St. Thomas University) to La Cuidad de Kennedy (the city of Kennedy), a barrio located outside of Bogotá. The poverty in Kennedy was unlike anything I had ever witnessed. Although the Uribe administration and supporters will tout the economic growth of Colombia over the past six years,[44] little impact has been felt in barrios such as Kennedy. Stepping into the barrios of Bogotá, one can see clearly why revolutionaries such as the FARC and ELN were once able to thrive. For example, there is no educational opportunity or employment, and poverty is the rule rather than the exception. In fact, one might even wonder why the youth of Kennedy are not picking up assault rifles and heading toward the Capital right now!

But even in the midst of cardboard houses, dirt roads, and seemingly no alternatives, a Catholic youth group, Genesis Rades, had formed within the past couple of years with the aim of improving their community. This youth group wanted to start a recycling project, in order to clean up the environment and establish a business that could make money, which could be invested in other social projects within the community. Essentially, there is little recycling in Latin America, although such an activity can be very profitable.[45] The youth group believes that this recycling programme could be the start of something big in their community, and, in turn, actually empower this neighbourhood and bring autonomy to the people. Perhaps, but not surprisingly, to date no NGO has funded this project, which focuses on social justice and community empowerment.

When speaking to these youth, one finds that they are not shy about letting anyone know they do not want neoliberalism in their community. These students clearly reject the neoliberal values that dominate the social scene in Colombia. What they want to build, in short, is a sense of community and social responsibility from below. And bearing that in mind, the question remains: does the most powerful aspect of civil society in Colombia - the NGOs - share these same values?

The answer put forth in this paper is clearly 'no'. The NGOs are being "guided" by the state and the market, and only serve to reinforce the realist agenda of the elites by not presenting a viable counter-ideology. And, as Petras stated, since the 1980s "NGOs turned from supporting the movements to collaborating with the government".[46] In the end, NGOs support neoliberal values such as individualism, self-interest, and the prevailing social arrangements. Clearly, this concept of civil society is neither civil nor social. Therefore, the conceptualization of civil society as acting like an intermediary is not only faulty but also dangerous, and a re-conceptualization of civil society is necessary for Latin America.

Accordingly, the focus on civil society in Colombia needs to originate at the community level and be centred on local empowerment. Such a shift in emphasis would place social and economic power into the hands of Colombians at the neighbourhood level. And, as Murphy and Caro argue in their new vision for civil society for Latin America, local planning and democracy from below can be the "motor of social development".[47]

Furthermore, a civil society that consists of democracy at the local level puts control into the hands of the people themselves by emphasizing that human praxis is the source of all creation. This understanding is contrary to the common belief throughout the Western philosophical tradition that a higher power - a reality sui generis - must organize people or else chaos will erupt. Clearly, this type of philosophy, which implies that the human being is selfish and malevolent, has been evident in Colombia where people find it extremely difficult to organize. In this sense, the traditional civil society still looks to large organizations, such as NGOs, to organize these communities from above. But a civil society based on local community empowerment can provide Colombians with the opportunity to organize themselves in a manner that is democratic, inclusive, and bereft of outside intervention. And with emphasis placed on participation at the local level, places such as Kennedy can begin to take control of their own destiny. Furthermore, these communities can become self-sustaining without dependence on the state, market, or anyone else. In the end, a counter-ideology can develop on the basis of democratic participation at a local level that is able to offer a real alternative to these standard options.

Essentially, this idea is what many scholars refer to as democracy "from below". The use of this term "from below" has been extremely popular in recent literature and many believe it is the only way to achieve democracy. For example, Wood discusses how people in South Africa and El Salvador were organized and mobilized and transformed their respective political economies "from below".[48] However, the conceptualization of democracy coming "from below" is still somewhat problematic. Specifically, this type of language conveys the message (although more veiled) that a hierarchical relationship exists within both the state and market even if the people are essentially guiding these facets of society. Unfortunately, this difficulty has not been pointed out in the literature.

In this sense, an image of society must be put forth that is more inclusive, and more important, implies that social space is actually "contested". For example, some scholars have used the idea of society existing as a montage or a collage, expressing the idea that a hierarchy does not have to exist, and that different perspectives can coexist in a manner that does not repress or overpower any particular component.[49] Civil society, which consists of a multitude of communities, replaces the state and market as an intricate web of relations that operate in a manner that is not conducive to despotism, but allows for the development of a democracy.

CONCLUSION

At the core of my argument is that the social imagery presented to Colombians creates a fatalistic mindset where change appears to be impossible. Furthermore, the rich and poor must always coexist or society cannot function properly; hence, the only option is to fit into the existing social order. With this imagery in place, the only space for civil society to operate appears to be in-between the state and the people. However, this social imagery is highly problematic and sends a realistic message to the people: they are unable to change their world and organize and govern themselves in a democratic fashion.

Accordingly, a re-conceptualization of civil society that emphasizes community empowerment along Gramscian lines should take place. To be sure, community building, such as the project in Kennedy, can bring social, political, and economic power to local neighbourhoods. A counter-ideology can be created and the people can organize themselves in a manner that is democratic, inclusive, and results in their ability to *resist* the state and the market.

NOTES

1. Noam Chomsky, *Profit over People: Neoliberalism and Global Order* (New York: Seven Stories Press, 1999).
2. Jose M. Vivanco and Maria McFarland Sánchez-Moreno, "Troubled times", *Progress Magazine* (February 2008).
3. Speech delivered at University of Miami, School of Business, Tuesday, March 4, 2008 by Santiago Montenegro, who served in President Álvaro Uribe's cabinet as General Director of Pension Fund Administrators during his first presidential term.
4. World Bank, "Colombia at a glance", http://devdata.worldbank.org/AAG/col_aag.pdf (accessed March 20, 2008).
5. Some scholars, and of course the elites, argue that an oligarchy does not exist in Colombia. This assumption is partially correct. In fact, due to the success of the peasants and the FARC, the oligarchy has been minimized in the agricultural sector. Nazih Richani in *Systems of Violence: The Political Economy of War and Peace in Colombia*, pp. 141-142 notes that as of 1998, the elites' share of the agricultural GDP (Gross Domestic Product) decreased to 13%. However, in other sectors, such as financial markets and the industrial sector, the elites' share of GDP has risen significantly. In this sense, the elites still maintain control over most of the economy in Colombia and an oligarchy still rules the land (just without necessarily owning it per se).
6. Emile Durkheim, *Suicide* (New York: Free Press, 1951).
7. Derrick Purdue, "Introduction: Dimensions of civil society", in *Civil Societies and Social Movements*, ed. Derrick Perdue (New York: Routledge, 2007), pp. 1-16; James Petras, "Imperialism and NGOs in Latin America". *Monthly Review* 49 (1997):10-17.
8. In particular, in the late 1990s, Colombia and the Clinton Administration developed "Plan Colombia". This plan is part of the "war on drugs" which focuses on ending the drug trade in Colombia; however, a number of scholars, such as Noam Chomsky, will argue that this is a veiled attempt to consolidate power and exterminate the revolutionaries. Billions of dollars have been given to Colombia to buy weapons and other materials

in order to carry out this plan.

9. Geoff Simons, *Colombia: A Brutal History* (London: Saqi, 2004), p. 18.
10. Ibid., p. 38.
11. Charles Bergquist, "Introduction: Colombian violence in historical perspective," in *Violence in Colombia* (Delaware: Scholarly Resources, 1992), p. 7.
12. Nazih Richani, *Systems of Violence: The Political Economy of War and Peace in Colombia* (New York: State University of New York Press, 2002).
13. Bergquist, "Introduction: Colombian violence in historical perspective".
14. For a detailed journey through the 2002 presidential campaign of Ingrid Betancourt, see the documentary, *The Kidnapping of Ingrid Betancourt*.
15. Harvey Kline, *Chronicle of a Failure Foretold: The peace process of Colombian President Andrés Pastrana* (Tuscaloosa: University of Alabama Press, 2007), p. 9.
16. Richani, *Systems of Violence: The Political Economy of War and Peace in Colombia*, p. 60.
17. Richani, *Systems of Violence: The Political Economy of War and Peace in Colombia*, pp. 61-62.
18. Richani, *Systems of Violence: The Political Economy of War and Peace in Colombia*, p. 62.
19. Kline, *Chronicle of a Failure Foretold: The Peace Process of Colombian President Andrés Pastrana*, p. 11.
20. Information obtained from the European Commission, http://ec.europa.eu/external_relations/colombia/intro/index.htm (accessed March 10, 2008).
21. Kline, *Chronicle of a Failure Foretold: The Peace Process of Colombian President Andrés Pastrana.*
22. Richani, *Systems of Violence: The Political Economy of War and Peace in Colombia.*
23. In this context, ontological realism, as Durkheim argued, implies that society exists in a fixed and static manner that does not allow for social change.
24. CNG is considered one of the most elite private schools in the entire country. The school is composed almost entirely of students from the elite class. English is the only language spoken on campus and the school aims to prepare these elite students for attending college abroad in English-speaking countries such as the U.S. Most of these students indicated they would be (or

planned to) attending American universities.

25. Calvin J. Larson, *Major themes in Sociological Theory* (Philadelphia: David McKay Company, 1977).
26. Durkheim, *Suicide.*
27. Chomsky, *Profit over People: Neoliberalism and Global Order.*
28. This is particularly evident in Africa. A number of scholars are debating the presence and direction of African civil society as an alternative. For instance, see Pádraig Carmody, *Neoliberalism, Civil Society, and Security in Africa* (New York: Palgrave Macmillan, 2007).
29. Purdue, "Introduction: Dimensions of civil society".
30. Gideon Baker, *Civil Society and Democratic Theory* (London: Routledge, 2002), pp. 4-5.
31. Ibid, p. 4.
32. Ibid, p. 5.
33. Robert Cox, "Civil society at the turn of the millennium: Prospects for an alternative world order." *Review of International Studies* 25 (1999):1-28.
34. Baker, *Civil society and Democratic Theory*. Antonio Gramsci, *Selections from the prison notebooks.* (London: Lawrence and Wishart, 1971), p. 238.
35. Civil Society International, "What is civil society?" http://www.civilsoc.org/whatisCS.htm (accessed March 10, 2008).
36. James Petras, "Imperialism and NGOs in Latin America." *Monthly Review* 49 (1997):10-17.
37. Baker, *Civil society and democratic theory*, p. 118.
38. Petras, "Imperialism and NGOs in Latin America".
39. Ibid.
40. Ibid.
41. Pádraig Carmody, *Neoliberalism, Civil Society, and Security in Africa* (New York: Palgrave Macmillan, 2007).
42. Franz J. Hinkelammert, *Critica de la razón utópica* (Spain: Desclée, 2002).
43. Carmody, *Neoliberalism, Civil Society, and Security in Africa.*
44. Speech delivered at University of Miami, School of Business, Tuesday, March 4, 2008 by Santiago Montenegro, who served in President Álvaro Uribe's cabinet as General Director of Pension Fund Administrators during his first presidential term.
45. An informative article on the profitability and rising popularity of recycling in Latin America was published by the Inter-American Developmental Bank and can be found at http://www.iadb.org/idbamerica/archive/stories/2000/eng/

JAN00E/e200g.htm.

46. Petras, "Imperialism and NGOs in Latin America".
47. John W. Murphy and Manuel Caro, "Un nuevo concepto de sociedad civil para/desde America Latina," in *La filosofia en la era de la globalizacion*, ed. Alejandro Serrano Caldera and John W. Murphy (Connecticut: Praeger), pp. 13-31.
48. Elizabeth J. Wood, *Forging democracy from below: Insurgent transitions in South Africa and El Salvador* (New York: Cambridge University Press, 2000).
49. Paul Gilroy, *The Black Atlantic* (London: Verso, 1993), pp. 7-10.

7

Contesting Neoliberal Globalization and State Sovereignty

Heather Gautney

INTRODUCTION

With the end of the Cold War, changes in the structure of national sovereignty and the emergence of supranational institutions have been accompanied by a redistribution of power among states, market actors, and civil society. After a half-century of intense polarization, the dual superpowers system gave way to a new arrangement that could accommodate a diversity of cultures and political systems under a unique layer of authority known as Empire. These changes are associated with the increasing dominance of neoliberalism, a political-economic system of development, which, by the end of the 1980s, had become so firmly rooted in the common sense, that it became synonymous with the term *globalization*.

The most salient characteristics of neoliberalism include privatization of public services, deregulation of industry, lowering of trade barriers, and reduced public spending on social services. Its underlying ethos reflects a view of human freedom as best realized through free market activity and unregulated competition, protected and implemented by the state. Its ideological content prefigures individuals as rational, calculating actors whose value is measured by their ambition, work ethic, ability to self-manage, and capacity to assume personal responsibility for the conditions of their lives, rather than focus on how their circumstances are socially produced.

On a global scale, neoliberal institutions like the World Bank, International Monetary Fund (IMF), and the World Trade Organization (WTO) have attempted, with a great deal of success, to extend the system to the far reaches of the globe, primarily by way of debt, structural adjustment, and "free" trade. Notwithstanding claims to a "small government" and democratic freedom, neoliberalism relies heavily on these regulatory institutions as well as individual states' "monopoly on the legitimate use of physical force",[1] to secure property rights, establish monetary policy, and exploit new markets. Despite neoliberalism's strong arm, a variety of resistance movements have emerged that are contesting neoliberal state sovereignty and its processes of internal and external legitimation. This chapter looks at the mechanisms and effects of neoliberal globalization and the interworking of a transnational social movement that made use of, but also challenged, state sovereignty by creating a new (but now increasingly prevalent) form of political community not bound by the nation-state.

NEOLIBERAL GLOBALIZATION: ORIGINS AND EFFECTS

In order to understand the dynamics of neoliberalism, one must first start with its predecessor and antithesis, Keynesianism, the prevailing economic paradigm in the U.S. (and beyond) from the 1930s to the 1970s. John Maynard Keynes was a British political economist and financier from Cambridge University who went against the grain of neoclassical, laissez-faire economics by promoting a macroeconomic paradigm of compromise between the state and private industry.[2] Despite initial resistance by the Roosevelt administration, Keynes' model served as an antidote to the massive unemployment and recession of the Depression era, and in the wake of planned economies in communist and socialist countries, the New Deal was his and FDR's way of stemming capitalist crisis.

Keynesianism sustained broad appeal amidst the devastation wrought by World War II and post-war reconstruction, and Keynes himself was present at the landmark UN Monetary and Financial Conference at Bretton Woods in New Hampshire in 1944. The goal of Bretton Woods was to prevent further conflict by restructuring international economic relations in such a way as to safeguard against another worldwide economic depression. This restructuring involved restoring order and rebuilding the post-war economy through the provision of loans for reconstruction and the development of new, cooperative economic systems that could operate on a global scale. To that end, Bretton Woods resulted in a series of international agreements that were designed to establish a stable system of international trade, based on fixed exchange rates calculated in U.S. dollars. It also gave birth to two key institutions charged with facilitating the development of a cooperative transnational economy: the World Bank and International Monetary Fund (IMF). The World Bank was established to provide and manage aid to individual countries for post-war reconstruction, while the task of fostering economic stability on a global scale was left to the IMF. The IMF was charged with preventing another economic depression by providing loans to stabilize the international trade system by helping countries' meet their balance of payments and facilitating trade agreements among them.

Despite the primacy of the Keynesian paradigm throughout the early and middle part of the 20th century, it was by no means unanimously accepted among economists, especially those seated within the neoclassical tradition. Keynesianism itself was not a pure science and American and European versions diverged over the issue of income distribution: U.S. neo-Keynesians accepted a view of income distribution and labour costs as best determined by market forces, while European post-Keynesians argued that income should depend on institutional factors, not only the cost and supply of labour and raw materials, but on labour bargaining power and environmental protections, which require government regulation. According to Thomas Palley, neo-Keynesianism's convergence with the neoliberalism over issues of wages, union activity, and fiscal policy may have opened the door for neoliberalism's ascendency, which was also abetted by the U.S. culture of individualism and powerful anti-unionism, epitomized in the passing of the Taft-Hartley Act and the violent repression of labour strikes by police.[3] Despite these differences, by the late 1960s and early 1970s, the system was beginning to fail in both contexts. Keynesians did not conceive that inflation and stagnation could go together, but the OPEC crisis increased the costs of production, and inflation occurred because of excessive demand, which resulted in economic and political crises around the world, thereby discrediting the demand side model.[4]

Neoliberalism was the brainchild of Friedrich von Hayek, an Austrian political philosopher associated with the Chicago School of Economics. In 1947, von Hayek formed a study group called the Mont Pelerin Society, which included such notables as Milton Friedman and Karl Popper. Members of the Society called themselves "liberals" to highlight their commitment to personal freedom and their antagonism to Keynesianism, which they equated with socialism. The philosophical basis for the Society's political economic programme was set forth in Popper's *The Open Society and Its Enemies* (1944), wherein he waged a vehement attack on (Marxist) historicism. Popper argued that Marxism provided a theoretical justification for authoritarianism and that efforts to predict or theorize historical laws should be considered as acts of oppression. An open society was one in which no single person held a monopoly on truth, one that enabled debate and the expression of a plurality of views. The rule of law, a democratically elected government, and a vibrant civil society were the stuff of an open society, as was respect for difference and multiculturalism.

In his *Objective Knowledge: An Evolutionary Approach*, Popper bases his "ontological pluralism" on the distinction of three separate, but overlapping worlds: the physical, the mental, and the intelligible (the realm of ideas). The world of ideas may be a product of the human mind (the second world), but once ideas are produced, they become autonomous – they can be disembedded from the historical conditions of their production. A second presupposition in Popper is that there are certain objective truths about the physical world that are not locatable in a particular class experience or historical moment. A closed society is one in which the evolution of ideas is thwarted by dogmatism. An open society, on the other hand, evolves moving away from dogma and toward "rational criticism" of existing theories by any and all of society's members, and the "fittest" ideas—focused on solving social problems—survive.

Neoliberalism advocates the "supply side" economics, which locates the seeds of economic growth in incentives for production and adjustments to income and taxes on capital gains. Contrary to Keynesianism's focus on "demand", neoliberals argue for a free market, maximal competition, free trade, deregulation, and trade liberalization.[5] Rooted in Popper's concept of the open society,[6] neoliberalism posits human freedom and dignity as bases for democracy, against the threat of fascism, communism, and other kinds of state control, with an understanding of freedom as best realized through free market activity and private property rights. Despite claims to a "small government" and its emphasis on democracy as constitutive of the good life, various theorists have demonstrated how neoliberalism relies heavily on state power and regulatory institutions like the IMF to protect property rights, set monetary policy in times of crisis, and develop new markets.[7]

One of the first experiments in applying the neoliberal model, for example, was staged in Chile in 1973 with the installation of the Pinochet regime, which was achieved by way of a violent military coup, covertly facilitated by the U.S. government. In his memoirs, Richard Nixon admits to having directed the CIA to "make the Chilean economy scream" in hopes of preventing the nationalization of the U.S.-owned copper companies in the region as well as other elements of Allende's socialist programme, including land redistribution. The Chilean economy was beset by hyperinflation at the time, as was much of the region, and CIA plots to instigate strikes in the trucking industry only further exacerbated the situation.[8] Once installed, Pinochet followed the programme of "the Chicago boys" (Chilean economists at the University of Chicago) and implemented a series of free market reforms: the economy was opened to foreign investment, state-owned enterprises sold to private companies, social welfare programmes abolished, and property and capital gains taxes cut. Directly against the neoliberal claim for minimal state involvement in economic affairs, the Chilean state imposed neoliberal reforms with brutal force. State repression against labour unions and left wing social movements established Pinochet as one of history's most brutal dictators.[9]

In other parts of the world, neoliberalism gained strength in the late 1970s and early 1980s by an entirely different set of methods, yet still by the heavy hand of state power. In Great Britain, Thatcher's electoral success, secured by the 1978 "winter of discontent", resulted in a veritable reign of terror against social welfare programmes and trade unions.[10] Her dedication to neoliberal reform was accompanied by an ideological programme, largely influenced by Popper and von Hayek, that involved dramatic appeals to the virtues of individual freedom - "there is no such thing as society, only individual men and women...and families". She rallied against unions by inviting foreign investment and competition, which resulted in the transfer of domestic industries, like automobile manufacturing, shipbuilding, and steel, into foreign hands. She also cut deals with foreign and domestic entrepreneurs to sell off state-owned industries, including airlines, telecommunications, electricity, transportation, and energy services. Much of the country's public housing was sold at low prices, feeding into the middleclass dream of owning a home, but during her ministry, unemployment rose to 10 per cent and trade unions were nearly wiped out.[11]

The same year that Thatcher was voted into office, Paul Volker became head of the U.S. Federal Reserve. Volker crusaded against inflation by undoing fiscal policy, which resulted in a surge in unemployment and interest rates that crippled debtor countries, especially those in Latin America. Volker remained in his post during the Reagan years and was one of the main authors of the administration's massive overhaul to the economy under the mantra of "Reaganomics". Reagonomics involved fighting inflation by way of fiscal austerity, corporate tax breaks, and deregulation, which involved removing price controls on energy, telephone, transportation services, and others. Labour took major hits during Reagan's presidency, including the landmark firing of 11,000 federal air traffic controllers. Low taxation encouraged investment and the development of new financial markets allowed many companies to move production to right-to-work states in the south or overseas to enjoy low labour costs—all of which severely disabled labour union activity in the United States, perhaps permanently. Reaganomics was abetted by an ideology that lauded the benefits of flexible work arrangements against the bureaucracy of labour unions, and associated unemployment with lack of ambition and personal responsibility. According to Reagan, the economic ills of the 1970s could be cured through entrepreneurial activity, a rollback of government involvement in economic affairs, and tax breaks at the top of the income scale, along with other corporate incentives. Wealth would simply "trickle down" to the masses. But it didn't: the Reagan era saw dramatic increases in poverty rates, income inequality, and homelessness[12] and the Savings and Loan crisis, a by-product of deregulation, cost the U.S. an estimated $160 billion.

In addition to solidifying the neoliberal paradigm on both sides of the Atlantic, the Reagan and Thatcher years brought about significant changes in the working of the World Bank and IMF. During this period, the World Bank moved beyond small-scale lending and went into the business of making structural adjustment loans, which often required strict austerity measures and market liberalization. The economic reforms initially conceived at Bretton Woods reflected a Keynesian approach that emphasized the role of the state in creating jobs and stabilizing markets, but in the 1980s this tendency was replaced by a free market approach to development known as the "Washington Consensus", which referred to the "consensus" among the IMF, World Bank, and U.S. Treasury over issues related to economic development and crisis management. More specifically, it signified their consensus in implementing the spread of neoliberal practices around the world, including privatization of public services and industries on a massive scale, lowering trade barriers for foreign investment and competition, deregulating markets, and imposing extreme fiscal austerity.[13]

The third major international financial institution—the World Trade Organization - was initially conceived in Bretton Woods, but was not inaugurated until January 1, 1995. It proceeds through rounds of trade negotiations among member countries and enforces those agreements, operating in close cooperation with the IMF and World Bank.[14] The North Atlantic Free Trade Agreement (NAFTA), for example, was prefigured by privatization and fiscal austerity efforts imposed by the World Bank in the 1980s as part of the Bank's first structural adjustment lending programme. Negotiated during Mexico's De la Madrid presidency, the terms crippled the nation and resulted in a surge of crime and severe lack of government spending on basics such as trash removal, health care, water, and transportation. In the 1990s under Salinas, Mexico was further privatized and public sector industries were sold off to foreign investors, including agriculture, which was a protected domain for the nation's peasant population. The wave of privatization starved the peasant population, but Mexican entrepreneurs made millions, if not billions, from the programme.[15] Oxfam International reported that in the seven years that followed the signing of NAFTA, foreign ownership of the banking system increased to 85 per cent while lending to Mexican businesses dropped from 10 per cent of the GDP to 0.3 per cent, severely affecting small businesses and rendering Mexico vulnerable to capital flight, as evinced by the "tequila crisis" in 1995, which spread to other parts of Latin America and the rest of the developing world.[16]

Trade liberalization under the auspices of the WTO and other Free Trade Agreements (FTAs) has negatively affected domestic industry in many parts of the world, especially agriculture in developing countries. Trade protections, such as high tariffs and import quotas that helped keep small producers competitive in local markets, were lost after the signing of the Agreement on Agriculture (AOA) in 1995, which forced open agriculture markets in these countries by banning quotas and lowering tariffs. Developed countries' agriculture markets were heavily subsidized, which lowered market prices and rendered developing countries' agriculture noncompetitive. These lack of protections essentially destroyed local production and wrecked havoc on social life in these regions. For example, in India, where the cotton industry has been plagued by low priced (subsidized) cotton imports and the high costs associated with Monsanto's monopoly on seeds (which self-destruct so they must be re-bought on an annual basis), the situation precipitated a wave of farmer suicides numbering in tens of thousands.[17]

In addition to trade liberalization, neoliberalism has been marked by dramatically increased activity in the financial sector, even among production-oriented companies. Lucrative financial services - insurance, credit, currency speculation - can make up for losses in production, and in the 1980s, finance was freed from the encumbrances of government regulation, which provided new opportunities for investment and enabled a freer flow of money around the globe. The results were staggering: "The total daily turnover of financial transactions in international markets, which stood at $2.3 billion in 1983, had risen to $130 billion by 2001."[18] Large fortunes have been made in the financial sector, especially through hedge funds and futures, but with speculation and risk as its mainstay, the rise also introduced a high level of volatility into the global economy as well as unprecedented opportunities for fraud.

In Argentina, for example, the domestic banking industry was dominated by foreign banks, a trend introduced during the presidency of Carlos Menem. In addition to lowering trade barriers and privatizing state-owned enterprises, Menem pegged the Argentine peso to the U.S. dollar as a way to control inflation and secure foreign investment. As in Mexico and elsewhere, unemployment in the country rose precipitously as did all measures of social inequality, but foreign investment continued to flow into the country at an average annual rate of 8 per cent from the middle of 1990 to 1994. In December 1994, however, the Mexican peso was devalued significantly as a result of the U.S. Federal Reserve's increase in interest rates under Volker, which set off alarm bells for investors around the world, especially those with stakes in Latin America. The Argentine banking system lost 18 per cent of its deposits, but maintained the peg to the U.S. dollar in accordance with the IMF's mandate for the country. When the East Asian crisis hit the global economy, foreign investors lost confidence in developing countries in general. As a result, the debt in Argentina doubled between 1994 and 2001 and interest payments soared into the billions. Despite a $6 billion IMF bailout, the banking system lost over 17 per cent of its deposits in 2001. With the country in dire straits, the IMF refused another bailout and the country defaulted on its loans. The government decided to restrict bank withdrawals and, in 2002, the peso was devalued. Savings accounts containing $3,000 or higher were frozen and dollar amounts were treated as pesos, which reduced the amounts of savings to a third of their previous value.[19] Massive social and political unrest ensued, with many pointing to the IMF and United States as instigators of the crisis.[20]

The same year as the collapse of the Argentine economy, another crisis hit the world of finance, this time within U.S. borders. While scandals were nothing new to the corporate world, Enron implicated some of the largest banks and corporations in the world, including Credit Suisse First Boston, Citigroup, Merrill Lynch, and Arthur Anderson, and manufactured an entire energy crisis in the state of California. One of the largest corporate bankruptcies in history, the "Crooked E" highlighted the pitfalls of wild financial speculation, risk, and political corruption endemic to neoliberal economics.

Enron executives were staunch advocates of deregulation and lobbied California politicians and the federal government to deregulate energy in the state. California fought deregulation for fear that it would cede too much power over price control to traders. In 1996, Governor Pete Wilson authorized the deregulation of the electricity utility in his state, but when the bill was implemented, it involved a complex system of rules to protect consumers from price increases. Enron's response to what it perceived as a lame attempt at deregulation was to locate exploitable loopholes. In 2000 and 2001, Enron created fake energy shortages and ran up prices for California utility companies, who, subject to price controls, were paying more for electricity than they could charge customers. Since California's utilities partially depended on the import of electricity from states like Oregon and Washington, a drought in the summer of 2000 reduced the amount of power available. Although CA's power supply was never less than the demand, its reserves were low enough that during peak hours Enron could manipulate supply and demand and force grid managers to buy electricity on the "spot market", which was extremely volatile and expensive. Traders would export energy out of the state of California, increasing demand, then resell it at a higher price back into the state. Or, they would increase perceived demand by staging fake maintenance shutdowns during peak hours. In short, they manipulated the demand for energy by manufacturing scarcity, then raised prices—from $24 to $40 per megawatt hour to $750 per megawatt hour overnight - and booked record profits. The price increases bankrupted local utility companies, and the rolling blackouts left many people, not to mentioned schools, hospitals, and other essential institutions, without electricity.

The debacle in California demonstrates the dangers of deregulation, but also the state's integral role in neoliberalism. Enron made its second largest campaign contribution to Congressman Phil Gramm, a key player in deregulating energy trading in California in 2001. It was also one of the largest contributors to the Presidential campaign of George W. Bush, and former U.S. Attorney General John Ashcroft received $57,499 in campaign cash from the company for his Senate re-election in Missouri in 2000. Texas attorney general John Cornyn received $158,000 of Enron's money in campaign contributions, among many others. Moreover, while Democratic Governor Gray Davis appealed to the federal government to set price controls on energy in the throes of the energy crisis, Enron President Kenneth Lay met with Vice President Dick Cheney and governor-hopeful Arnold Schwarzenegger to lobby for continued deregulation. Amidst significant public outcry, Gray declared a state of emergency and appealed directly to the newly elected president, George W. Bush for assistance and price control. Bush put the issue back to Davis, but when the Democratic Senate imposed price controls in the state, he and Lay effectively shifted the blame on to Davis, which opened the door for Schwarzenegger to assume the role of governor. The energy crisis manufactured by Enron lasted for one year and cost the state $30 billion dollars.[21]

NEOLIBERALISM AND LEGITIMACY

In *A Brief History of Neoliberalism* David Harvey argues that the spread of neoliberalism should be understood, in large part, as a political project aimed toward a restoration of the ruling class that makes use of state power and regulatory institutions like the WTO and IMF, but also by way of ideological measures aimed at producing consent. Wendy Brown traces the system's political history to the advent of liberalism in the 19th century, the political order that replaced class privilege with modern forms of constitutional democracy rooted in "abstract individualism", i.e., a view of the human selfhood as given, rather than constituted in complex social relations.[22] Remembering Popper, liberalism posited the individual as a rational actor, whose humanity was defined and predicated on his ability and freedom to choose. While neoliberalism has maintained a sharp focus on the individual as such, it diverges from liberalism in that it does not consider rational (economic) behaviour as given. As we have seen in the preceding pages, it manufactures institutions, policies, and crises to facilitate and ensure its function. Moreover, while liberalism once involved the protection of private property by states, the neoliberal state of today is controlled and regulated by the market, which deploys it, when necessary, in the form of monetary policy and deregulation, welfare and housing reform, and even war.[23] Brown aptly terms this force "neoliberal political rationality", which first and foremost involves the submission of politics and all other aspects of social life to the logic of the market to considerations of efficiency, utility, and profitability. While not all action can be efficient and calculable, neoliberal political rationality evaluates it in these terms, and as such, has become the basis for decision-making at all levels of society.

In the context of this new relationship, the state does not require legitimation; its success is gauged in terms of its adherence to the standards of the market, which seeks to remake individuals in its own image.[24] Alongside issues of state sovereignty and state-centred political power, Brown looks at the ways in which the neoliberal state forms its subjects. Drawing from Foucault's lectures at the Collège de France, she identifies this relationship as a mode of *governmentality:* "techniques of governing that exceed and express state action and orchestrate the subject's conduct toward him - or herself". She points to neoliberalism's tendency to prefigure individuals as rational, calculating actors whose value is measured by their capacity to self-manage and "provide for their own needs and service their own ambitions".[25] As evinced by developments in U.S. welfare and housing reform in the last decade, which relied heavily on public perceptions of welfare recipients as "lazy, promiscuous, government-dependent baby machines",[26] this model reduces and depoliticizes social life into series of individual pursuits and cost-benefit analyses, rather than toward social responsibility and ideas of the good life as collectively defined.

In reference to western liberal democracies like the United States, Brown laments neoliberalism's foreclosure of what she calls the "interval" between the neoliberal political rationality of capitalism and the ethics of liberal democracy. In liberal democracies, NGOs and civil society organizations legitimate the capitalist system to some degree, but some have served as checks and sources of resistance over issues of social justice and "ethical individualism". She identifies a trend away from the ethical individualism characteristic of liberal democracy, toward a market rationality entirely disembedded from social relations, and as such, without limits in terms of the means it will apply in realizing its goals.

Take, for instance, the case of the Iraq War and the Bush administration more generally. In September 2000, just four months before George W. Bush was installed as president, the

Project for the New American Century released its landmark "Rebuilding America's Defenses for a New Century" report, which overtly detailed U.S. conservatives' blueprint for securing U.S. political and economic hegemony by way of extreme shows and use of force. Since the war in Kosovo, if not before, the American neoliberal state, along with the global network of the Great Powers' national governments and leading institutions of transnational capital, has made use of humanitarian justification to shield itself from the turbulence associated with military dictatorships and the widespread corruption characteristic of its client governments, and as a way to justify IMF and World Bank policies. In their seminal book *Empire*, Hardt and Negri have theorized this relationship in terms of a universal ethics of "peace", which involves deployments of force rationalized on the basis of an order that transcends the interests of individual states, posing itself as the humanitarian protectorate of the species. Humanitarian justification alone, they point out, is not a sufficient basis for the existence and extension of Empire's coercive apparatus, however; Empire's legitimacy also wrests on its ability to apply force *effectively*.[27]

CONTESTING NEOLIBERAL GLOBALIZATION AND STATE SOVEREIGNTY

Despite neoliberalism's extensive reach, by hook or by crook, it has also given birth to new forms of resistance. In the previous decade, a broad variety of social movements and advocacy groups have attempted to contest the authority of the neoliberal paradigm of globalization and its terms of legitimacy through direct confrontation with financial institutions like the IMF, but also by creating new social and cultural institutions and political practices, guided by grass roots democratic principles. While state agents play a role in opposing neoliberalism—in South America, for example—many of today's movements do not locate the state at the centre of their politics nor see it as a source of alternatives. Instead, many of them identify as agents of globalization unbound by national politics, identity and borders. As a result, they are forging political communities based on shared experiences, often oscillating between the local and the global, rather than defining their political involvements according to national interests or understanding their rights in strictly juridical terms.

The Zapatista uprising against NAFTA in January 1994, for example, marked a decisive moment in the development of a global resistance to neoliberalism. Against the backdrop of decades, really centuries, of peasant dislocations, the Mexican government repossessed settlement land in the Lacandon Jungle in the name of bioconservation and, leading up to the signing of NAFTA in 1994, deregulated corn imports and protections on the price of coffee, which tanked the local economy. Shortly after, the Zapatistas—indigenous people of Chiapas—confronted the Mexican government, garnering widespread support among Mexicans as well as the international community.[28] According to Naomi Klein, "the strategic victory of the Zapatistas was to insist that what was going on in Chiapas could not be written off as a narrow 'ethnic' or 'local' struggle—that it was universal. They did this by identifying their enemy not only as the Mexican state but as 'neoliberalism'".[29]

The Zapatistas' broad, "universal" appeal to oppose neoliberalism, ability to rescale an indigenous struggle in global terms, and clever use of the Internet not only spurred *The New York Times* to declare it the world's first "postmodern revolutionary movement", but provided a necessary spark for a linking of anti-neoliberal activism across national borders and local communities. As the following case study indicates, a similar tendency emerged in Vieques, Puerto Rico in which an indigenous struggle was redefined, over the course of several decades, in terms of shared experiences of dislocation that ultimately defied the nationalist framework imposed on it by mainstream Puerto Rican politicians.

THE CASE OF VIEQUES[30]

Vieques is a small island-municipality of Puerto Rico that was occupied by the U.S. Navy for over 60 years. Following the Spanish-American War in 1898 and the acquisition of Puerto Rico, the U.S. government replaced the autonomous government established by the Spaniards with a military administration, disregarding the quest for self-determination by anti-Spanish resistance movements. The military occupation of Puerto Rico, imperialist in tone, aimed to securing military outposts along major trade routes and exploit local resources, rather than building local administrative apparatuses characteristic of colonial states.[31] Unusual in such dependencies, in 1917 Puerto Rican residents were given citizenships rights, a Puerto Rican Bill of Rights, and a representative local government and bicameral legislation, conditioned by U.S. Presidential veto power. While the appointment of governors was initially determined by the U.S. President under the 1900 Foraker Act, a 1947 amendment to the Jones Act provided for the election of governors by universal suffrage, and in 1952, Puerto Rico was established as a Commonwealth.

While this trajectory reinforced popular myths about the U.S. as a "reluctant empire", U.S. government officials revealed their colonialist disposition in racist and paternalist terminology that identified Puerto Ricans as "a subject race in need of guardianship, tutelage and democratic mentorship".[32] Moreover, the exploitation of sugar plantations by the Spanish was reinforced under U.S. occupation in a way that largely benefited U.S. sugar refineries, while severely inhibiting Puerto Rican growers' and local coffee planters' ability to compete on the global market. Ownership of the land remained highly concentrated, and in the 1920s, four U.S. corporations controlled half of the island's sugar production, while the number of landless peasants continued to grow. During this period, thousands of Puerto Ricans were recruited to serve in the U.S. army.

In the 1930s, military presence on the island increased substantially as a result of the strategic imperative to protect routes to the Panama Canal. Thousands of acres of land were expropriated to build military installations and in Vieques, the military occupied two-third of the island. With the onset of World War II, large sections of the nearby island of Culebra, and later, Vieques, were used as training grounds and shooting ranges for the U.S. Navy and its NATO allies. While the rhetoric of individual liberties manifest in the granting of limited civil and political citizenship rights for Puerto Ricans, these developments were abstracted from many Puerto Ricans' actual life conditions, and thereby failed to address the unremitting disempowerment, economic expropriation, and racialized subordination they suffered.

Puerto Rico's peculiar position as a "non incorporated territory" of the U.S., and the colonial structures that underpinned these relationships, stimulated the emergence of various strands of nationalist politics, split between *independentistas* that argued for Puerto Rican national sovereignty and those that sought full incorporation as a state in the Union. *Independentistas* were marginalized as an electoral force, in part because the creation of Commonwealth status in 1952 addressed the demands of more moderate nationalists, such as the Partido Popular Democrático (PPD), whose leader, Muñoz Marín, became the first elected governor of Puerto Rico in 1948. It marked an important turning point in Puerto Rican politics because it helped make nationalist movements part of the local political establishment, despite the rise of the pro-statehood Partido Nuevo Progresista (PNP) in the late 1960s and the marginalization of the Partido Independentista Puertorriqueño (PIP).

During this period, the U.S. supported the moderates through economic development programs that helped "contain" communism after the Cuban Revolution of 1959, presented as integral to the promotion of democratic ideals and as justification for continued military presence. "Operation Bootstrap" involved massive investment in infrastructure and capital intensive manufacturing for which Puerto Rico became a laboratory for export-oriented industrialization. At the same time, the formation of a local working class out of landless workers, which could have become a source for radical politics, was prevented by the massive migration of Puerto Ricans to work as cheap labour in urban centres in the U.S. or fight in U.S. wars in Korea and Vietnam. The outflow of more than 600,000 Puerto Ricans between 1940 and 1960, mainly low-skilled, low-wage rural labour, meant that Puerto Rico's class composition was cleared of its proletarian elements.

The experience of the Puerto Rican diaspora in the U.S. enabled a redefinition of national identities and new forms of cultural nationalism to withstand the harsh social and economic conditions of the ghettos. Ideas of Puerto Ricanness that were part of the ideological baggage of most of the elites now governing the islands, personified in the pro-Commonwealth position of defending the authenticity of Puerto Rican culture, became the target of substantial disillusionment. A new Puerto Rican nationalism emerged as a result, characterized not so much by the idea of "national liberation" as witnessed in anti-colonial struggles in the "developing" world, but rather, by the construction of a transnational Puerto Rican identity that included the experience of Puerto Ricanness in the U.S.[33]

Nowhere else in Puerto Rico have the colonial features of economic exploitation been more apparent than in Vieques. The island has been historically dependent on sugarcane production, and patterns of land ownership have left most peasants in conditions of extreme poverty. In the decade preceding the Navy's takeover in 1940, 95 per cent of the rural population was landless and two sugar corporations controlled 71 per cent of the land.[34] The Vieques municipality has always been among the poorest in Puerto Rico, and in 1935, it had the highest male unemployment rate in the territory. Migration to St. Croix, whose economy was also based on sugarcane, rapidly became a major source of income for Vieques residents to the extent that the island's complete depopulation was considered a realistic prospect by the end of the 1930s.

During the 1930s, relations of production on the land were still characterized by the *agrego* system. The *agregados* were landless peasants who lived on the sugar plantations exchanging diverse forms of labour for limited use of the land, without property rights. Initially defined as crop-sharing or labour-sharing agreements, *agrego* relations came to be increasingly mediated by a monetary wage, and the *agregados* became a rural working class whose residence on the land depended entirely on the landowner's will. Despite the precarious nature of this relationship, *agregados* were attached to the land by way of subsistence activities, such as fishing and the gathering of food crops and wood, in addition to cultivating their own small plots. To further complicate the situation, plantation owners often imported *jornalero* migrants as seasonal workers from the Puerto Rican mainland.

In 1942, the Puerto Rican legislature gave two-third of the island to the U.S. Navy to be used as facilities for its fleet. A large portion of the population of Vieques was relocated to a narrow, barren strip of land in the centre of the island, without ownership titles. Military occupation and the associated expropriations accelerated the decline of the sugar-based economy, which not only deepened Viequenses' impoverished conditions, but dealt a fatal blow to *agrego* sustenance relations. Economic development programmes on the mainland of Puerto Rico bypassed Vieques, which was also politically marginalized in Puerto Rican politics, at least for the time being.

The Navy's arrival to Vieques was part of a larger plan to establish a military complex in Puerto Rico that connected the main island with the eastern islands of Culebra and Vieques. Once World War II came to a close, the Navy refused to return the expropriated land to its inhabitants, and in 1947, more land was expropriated. In the meantime, the population of Vieques dropped from 10,000 to 7,000, spurring discussion of a mass relocation of all Vieques residents to St. Croix. The social impact of the expropriation was devastating. While landowners received monetary compensation by the acre, *agregados* were handed a miniscule lump sum for their homes and belongings that in no way could compensate for the loss of their subsistence activities. The whole process, in fact, was conducted in repressive and often brutal ways. Evictions could take place at 24-hour notice, homes were bulldozed, and inhabitants forcibly expelled.

The Navy's 1947 strategic plan for Vieques was to use the island as a training installation, fuel depot, and bombing range. Early resistance movements against the military occupation of the island were largely articulated as a defence of the local community and culture. In the 1950s and 1960s, this message was predominantly voiced by figures in the local government, but in the 1970s grass roots mobilization started to grow, especially among Vieques' fishermen communities. Many Viequenses were not opposed to the Navy's presence in the first decades of the occupation. Faced with the century-long economic and social decay of the island, the Navy represented a lesser evil or even a promise of economic development and investment. Events in the nearby island of Culebra, however, played an important role in changing this view. Heavy bombing severely damaged Culebra's island community, and in the 1970s, residents expressed their opposition in overtly anti-Navy, anti-colonial terms. The subsequent decision by the Navy to suspend exercises on Culebra led to intensified bombing on Vieques, thereby aggravating their already desperate plight. In addition, mainstream political parties in Vieques became more antagonistic toward the U.S. military as a result of plans to ease restrictions for air force exercises. More important, Vieques' own fishermen were politicized, which helped transform widespread resentment into community action.

Vieques' fishermen were especially affected by the land expropriations and environmental devastation associated with the bombings, which threatened their economic resources and community life. In the context of intensified military presence, politically moderate fishermen cooperatives became a vehicle for political activism; their direct action tactics were at the centre of resistance both in the 1978 "fishermen's war" and subsequent waves of mobilization. These early efforts at organizing, however, were frustrated by the encroachment of mainstream party politics. While the opposition to the Navy occupation spanned the entire political spectrum, politicians would later turn the issue into a polarized debate about Viequenses' patriotism and allegiance to the United States, a polarization that allowed radical elements to be branded as communist agitators and destroyed the movement. While the fishermen emphasized the cultural and symbolic dimensions of the struggle, rooted in popular outrage over the destruction of forms of life that depended on access to common resources, grand narratives of Puerto Rican nationalism, including the *independentistas*, and U.S. patriotism proved to be disabling and divisive for the Vieques community.

The economic and environmental rehabilitation plan, known as the Fortín Accord, signed in 1983 by the Navy and the Commonwealth government, was hailed as a solution to the island's problems. The Navy's presence was accepted in exchange for its commitment to improve economic conditions, but its subsequent failure to act triggered periodic waves of opposition. The 16 years that followed were characterized by an undercurrent of activism that occasionally erupted in direct confrontations with the Navy. Notable was the 1989 movement for land reappropriation known as "land rescue", which was conducted by the Crusade to Rescue Vieques (CRV). Even though the "land rescue" campaign rapidly devolved into land prospecting, this phase symbolized a new way of organizing based on occupation and resistance against evictions.

In 1993, the Committee to Rescue and Develop Vieques (CPRDV) was formed, whose aim was to build a broad-based movement. The avoidance of direct confrontation tactics by the Committee sheltered it from accusations of anti-Americanism that plagued the CRV. Its birth signaled a new style of political activism that remained detached from broader ideological issues of state sovereignty and was more open to building coalitions and communities at the grass roots level. Moreover, the CPRDV continued the fisherman's tradition of cultural activism and used symbols of past expropriations to build a shared discourse that helped shape the community's sense of abuse and outrage. Together with local cultural institutions, for example, the CPRDV organized an excursion to the sites of the old sugar *centrales*, factories that represented the social structure that existed prior to the Navy's occupation. Moreover, environmental problems emerged in this period as a central concern that linked Vieques to the broad-based environmental movement. During the 60 years of military occupation the residents of Vieques lived down wind from targets that were bombed up to 200 days per year. Weapons used included napalm, Agent Orange, chemical weapons and, since 1999, by admission of the US. government, depleted uranium. Toxic particles and debris contaminated the drinking water, as well as the air and soil. Levels of pollution for carcinogenic substances such as cadmium, arsenic, and lead exceed legal limits by percentages that range between 100 and 200 per cent. In 2003, the Vieques population was showing rates of cancer, scleroderma, lupus, thyroid deficiencies and asthma, far greater than the rest of Puerto Rico, while infant mortality was 55 per cent higher.[35]

On April 19, 1999 during a training session, two bombs went off-course killing David Sanes Rodríguez, a Puerto Rican security guard employed by the Navy. The event caused an uproar on Vieques and the mainland, and was followed by a campaign of civil disobedience in which residents acted as human shields, and encampments where built on the bombing range. The mobilization halted military exercises for more than a year. Meanwhile, the Clinton administration began inquiries into the Navy's presence on the island and the Puerto Rican government adopted a political stance that favoured its withdrawal. Vieques gained unprecedented visibility: in July, 1999, 50,000 people marched at the Roosevelt Roads Naval Station, and in February, 2000, between 85,000 and 150,000 staged the "Peace for Vieques" march in San Juan. In November 2000, Vieques Libre hung a "Free Vieques" banner alongside the Vieques and Puerto Rican flags from the Statue of Liberty in New York City.

The widening of protest also catalyzed one of the most conservative sectors of the Puerto Rican society, the churches. Traditionally enmeshed in party politics, the churches were drawn into the political opposition to the Navy by the outrage following Sanes' death and by the increasing amount of information being made available about the impacts of the bombing on the environmental health of Vieques. Religious leaders began to identify Vieques as a global human rights issue. For example, in 1999—when pro-statehood Governor Rosselló signed an agreement with U.S. President Clinton that authorized the continuation of bombing after a one-year pause in exchange for monetary compensation—church leaders denounced it as immoral and an "abuse of power". Since Rosselló had at one point championed the anti-Navy position, the agreement was viewed by most as a betrayal and indicative of an unbridgeable divide that separated the movement from mainstream nationalist politics in San Juan. At the same time, the churches provided a renewed legitimacy to civil disobedience, in its non-violent variant, among large strata of the civil society.[36]

Perhaps the most significant discontinuity with past waves of resistance was the linkage established between the struggle in Vieques and the Puerto Rican diaspora on the U.S. mainland. The experience of Puerto Ricans in the U.S. has always been shaped by a politics of exclusion that reflects and reinforces the poor living conditions of many Puerto Ricans. Puerto Ricans, especially in New York, have gravitated toward the Democratic Party, but their political identities have largely been shaped by the social and economic problems experienced at the community level. The radical social movements that emerged among later generations of Puerto Ricans in the U.S. during the 1960s blended Puerto Rican *independentista* nationalism with influences from the Black Panthers, and civil rights and anti-war movements. In Vieques, the diaspora continued to reinforce the construction of Puerto Ricanness as a condition of a colonized people, rather than as inhabitants of a nation with a specific territory, thereby exceeding the terms of resistance and representation imposed by traditional party politics.

The fact that the movement in Vieques successfully challenged Navy operations immediately following Sanes' death and forced the U.S. government's hand in negotiating solutions probably contributed to the increasing interest with which Puerto Ricans in the U.S. viewed the struggle in Vieques. Vieques represented a common grievance of all Puerto Ricans that did not fit within the U.S. government's convenient image of them as divided over political allegiances associated with the status question. In fact, the linkage between Vieques and the diaspora acted in much more complex ways. On the one hand, it helped to frame the discourse of resistance in national terms, bringing to the fore the latent Otherness that constituted Puerto Rican relations with the U.S. On the other hand, this nationally framed discourse exceeded the idea of the nation as a territorially bound identity. This element is what ultimately facilitated solidarity between the anti-Navy movement in

Vieques and other anti-militarist movements around the world, such as those in Hawaii, South Korea, and the Netherlands.

CONCLUSION

In April 2003, the U.S. Navy announced its withdrawal from Vieques amidst a generalized political opposition that by then had come to include prominent figures in the broad U.S. left. Episodes like the imprisonment of Al Sharpton for 90 days for civil disobedience, the involvement of prominent Puerto Rican celebrities like Ricky Martin and Rosie Perez, and the multi-million dollar class action lawsuit started by the John A. Eaves law firm on behalf of 55 Vieques cancer patients, added to the embarrassment of the U.S. government and made the presence of the Navy indefensible. The announcement signaled a glowing victory for the anti-military movement, but one that has proven bittersweet: Most of the territory occupied by the Navy was transferred to the U.S. Fish and Wildlife Service, and Viequenses were still denied access to more than half of their land. Moreover, much of the island remains severely contaminated from the bombing, its waters littered with live ordinance, and inhabitants steeped in legal battles over clean up and health-related compensation.

The neoliberal approach to the Navy's legacy in Vieques is a repetition of existing patterns of domination that define life as an abstract entity, whose protection (rights) or expropriation is decided by the powers of the state. As neoliberalism posits individuals as self-managed "autonomous" citizens-consumers, it also annihilates or renders illegitimate forms of life that cannot or will not be converted into its framework. But material life is an articulation of sensuous relations and emotional attachments that ultimately exceed such abstractions and find grounding in struggles over collective life. While the Vieques movement did not ultimately re-acquire the expropriated land, it did successfully contest the political construction of citizenship within the U.S. government's discourse of rights that disempowered Viequenses and stifled radical voices within Puerto Rican politics. The focus on the reappropriation of land and the practice of squatting provided the movement with an alternative citizenship discourse that challenged the state's construction of rights. Even when the struggle was couched in a rights-based discourse, Viequenses' rights were ultimately affirmed through the exercise of collective power and direct action. This new citizenship discourse and practice was linked to a redefinition of the political community away from a territorially bounded nation. Although the imagery of the movement and of solidarity within the diaspora remained somewhat "national" in character, they nonetheless built an open, borderless political community based on a common experience of expropriation, rather than on the myth of the nation.

NOTES

1. Max Weber, Max. "Politics as a Vocation" in *From Max Weber: Essays in Sociology*, edited by H.H. Gerth and C. Wright Mills. (London: Oxford University Press, 1958).
2. Thomas I. Palley, "From Keynesianism to Neoliberalism: Shifting Paradigms in Economies." in *Neoliberalism: A Critical Reader*, edited by Saad-Filho and Johnston, (London: Pluto Press, 2005), p. 20.
3. Thomas I. Palley, "From Keynesianism to Neoliberalism: Shifting Paradigms in Economies." in *Neoliberalism: A Critical Reader*, edited by Saad-Filho and Johnston, (London: Pluto Press, 2005), pp. 20-22. Also see Frances Fox Piven and Richard A. Coward, *Poor People's Movements: Why They Succeed, How They Fail*, (New York: Vintage Books, 1979).
4. David Harvey, *A Brief History of Neoliberalism*, (London: Oxford University Press, 2005).
5. Thomas I. Palley, "From Keynesianism to Neoliberalism: Shifting Paradigms in Economies." in *Neoliberalism: A Critical Reader*, edited by Saad-Filho and Johnston, (London: Pluto Press, 2005), pp. 21-22.
6. Popper's work informed that of more contemporary works, such as George Soros' "Open Society Institute" and Friedman's *Capitalism and Freedom* (1962).
7. Wendy Brown, "Neoliberalism and the End of Liberal Democracy." *Edgework: Critical Essays on Knowledge and Politics*, (New Jersey: Princeton University Press and Oxford, 2005). Also see David Harvey, *A Brief History of Neoliberalism*, (London:

Oxford University Press, 2005) and Bob Jessop, "Liberalism, Neoliberalism, and Urban Governance: A State-Theoretical Perspective." *Antipode*, 34, 2002, pp. 452-472.

8. Monte Reel and J.Y. Smith, "A Chilean Dictator's Dark Legacy." *The Washington Post*. December 11, 2006.
9. Alejandro Colas, "Neoliberalism, Globalization and International Relations" in *Neoliberalism: A Critical Reader*, edited by Saad-Filho and Johnston (London: Pluto Press, 2005).
10. David Harvey, *A Brief History of Neoliberalism*, (London: Oxford University Press, 2005), pp. 57-58. Also see Tim Dowling, "Coming soon - (another) Winter of Discontent?" *The Guardian*. October 4, 2006.
11. David Harvey, *A Brief History of Neoliberalism*, (London: Oxford University Press, 2005). Also see Susan George, "A Short History of Neoliberalism." Paper presented at the Conference on Economic Sovereignty in a Globalizing World, Bangkok. March 24-26, 1999.
12. Jerry Kloby, *Inequality, Power, and Development: Issues in Political Sociology*, (New York: Humanity Books, 2003). Also see William H. DiFazio, *Ordinary Poverty: A Little Food and Cold Storage*, (Philadelphia, Temple University Press, 2006).
13. Thomas I. Pallcy, "From Keynesianism to Neoliberalism: Shifting Paradigms in Economies." in *Neoliberalism: A Critical Reader*, edited by Saad-Filho and Johnston, (London: Pluto Press, 2005), p. 25.
14. Jonaldo Munck, "Neoliberalism and Politics, and the Politics of Neoliberalism" in *Neoliberalism: A Critical Reader*, edited by Saad-Filho and Johnston, (London: Pluto Press, 2005), p. 61.
15. David Harvey, *A Brief History of Neoliberalism*, (London: Oxford University Press, 2005), pp. 101-103.
16. Emily Jones, Oxfam International Report. "Signing Away the Future: How Trade and Investment Agreements between Rich and Poor Countries Undermine Development", March 2007.
17. Shiva, Vandana. *Earth Democracy: Justice, Sustainability and Peace*, (London: Zed Books, 2000). Also see Walden Bello. "The Forum at the Crossroads," Foreign Policy in Focus. www.focusweb.org/the-forum-at-the-crossroads.html?Itemid=1, dated May 9, 2007, (accessed June 2007).
18. David Harvey, *A Brief History of Neoliberalism*, (London: Oxford University Press, 2005), p. 161.
19. David Harvey, *A Brief History of Neoliberalism*, (London: Oxford University Press, 2005).

20. *The New York Times* referred to the neoliberal paradigm of development in Argentina as "a failed economic experiment" citing the United States and IMF as largely responsible for the crash. See Larry Rohter, "Consequences for the United States in Argentina's Collapse". *New York Times*, December 25, 2001.
21. Bethany McLean and Peter Elkind, *Smartest Guys in the Room: The Amazing Rise and Scandalous Fall of Enron*, (New York: The Penguin Group, 2003).
22. Wendy Brown and Janet Halley, *Left Legalism, Left Critique*, (Durham: Duke University Press, 2002).
23. Wendy Brown, "Neoliberalism and the End of Liberal Democracy." *Edgework: Critical Essays on Knowledge and Politics*, (New Jersey: Princeton University Press and Oxford, 2005). Also see David Harvey, *A Brief History of Neoliberalism*, (London: Oxford University Press, 2005).
24. Wendy Brown, "Neoliberalism and the End of Liberal Democracy." *Edgework: Critical Essays on Knowledge and Politics*, (New Jersey: Princeton University Press and Oxford, 2005). Also see Ronaldo Munck, "Neoliberalism and Politics, and the Politics of Neoliberalism" in *Neoliberalism: A Critical Reader*, edited by Saad-Filho and Johnston, (London: Pluto Press, 2005), p. 61.
25. Wendy Brown, "Neoliberalism and the End of Liberal Democracy." *Edgework: Critical Essays on Knowledge and Politics*, (New Jersey: Princeton University Press and Oxford, 2005), pp. 42-44.
26. See Barbara Ehrenreich. 2004. "The New Cosby Kids", *The New York Times*, July 8, 2004.
27. Michael Hardt and Antonio Negri, *Empire*, (Boston: Harvard University Press, 1999).
28. Manuel Castells. *The Information Age: Economy, Society and Culture, Volume II: The Power of Identity* (Oxford: Blackwell Publishing), pp. 72-81.
29. Naomi Klein, "Farewell to the End of History: "Organization and Vision in Anti-Corporate Movements." *A World of Contradictions*. Panich, Leo and Leys, Colin (eds.) (New York: Monthly Review Press, 2002).
30. A study of the Vieques movement was conducted with Franco Barchiesi in 2003 and published in Italian in "Vieques O Muerte: Transnational Movement and the Politics of Diaspora," *DeriveApprodi*, no copyright.
31. H. Magdoff, *Imperialism without Colonies*. (New York: Monthly Review Press, 2003).

32. A. Barreto, *Vieques, the Navy and Puerto Rican Politics* (Gainesville: University Press of Florida, 2002), p. 14.
33. Negron-Muntaner and Grosfoguel, (eds). *Puerto Rican Jam: Rethinking Colonialism and Nationalism*, (Minneapolis: University of Minnesota Press, 1997).
34. K. McCaffrey, *Military Power and Popular Protest: The U.S. Navy in Vieques, Puerto Rico*, (New Brunswick, NJ: Rutgers University Press, 2002).
35. Dominicans for Justice and Peace et al. *Questions of Human Rights Violations in Vieques*, 59th Session of the UN Commission for Human Rights, Geneva, March 17 – April 24, 2003.
36. A. Barreto. *Vieques, the Navy and Puerto Rican Politics.* (Gainesville: University Press of Florida).

8

The Dialectic of Labour and Capital in Globalization

How the Historical Formation of the American Labour Movement Influenced the Course of Globalization

Michael Roberts

INTRODUCTION

Talk of globalization invariably turns to the issue of the mobility of capital and the dramatic rise of corporate power relative to the nation state. Critics of globalization, like Ralph Nader point to institutions like the World Trade Organization (WTO) – an international governing body not beholden to those who bear the brunt of its policies because the policy makers are not elected – as evidence that corporate interests are increasingly at odds with the democratic polity worldwide.[1] The mobility of capital and corporate dominance has both reduced the role of the nation state to primarily policing functions – by robbing the state of revenue for social programmes through massive tax cuts for the wealthy - and worse, cast doubt on the very possibility of democracy in the new world order. And yet, some critics of globalization insist on returning to the nation state to reverse the process of the outsourcing of jobs, draconian cuts to spending on social programmes like housing, job training, education and health care and the demise of democracy more generally. There seems to be a call for a return to the "golden years" of Keynesian economic policy at the federal level of government, which includes, as a crucial component, a "corporatist" labour relations strategy that promotes a "partnership" between labour and capital, where both sides are obligated to promote the well being of the whole by way of grounding "common" interests in a social compact regulated and enforced by the state.[2] In short, "bring back the social compact!" or "bring back the New Deal!" seems to be the rallying cry of many critics of globalization.[3]

We have come a long way since the 1960s when dissent meant a *critique* of the Keynesian welfare state. Now dissenters of federal policies and critics of globalization defend that which they used to criticize. Even if the irony is not lost on the critics of globalization that it was a Democrat who demolished the American welfare state when Bill Clinton signed the welfare "reform" act in 1996, critics today still call for a return of the welfare state they once used to criticize. For example, Harold Meyerson – a student of former Secretary of Labour, Robert Reich - argued in a recent editorial in the *Washington Post* that globalization has led to a "shattering" of the American identity, which for him is the result of the undoing of the New Deal. "The big story here," writes Meyerson, "is the shattering of America's sense of a common identity in a time when the economy no longer promotes the general welfare. The world the New Deal built has been destroyed, and we are, as we were before the New Deal, two nations."[4] Perhaps, but the question is: what would it mean to bring back the New Deal, and is that the best response we can think of for the problems we face in the context of globalization? And what of all the criticism of the New Deal and the welfare state that took place in previous decades? Are they no longer relevant?

Part of the problem with standard critiques of globalization is that the power of corporations and the ease with which capital is able to move around the globe has been somewhat exaggerated by critics of globalization, because there has been too much focus on the *effects* or consequences of globalization – destruction of the environment, the race to the bottom that defines the insatiable corporate appetite for cheaper and cheaper labour and zero workplace or environmental regulations, the growth of worldwide abject poverty, the loss of good paying jobs in the so-called "first" world, etc. - and less on the conditions that have made globalization of business since the Second World War possible in the first place.[5] Corporate power is too often taken as *given* when we examine the effects of globalization, which leaves a blind spot concerning its conditions of possibility. It is true that many scholars have examined how the decline of the New Deal has contributed to the acceleration and shape of globalization, but there has been less analysis of how corporate strategies in globalization have been shaped by the particular historical formation of the U.S. labour movement. In the worst case, this gap in theoretical perspective can lead to the reification of corporate power inhibiting our capacity to imagine all the possible alternatives to the social formation of capitalism we face today.

It must first be understood that, historically, the mobility of capital since the early 1970s has been a *response* by capital to a *particular* historical formation of the American labour movement. Perspectives that make a fetish of corporate power, however, miss this crucial point, because it is assumed a priori that capital is always in the driver's seat and that labour is always already the dependent variable in any particular social formation under capitalism. On the contrary, a close study of labour history reveals that capital does not always have the upper hand in the class struggle.[6] Ironically, in the U.S. case, it was the world view and practices of certain labour leaders that situated labour as a dependent variable, not capital. In the American labour movement, it was the "corporatist" labour leaders who situated labour as a dependent variable after the formation of the New Deal. Indeed, the New Deal institutionalized labour as a dependent variable in the Keynesian social formation that some critics call "late" capitalism.

"Corporatism" here does not refer to a business organization – corporation – but to a labour movement ideology that emphasizes a cooperative strategy between capital and labour as well as the import role of a Keynesian welfare/warfare state that promotes "full employment" through deficit spending. In the corporatist strategy the labour movement depends upon the federal government to spend money and build up the public sector. In "corporatism", workers are defined not as a social class, but as "producers" and they share this identity with management. Society in a corporatist framework is viewed as a composition of a variety of economic groups that each performs a vital function for the system as a whole.[7] The defining characteristic of the corporate ideology is that workers and management have an equal stake in steady, predictable and efficient production.

The triumph of corporate ideology in the American labour movement was, in the 1930s, a radical change in direction for the labour movement. The legacy of corporatism in the American labour movement has had a significant impact on the development of globalization, in so far as this tradition in American labour has contributed to the ease with which American corporations have been able to both destroy the manufacturing infrastructure of the United States, and shred the social fabric. Perhaps most troubling is that the liberal left today – including influential public intellectuals like Robert Reich - advocates for policies that ironically continue to increase the power of global capital rather than contain or challenge it. I argue below that corporatism was and is a weakness in the American labour movement that capital has been able to exploit and continues to exploit today.

Critics of globalization do point to the need for a contemporary global labour movement; rightly so, but it remains mostly unknown that not only was there once a global labour movement - launched by the shorter hours movement with the institutionalization of the international labour holiday "May Day" at the end of the 19th century - but that the social democratic left, together with a particular tradition *within* the labour movement conspired to destroy that movement.[8] Walter Reuther, the leader of the UAW, and perhaps the most influential labour leader in American 20th century history, opposed the shorter hours movement, and stamped it out both within his own union, but also in the labour movement as a whole, which after the Second World War became a "corporatist" movement as well as an appendage of the Democratic party and the Keynesian welfare/warfare state. Reuther's corporatist vision was in competition with an older tradition in the labour movement, sometimes referred to as syndicalism.

The syndicalist tradition of the American labour movement , which focused on controlling the supply of labour to capital via shorter working hours understood that labour markets were *created* by the changing relations between labour and capital and that leverage over capital was made possible by creating a labour market where labor is always in short supply. Critics of globalization are correct to deconstruct the metaphysics of the "free" market discourse that apologists of globalization rely upon to perpetuate the myth of the inevitability and desirability of globalization, by revealing the fiction of so-called "free" markets. Markets do not exist a priori or in themselves. Markets are created by powerful institutional actors.[9] Capital always intervenes in the creation and manipulation of markets when it is to the advantage of capital to do so, and if and when the state or labour unions intervene to shape and create a market situation that benefits labor, then capital cries foul play.[10]

The syndicalist tradition in the labour movement understood this dynamic quite clearly. Indeed, the social construction of the labour market was framed as the *goal* of the labour movement through the implementation of shorter hours of work. We need to reconsider what we lost when syndicalism was marginalized in the American labour movement, and when shorter hours of work dropped out of the American political discourse. In short, it is important to supplement philosophical deconstructions of the bourgeois metaphysics embedded in the discourse of "free" markets with an historical understanding of the *praxis* of the syndicalist labour movement that once flourished in the United States and worldwide prior to the New Deal.[11]

Globalization of American business, in the specific form that it has come to be – in terms of outsourcing of jobs, automation and the over-supply of labour worldwide - is as much the result of the institutional history of the American labour union bureaucracy and the policies of the liberal/left as it is the corporate quest for profit based upon growing avarice. Another way to say this is that capital's incessant drive toward accumulation at any cost and the relentless quest for surplus labour is the necessary but not sufficient condition for the specific formation of globalization that we have today. It can be taken for granted that capital must accumulate and must develop strategies for creating surplus labour, but what cannot be taken for granted is the various *obstacles* to capital accumulation that are always empirical questions for history. It is the particular *relationship* between labour and capital and the specific form of struggle between these two groups that gives rise to the particular shape of a social formation under capitalism. We must analyze both sides of this relationship to get an adequate understanding of globalization today. Things could have been much different; the history of globalization is a contingent determinate, rather than necessary or inevitable history.

This is an important point to make, because too often "critics" of globalization ignore this point due to a reification of corporate power. That leaves us with very limited ways for developing an adequate response to the problem of globalization. Serious mistakes were made by the American labour movement and the social democratic left, but we have yet to learn from them, which is why public intellectuals like Meyerson are calling for a rather uncritical return of the New Deal. The lack of historical understanding of the particular historical formation of the American labour movement contributes to misdirected policy suggestions today. Past mistakes have made it easier for corporate interests to shape the global economy to suit their desires. In short, the legacy of American labour union practices since the New Deal together with liberal/left government policy has allowed global businesses to succeed without really trying. The following pages offer a preliminary way to look at the globalization question without taking corporate power a priori as well as a way to question the received wisdom of bringing back the New Deal in the United States.

SYNDICALISM VERSUS CORPORATISM IN AMERICAN LABOUR HISTORY

The American labour movement has developed historically along two different paths, which have at times overlapped in the same institution. The two different strategic paths are: the syndicalist direction on the one hand, and a corporatist direction on the other hand. Syndicalism and corporatism are based upon different principles, but historically each framework for action has developed under unique historical conditions in the U.S. that have shaped the two traditions in particular ways. Both of these traditions in the labour movement have had a direct impact on how globalization of American corporate power has taken shape since World War II. The important historical eras in which these traditions took shape are – for syndicalism - the era between the Civil War and the New Deal, and – for corporatism - the years roughly between the First World War and the 1950s. These two traditions – in different ways - have had an impact on how American business has gone global.

In various historical studies of the American labour movement, scholars have indicated that the U.S. labour movement has been bifurcated between the so-called "pure and simple" or "business unionism" of the American Federation of Labor (AFL) under Samuel Gompers and "social unionism" or "social movement" unionism linked to the Congress of Industrial Organizations (CIO) and to Sidney Hillman in particular, who was the leader of the textile workers during the 1920s and 1930s. The AFL version of unionism has, by and large, been coded as "conservative" and the version of Hillman's unionism has been coded as more "progressive". The AFL has been criticized, rightly so, for failing to make unionism a broad social movement including all workers. Instead, the AFL had a very insular view, focusing only on the well being of their members, rather than all workers. I do not disagree with this criticism, but the history of the American labour movement is more complicated than this view that splits the labour movement into conservative and progressive traditions.

Rather than appropriate that framework, I find it more useful to understand the competing traditions of the American labour movement in terms of syndicalism and corporatism. The syndicalist tradition was more prominent among the craft unions of skilled workers that constituted the membership of the AFL and the "unskilled" casual labourers of the International Workers of the World (IWW, also known as the "wobblies") of the period – roughly speaking - between the end of the 19th century and the New Deal. The IWW had a relatively brief influence on labour organizing in the first decades of the 20th century, eventually losing out to the AFL, which is an older institution dating back to 1886.[12] Still, the IWW was a classic syndicalist organization, and for that reason deserves attention. There were important differences between the IWW and the AFL, but they shared the core principles of syndicalism.

Syndicalism as a labour union *praxis* involves two components: first, syndicalism understands the focus of labour union action to be the shop floor. The terrain upon which labour meets capital and struggles with capital is within the context of the labour process. Syndicalism does not seek access to the state to mediate the conflict between labour and capital. Withdrawal from the labour process by means of the strike is the main mechanism of leverage over capital and the principal tactic relied upon in syndicalist labour strategies. Second, syndicalism understands that in conjunction with a campaign of struggle over the conditions that structure the labour process - including working conditions, hours of work and wages - labour must maintain a short supply of itself through the fight for shorter hours of work. A strike can only be successful as long as workers who go on strike cannot be replaced by scabs. Shorter hours make up the strategic framework that situates the practice of strikes. Furthermore, the struggle with capital is an ideological one as much as a "material" one, in so far as labour leaders must also struggle over the discourse of political economy.

The syndicalists had their own organic intellectuals that provided both principles for action as well as reflection upon the validity of those principles.[13] The ideological struggle involved the justification for the existence of unions in the first place, which involved a struggle over the language of political economy. Labour leaders in the AFL during the late 19th century intervened in the development of economic theory by making a case that Adam Smith himself – the prophet of free market capitalism – defended the existence of unions because rising wages across the board is crucial for economic growth.[14] The discursive struggle also involved a legitimation of strategies of intervention in and the shaping of labour markets in the name of more leisure time. Thus, the ideological struggle was both a means to develop a sound strategy for labour's engagement with capital, and a prescription for the "good" society. Shorter hours of work are both a means and an end. More leisure time is an end-in-itself, and the way to achieve it is through reducing the hours of work to get leverage over capital. These were the core principles of syndicalism. Much of the 19th-century history of labour relations in both the U.S. and the U.K. was animated by the struggle for shorter hours of work, from the 12-hour day, which was the norm at the beginning of the 19th, century to the 8—hour day, which was becoming the norm by the close of the century. The middle chapters of *Capital: Volume 1*, by Marx are an extended theoretical analysis of the implications of this movement for the development of capitalism. Marx argues that capitalism took its particular form in response to this decades-long movement for shorter hours in both the United States and the United Kingdom. The fight for shorter hours was understood by Marx as the engine that drives technological development and economic growth. This was also the understanding of labour movement intellectuals like George McNeil, who published his classic treatise on the subject, *The Labor Movement : The Problem of Today* in 1888. As I will discuss below, the New Deal and corporatist labour leaders crushed the shorter hours movement and marginalized the discourse.

Although the IWW and the AFL shared these principles, the AFL took a much more conservative, and ultimately unsustainable path because the AFL developed a syndicalism based upon exclusion of workers from certain labour markets. The IWW was perhaps more "radical" than the AFL and they were a prime example of a labour union that was based upon syndicalist principles that fostered inclusion.[15] Unlike the AFL, which fought for labour contracts, they refused labour contracts because they argued that contracts took away the power of the strike, and they understood that markets are spaces of interventions not entities that exist a priori outside of and independent of actors. Syndicalism per se does not guarantee "success", because the core principles were given particular shape by particular historical conditions, which included "choices" made by labour leaders that provoked a particular response by capital.

Another important difference between the AFL and the IWW, however, was that not only did AFL unions fight to secure labour contracts with their employers, whereas the IWW did not, but also the AFL's strategy to reduce the supply of labour was based upon the *exclusion* of the Other from the labour market altogether. To reduce the supply of labour, the AFL fought to restrict membership within the federation of unions it governed – which meant the exclusion of women, ethnic minorities like the Irish and Southern Europeans as well as blacks from apprenticeship programmes in the trades where their unions were active. The AFL also fought for a federal policy of keeping immigrants out of the U.S. In short, one way to reduce the supply of labour is to *remove* bodies from the labour "market". This kind of syndicalism is unique to the AFL, and it can be thought of as an exclusionary syndicalism. The exclusion of the Other by the AFL resulted in a peculiarly conservative historical formation of syndicalism in the U.S., because it was grounded in xenophobia and nationalism.

Removing bodies from the labour market is ultimately unsustainable, however, and the conservative, exclusionist version of syndicalism practised by the AFL failed because capital responded to this historical formation of the labour movement by moving the jobs to the workers. It is in the interests of capital to increase the supply of labour, and if capital cannot bring more workers into the domestic labour market, then capital either brings the jobs to workers outside of the U.S. or deploys labour-saving machinery that both makes existing workers more "productive" and increases the labour supply within the U.S.[16] Of course, concomitant with the shipping of jobs overseas, capital also moves jobs to non-union locations *within* the U.S. The exclusionist version of syndicalism practised by the AFL worked only as long as the AFL could influence the government to restrict immigration, the best example being the Chinese Exclusion Act of 1882 and the congressional legislation that restricted the flow of Eastern and Southern immigrants after 1920.[17] The AFL was not alone among workers' organizations that fought to keep foreign workers out of the U.S. The Socialist Party in the U.S. also fought to keep immigrants out. Morris Hillquist, one of the leaders of the Socialist Party argued in 1917 that "the Socialist Party of the U.S. favors all legislative measures tending to prevent the immigration of strike breakers... and the mass importation of workers from foreign countries brought about by the employing classes for the purpose of weakening the organization of American labor and lowering the standard of life of American workers".[18]

Thus, the main strategy for American exclusionary syndicalism during the late 19th and early 20th century was to restrict the global mobility of labour. As I will argue below, capital's response to the restriction on the global mobility of labour was to make capital more globally mobile. For the capitalist, if you can't bring the worker to the job, then bring the job to the worker. If capital faced obstacles in its efforts to flood the U.S. with surplus workers, then the response of capital has been to take the jobs to the surplus population of workers outside the U.S., on the one hand, and to automate jobs within the U.S. out of existence altogether on the other hand. Both strategies create, manipulate and exploit the surplus population of labour. The version of syndicalism based upon exclusion of the Other ultimately failed for these reasons. The labour unions did not only fail their own members, of course. Rather, they failed workers worldwide.

The AFL also advocated shorter hours, but because they focused on a strategy for keeping bodies out of the labour market, and devoted more resources to fighting for exclusion than organizing campaigns for shorter hours, they helped to ensure their own demise. The chickens have come home to roost for conservative labour leaders in the exclusionary syndicalist movement. Only an international movement for shorter hours of work could be a sustainable movement in the face of a growing global surplus of labour because it gives everyone a job who needs one and higher wages and more leisure time for all workers. Historically, shorter hours have been extremely popular with workers and it is an inherently inclusive strategy.[19]

Gomper's unique exclusionist syndicalism ironically involved the state when it came to keeping the Other out of the American labour market, and this diversion led the AFL away from the historic struggle for shorter hours that defined the 19th-century labour movement.[20] The question of exclusion worked hand-in-hand with the creation of a national identity for American union workers. To be an American union worker meant that you were not black, not a woman, not a Southern European, not an Asian, and on down the line. Exclusion was, in part, legitimated by the American labour movement in terms of race and ethnic identity.[21] Of course, racism cannot be reduced to the labour question. The problem of race, as DuBois made clear early in the 20th century, was largely independent of the labour question, although DuBois himself insisted that the failure of Reconstruction in the U.S. cannot be understood without a consideration of the labour question.[22] A kind of syndicalist strategy based upon shorter hours of work is more sustainable than an exclusionist strategy of keeping people out, because not only is it nearly impossible to keep out people who need jobs, but also because capital can make alliances with the excluded groups *against* labour when labour seeks to exclude the Other. We see that today with the Bush Administration's push for "guest worker" programme for "illegal" immigrants in the U.S.

The virtual abandonment of the struggle for shorter hours and its replacement by lobbying the state for restrictions on immigrant labour was a very serious mistake in strategic terms, but it also begs the question of the race problem in the labour movement. American union workers have developed a unique identity for themselves that was constructed by race and nation and this identity has seriously crippled the effectiveness of the movement.[23] These particular historical conditions – exclusionist syndicalism – exposed a very serious weakness present in the labour movement, and capital *exploited* this weakness by not only fostering racial divisions among American workers by using racial and ethnic "minority" strike breakers on a frequent basis before the New Deal, but also capital moved jobs to the excluded Others to break the back of American labour. Exclusionist syndicalism existed in the AFL up until the 1960s when the federal government forced the AFL to integrate its racially segregated locals after passage of the Civil Rights Act of 1964. If the AFL was able to restrict the mobility of labour in the late 19th and early 20th century, corporate power responded to the relative immobility of labour with the increasing mobility of capital. This response by capital was made possible, in part because the American labour movement gave up its struggle for shorter hours in the 1930s.[24]

The IWW on the other hand, had an *inclusive* strategy of syndicalism that emphasized the importance of including the Other. They actively organized blacks and other racial and ethnic minority groups, because they realized that employers frequently used blacks and other racial and ethnic groups as strikebreakers to both break particular labor unions they were struggling against and to create racial tension among workers in general as a means to divide and weaken the labour movement as a whole.[25] But including more people in the labour process and into your union requires a strategy of shorter hours, otherwise no leverage over capital is possible since excess workers can be used as strike breakers. Shorter hours was understood by the syndicalists of the IWW as the mechanism to overcome this problem. In other words, if more people are brought into the labour process and the labour market, then the only way to reduce the supply of labour in the "market" is for each individual to withdraw the amount of time they give to work.

At the turn of the century, it was still uncertain which way the labour movement would go: either toward an exclusionist syndicalism, or toward an inclusionist syndicalism based on shorter hours. Both of these paths were present during the years between the Civil War and the New Deal. Unfortunately, the exclusionist position, which manifested in anti-Immigrant legislation became dominant in the AFL, and explains, in part how globalization took shape after WWII. The IWW version of "inclusionist" syndicalism was not exclusively the dominion of the wobblies, because there were AFL members and leaders who continued to push for shorter hours, but the AFL was seriously crippled by racism and nationalism. The AFL could never sustain a successful shorter hours campaign as long as they remained a racist and xenophobic institution. The AFL was also self-limiting because their strategy of organizing focused on individual employers rather than entire industries, as was the wobblies' strategy.[26]

The other tradition in the American labour movement is the corporatist tradition, which was and remains the dominant point of view among the unions in the Congress of Industrial Organizations, after the formation of the CIO in 1935. Although elements of "corporatism" were and are shared by labour leaders in both the AFL and the CIO, corporatism was most prevalent in the UAW in particular under Walter Reuther, and among the textile workers who were led by Sidney Hillman. Corporatism, as a labour movement strategy seeks a "voice" in the management of production rather than "exit" from production, which is the syndicalist strategy.[27] The exit strategy of syndicalism builds leverage by withdrawing labour from the "market", whereas corporatism seeks more power and influence over the management of production. Corporatism seeks joint management of production between labour and capital as a strategy, and the strategy is grounded in principles that frame a common interest between capital and labour as "producers". The state is included in the corporatist perspective as a "neutral" third party to mitigate conflict between labour and capital and ideologically, the state serves to create a discourse that insists that the interests of capital and labour are the same, because both sides serve the national interests as "producers". With the creation of the New Deal, labour came to depend upon public spending by the state to maintain "full employment". In this strategy the focus is on the demand side, rather than the supply side. In syndicalism the strategy is to restrict supply of labour via the strike and shorter hours. In corporatism, the strategy is to lobby the government for public spending programmes that create jobs, thereby increasing the demand for labour. Syndicalist and corporatist labour strategies both seek interventions in the labour market, but from opposite sides. One seeks to restrict supply, the other seeks to boost demand. The crucial difference, however, is that syndicalism is an independent labour movement that acts directly upon capital with its own members. Corporatism, on the other hand depends upon the mediation of the state, and seeks to have the state represent the interests of labor. In corporatism, labour's intervention in the labour market is indirect, mediated by the state. In this way, corporatism as a strategy makes labour a dependent variable, existing precariously only as long as the state remains a "friend" of labour.[28] Corporatism is only sustainable as long as labour can depend upon the government to create jobs and actively adjudicate conflicts between labour and capital. In the current political climate in the United States, neither of these conditions exist.

We have seen that this strategy has also been unsustainable, since beginning in the early 1970s the federal government abandoned Keynesianism for neo-liberalism, which has been disastrous for labour.[29] Again, capital has been able to exploit a weakness present in the American labour movement, only in this case the weakness was present in the corporatist dimension of the labour leadership. When the labour union leadership attached itself to the state and situated labour as a dependent variable, it revealed a very serious weakness, as capital was able to retake the state under Reagan and use the state to attack labour, as when Reagan infamously fired the nation's air traffic controllers in 1981. But the labour union bureaucracy continues to spend enormous amounts of money lobbying Congressional leaders instead of putting those resources towards organizing new members, or pushing for an independent labour party.

In addition to seriously weakening the labour movement by situating labour as a dependent variable, corporatism also became very conservative as a labour movement strategy, although in a different way than exclusionary syndicalism. Corporatism as a labour movement strategy became conservative because it latched on to the warfare state and the military industrial complex after World War II. Union members benefit indirectly from huge contracts given to the corporations that drive the war machine, which is why the AFL-CIO leadership never came out against the Vietnam War. Nor can the labour movement take a stand on wasteful military spending more generally.[30]

The other conservative dimension to the labour union bureaucracy is that it cannot take a stand on environment issues because jobs take precedence over the environment. Because corporatist oriented labour leaders have made labour dependent on the state to generate jobs, and because the labour movement has given up even discussing shorter hours as a strategy to create jobs, the labour union leadership cannot take a progressive stand on environmental issues, believing that they must hold the line on all existing jobs. Jobs, jobs, jobs and the creation of jobs via state spending is all that the corporatist-oriented leadership are capable of advocating in the name of workers. Shorter hours, however, could be environmentally sustainable. If labour were to fight for shorter hours of work, then demand for labour could go up and we could cut back on industries that destroy the environment. Labour could take a progressive stand on the environment only if the leadership structure returns to the fight for shorter hours of work.

So in the AFL-CIO formation, we have two kinds of conservatism and two specific kinds of weaknesses exploited by capital, exclusionary syndicalism on the AFL side and corporatism on the CIO side. Both of these traditions existed in the house of labour when the AFL-CIO merged in 1955, and globalization in the form we see it now, was and remains capital's exploitation of the weaknesses that were already present in the labour union bureaucracy. On the one hand, capital exploited the weakness of exclusionary syndicalism by taking jobs to those excluded from the labour market by the AFL. Capital also made alliances with the excluded *against* labor within the borders of the U.S. President Bush's administration has been pursuing this strategy with immigrants today. Of course, Bush is not a friend of immigrant workers per se, because the Bush administration opposes amnesty for immigrant workers, but nonetheless, Bush has tried to present his administration as friendly to immigrants, only as "guest" workers, not citizens. The Bush administration is clearly manipulating the immigration issue to the advantage of capital. Still, it's not only a question of strategy. The AFL's exclusionary syndicalism was a terrible strategy, but beyond that, the AFL's position on the Other is also morally bankrupt, because the AFL-CIO has not been able to take a progressive stand on either immigration or the disastrous effects of U.S. imperialism on the populations of human beings worldwide. On the other hand, capital responded to the weakness of corporatist strategies but dismantling the state and reducing it to a mere police apparatus. Again, it is not simply a question of bad strategy. The CIO leadership made a serious mistake by placing labour in a subordinate position to the state, because it made the labour movement weak, but beyond that depending upon the state to create jobs meant that the AFL-CIO leadership could not afford to bite the hand that fed them, namely the military-industrial complex. There is a troubling moral dimension here as well. The AFL-CIO essentially muzzled itself since it has been unable to take a stand against imperialism. Union members have historically benefited from the military industrial complex making it structurally difficult to oppose U.S. imperialism.

CONCLUSION: THE CURRENT SITUATION

While the labour movement today – if we can still refer to the AFL-CIO as a "movement" – does not have much, if any, significant presence in national culture and politics, the voices of exclusionary syndicalism and corporatism are still very present in our media and public discourse. On the side of exclusionary syndicalism, we have Lou Dobbs the host of CNN's news programme, Lou Dobbs Tonite and on the side of corporatism we have Robert Reich the former Secretary of Labor under President Clinton and currently Professor of Public Policy at the Goldman School of Public Policy at the University of California at Berkeley.

Dobbs is an interesting case because he was formerly host of CNN's major business show, *Moneyline*, where he presented the free market point of view on the economy. On that show, Dobbs took the side of investors on Wall Street. Only recently has Dobbs come out as the main media representative of working people in the U.S., the demographic he refers to as the "middle class". Dobbs has since 2003, when he became host of his own show, *Lou Dobbs Tonight*, shed his fiscal conservative skin, to become a self-described "independent populist" and critic of "the excesses of capitalism". In his book *War on the Middle Class*, Dobbs says that he still "believes strongly in free enterprise", but he also "strongly rejects unfettered capitalism".[31] Dobbs, like most critics of globalization, points to the eclipse of democracy and freedom as the most pernicious by-product of globalization. "What was for almost two hundred years a government of the people," writes Dobbs, "has become a government of corporations."[32] Dobb's rather sanguine view of the previous 200 years of American governance notwithstanding, his view of the demise of democracy seems radical in some circles, but his definition of himself as a populist is troubling because he has become a right wing populist, although not as extreme as Pat Buchanan. It speaks volumes about the state of disarray on the left, that the two most vocal and recognizable public figures who speak the most frankly about the erosion of good paying jobs, and who are the most critical of corporations are right-wing populists like Buchanan and Dobbs.

Unfortunately, Dobbs has developed an exclusionary syndicalism, because he advocates restrictions on immigration. Although Dobbs rejects socialism and considers himself pro-capitalist, his position on immigration echoes that of Hillquist – the Socialist Party activist - from a century before. "The exploitation of illegal workers must end," writes Dobbs. "Every reputable nonpartisan economist acknowledges that pay for those who work at the lower end of the pay scale are adversely affected by the flood of illegal aliens into this country...if we are to reform our immigration laws, we must first secure and control our borders."[33] Dobbs is sympathetic to workers who are exploited - even immigrants - but he sees closing our borders as the only solution to falling wages in the U.S. Dobbs' nationalism, which is the core of his right-wing populist perspective, prevents him from considering amnesty for immigrants. It might also be the case that Dobbs cannot not imagine any other option - besides closing our borders - because he has never been exposed to the discourse of shorter hours...***perhaps***.

The demise of the discourse of shorter hours in the 1930s has left us with public figures like Lou Dobbs as one of the few voices for American workers, but followers of Dobbs are doomed to fighting an unsustainable and immoral battle. People who are desperate for income find ways to get into the United States, no matter what the obstacles. More important, it is immoral to tell people they cannot and should not expect to get their share of the global economic pie. Only a global shorter hours' policy can be a sustainable strategy because it is inclusive. There are no public intellectuals today that advocate shorter hours.[34] Instead, public intellectuals that position themselves as friends of labour advocate for job training programmes. The most recognizable figure is Robert Reich, former Secretary of Labor under President Clinton.

Reich's intellectual roots are in corporatism. Unlike Lou Dobbs, who sees the issue as a supply problem (too many workers), Reich focuses on the demand side of the equation, namely, how to increase jobs for skilled workers, what he calls "symbolic analysts". And in the tradition of corporatism, he views the interests of labour as the same as the interests of capital: both sides are producers, part of the same team. He views the period from the end of World War II and the 1970s as the golden years of the American economy where capital and labour coexisted peacefully and worked together to ensure economic growth and a rising standard of living for all American workers. In his book *The Work of Nations*, Reich argues, "Between 1950 and the early 1970s, the American economy as a whole began to exemplify this principle. Labor, business, and the broader public, through its elected representatives, tacitly co-operated to promote high volume production; the resulting efficiencies of scale generated high profits; some of the profits...were returned to the production workers and middle-level managers in the form of higher wages and benefits. As a result, larger numbers of Americans entered the middle class..."[35]

For Reich, things have changed drastically since the early 1970s, as automation and outsourcing have virtually eliminated good paying jobs in the manufacturing sector. What we are left with, according to Reich is a polarized job market, between low-wage, low-skilled jobs and high-skilled high tech jobs in industries based upon computer technologies. Workers in these high-end jobs manipulate symbols and information. Reich refers to these workers as "symbolic analysts". For Reich, what the federal government needs to do is create more opportunities for people to get these kinds of jobs, which is what places him in the tradition of corporatism and Keynesianism. He argues for state intervention in the economy to create more of these kinds of jobs. Reich acknowledges that it would be a huge task to return to a Keynesian policy of job creation and full employment based upon expanding the public sector, because that would require raising taxes, which is extremely unpopular in today's political climate in the U.S. But even if that obstacle were surmounted, there remains a serious flaw in Reich's strategy.

Reich observes that "symbolic analysts" command much higher wages relative to workers at the bottom of the labor market, because "symbolic analysts" are in short supply. "Symbolic analysts... are in such great demand," writes Reich, that "they have difficulty keeping track of all their earnings."[36] He also notes that the opposite is the case with two other groups in the labour market, routine production workers and in-peson service workers. "For the other two major categories of worker," Reich writes, "the law of supply and demand does not bode well. Routine producers, confronted with an immense and rapidly growing pool of unskilled and semiskilled laborers worldwide, find their incomes slipping and their jobs disappearing."[37] Semiskilled and unskilled workers in the service sector are also facing poor labour market conditions, just like semiskilled workers in the manufacturing industries. According to Reich, "In-person servers... [have to compete with] workers who otherwise would have entered into routine production [if it were not for] from immigrants and labor-saving machinery."[38]

Having noted that it is the relative scarcity of symbolic analysts that explains their relative high wages, and the relative high supply of semiskilled an unskilled workers in routine production and service industries that explains their low wages, Reich goes on to argue that the government should pursue a jobs training programme to create more symbolic analysts, as a way to lift up those who are stuck in low-paying jobs. Reich inexplicably overlooks the contradiction in his strategy, namely that educating more workers to become symbolic analysts will eventually drive wages down for this group of workers. Instead, Reich argues that blue collar union workers who have lost their jobs in the manufacturing industries can be re-tooled for symbolic analyst jobs. "In principle," writes Reich, "all of America's routine production workers could become symbolic analysts and let their old jobs drift over seas to developing nations." [39] Apart from Reich's rather problematic view that it is ok to ship the less desirable jobs overseas to the developing world – why is it ok that *the Other* be expected to perform the less desirable work? – Reich seems to forget his own point about symbolic analysts. Their high pay is a result of their short supply. Training more workers on the other hand, would increase the supply, and reduce their wages. Reich's solution to this problem is massive public investment to create jobs for the newly trained symbolic analysts. "A large pool of symbolic analysts within the nation would require substantial additional investments in universities, research parks, airports and other facilities conducive to symbolic-analytic work."[40] Apart from the rather vague conception of "other facilities" – what would these be? – Reich is rather optimistic that the investments necessary to create these jobs. Can we count on this investment in the current climate of globalization, when corporations can find symbolic analysts for less in developing countries? Furthermore, Reich is aware the labour-saving technologies threaten to replace workers in all industries – including in the industries that employ "skilled" workers - and yet he continues to push for job training programmes to flood the labour market with more educated and skilled workers. Nobody would argue against education, but maybe we should consider severing education from the labour market and return to the much older conception of education for education's sake, as was the case in traditional, pre-capitalist societies.

The main weakness of Reich's argument is that somehow the United States has a monopoly on symbolic analysts. This is not a tenable argument to make, as we have already seen the outsourcing of symbolic-analytic jobs from the U.S. to so-called developing countries like India and China. Most troubling, however, is that Reich does not see the glaring contradiction in his strategy. When he describes why symbolic analysts command high wages, he says it is a result of the relative scarce numbers of people that perform this kind of work. But when he switches over to a discourse of what to do about the low pay of other workers in routine production and service industries, he claims that it is the nature of what workers do – rather than the market – that explains their high wages. In other words, symbolic analysts make a decent wage because they are in demand. Reich notes this, but then he makes a serious shift of argument by implying that it is the skill per se, or the type of work that accounts for the high pay of symbolic analysts rather than their relative supply in the labour market. The labour market does not respond to skill per se, but the relative supply of a given skill. If we train more people to become symbolic analysts, then we would be undermining their position in the labour market. This strategy, like Dobbs' strategy, is not sustainable.

Today the AFL-CIO seems to support both Dobbs' position and Reich's, which reflects the troubled and confused legacies of exclusionary syndicalism and corporatism still present in the labour union bureaucracy. On their homepage, the AFL-CIO advocates for more public funding for job training and job creation strategies. This is a reflection of the lingering corporatism in the bureaucracy. On the other hand, reading the main media sources of the AFL-CIO – which is also available online – it is clear that the leaders of the AFL-CIO are in conflict about the immigration question. The rank and file demographics of union workers has changed substantially in the past few decades, and the AFL-CIO has recently responded to workers of colour and women, but they remain ambivalent about the immigration question, which reflects a lingering exclusionary syndicalism. While the AFL-CIO argues that immigrants who are in this country should be allowed to become citizens and have the same workplace rights as workers who are U.S. citizens, the emphasis is upon workers who are "already here", which implies that the AFL-CIO is ambivalent about the continuing stream of workers coming into the U.S. because they understand that flooding the labour market will drive down wages. Indeed, in his testimony before Congress on the recent immigration reform bill, Richard L. Trumka, Secretary-Treasurer of the AFL-CIO implied that immigration should only occur in the first place, when there is a labour shortage in the U.S. Otherwise, it is implied that we should keep immigrants out. It seems the AFL-CIO is torn on the question of immigration: on the one hand, they want citizenship status for "illegal" immigrants who are already here so those immigrants can join labour unions, on the other hand the AFL-CIO argues that unless there is a labour shortage, the U.S. should discourage immigration.[41]

The AFL-CIO is similarly troubled about job training issues. On a recent blog, the AFL-CIO criticizes the Bush Administration's lack of serious commitment and funding for job training programmes. The author of the blog article, Mike Hall, criticizes Bush's Secretary of Labor Elaine Chao for saying, "Workers are empowered to take control of their own training experience".[42] The union bureaucracy takes the position that the federal government is obliged to help workers find new jobs. It seems that the only way the union establishment can imagine job creation is via government spending, either directly creating jobs in the public sector, or indirectly in the private sector through funding research and development. But training more workers to become skilled only floods the labour market with skilled workers and drives down the wages for skilled workers. How can that be a sustainable strategy for workers, either in the U.S. or worldwide?

All of the main issues that face workers and unions today, namely immigration, outsourcing of jobs, and automation are all issues that have faced working people world wide since the 19th century. During the 19th century, organic intellectuals developed a discourse and political strategy based upon shorter hours of work to address all of these issues. And, shorter hours was immensely popular with workers worldwide who were able to develop a global labour movement based upon the principles, and they did this in spite of a relative lack of communication technologies that we have today. This points to the enormous demand for, and extraordinary popularity of shorter hours among workers that an international movement emerged almost immediately after the call for May Day in the late 1880s. We must reconsider that tradition if we are to adequately face the problems of globalization. First, however, all of us on the left need to face up to our mistakes and instead of going back to the New Deal, we must move forward to the future and revive the shorter hours of work movement on a global scale. Only then can we begin to mount a sustainable response to globalization. In the meantime, we continue to help global business succeed in exploiting labour without much, if any resistance.

NOTES

1. See Ralph Nader, *The WTO: Five Years of Reasons to Resist Corporate Globalization* (New York:Seven Stories Press, 2000).
2. "Corporatism" refers not to corporations per se, but to a tradition in the labour movement that advocates a "voice" for unions in the production process. In the "corporatist" tradition, labour is understood as a "junior partner" in the management of the production process. In the American labour movement, leaders like Walter Reuther of the United Automobile Workers – which was a CIO union - were among the major advocates of "corporatism", and they worked hard to marginalize the competing tradition of syndicalism that had been the dominant

point of view of the older AFL labour unions under the leadership of Gompers.

3. See Piven and Cloward, *The Breaking of the American Social Compact* (New Press, 1997).
4. Harold Meyerson, "Rise of the Have-Nots: Why More Americans Are Feeling Shut Out of Good Times," *Washington Post*, September 27, 2007.
5. A good example of this point of view is Schaeffer's book *Understanding Globalization: The Social Consequences of Political, Economic, and Environmental Change* (Rowman and Littlefield, 1997). Of course, there are those who are unaware of the consequences of globalization, and that problem must be addressed, but the focus on effects tends toward the creation of perspectives that see the solutions as obvious and straightforward, namely a return to the past: the Keynesian state.
6. The middle chapters of *Capital: Vol. 1*, by Marx are a superb example of a theoretical explanation of the relationship of capital to labour that does not assume a priori the dominance of capital as always already.
7. Emile Durkheim's "functionalism" in sociology is a good example of this point of view on the structural characteristics of industrial society.
8. May Day is Labour's legitimate holiday, but the U.S. government co-opted the holiday to remove it from the radical tradition of the shorter hours movement. Labour Day is now celebrated in September and the "values" that are celebrated have to do with the so-called "dignity" of work as opposed to celebrating leisure, which was the original raison de' etre of May Day. May Day developed organically out of the American labor movement and became an international holiday which spearheaded an international labour movement for shorter hours. Today, unfortunately, the history of the movement for shorter hours seems no longer part of our collective memory in the U.S.
9. See Karl Polanyi, *The Great Transformation* (Boston: Beacon Press, 2nd Edition, 2001).
10. See Karl Marx, Chapter 10: "The Working Day," in *Capital Volume One*, translated by Ben Fowkes (Penguin, 1976).
11. For an interesting explanation for the end of the shorter hours' movement, see Ben Hunnicutt, *Work Without End*: Abandoning Shorter Hours for the Right to Work (Temple University Press, 1988).
12. See Howard Kimmeldorf *Battling for American Labor* (University

of California Press, 1988).

13. George McNeil's *The Labor Movement, the Problem of Today*, (A.M. Bridgman & Co., 1888) is a good example of a point of view of an organic intellectual of the labor movement during the era the early years of the AFL.
14. See Glickman, *A Living Wage* (Cornell University Press, 1997).
15. See Mike Davis, "The Stop Watch and the Wooden Shoe," in *Radical America* 9, no. 1 (Jan-Feb., 1975): pp 69-96, for an excellent analysis of the syndicalist practices of the I.W.W.
16. See Marx, Chapter 25 of Capital Vol. One, and H.J. Habakkuk, *American and British Technology: the Search for Labor Saving Inventions* (Cambridge University Press, 1962).
17. See Alexander Saxton, *The Indispensable Enemy: Labor and the Anti-Chinese Movement in California* (University of California Press 1971) for an extended analysis of labour's role in the anti-Chinese movement of the late 19th century.
18. Hillquist's quote is from Aronowitz, *False Promises* (Duke University Press, 1992) p. 143.
19. See Roediger and Foner, *Our Own Time* (Verso, 1989).
20. See Gwendolyn Mink, *Old Labor and New Immigrants in American Political Development: Union, Party, and State, 1875-1920* (Cornel University Press 1990).
21. See David Roedigger, *The Wages of Whiteness* (Verso, 2nd edition, 2007).
22. See DuBois, *Black Reconstruction in the United States* (Free Press, 1998).
23. Ibid.
24. See Hunnicutt, *Work Without End*.
25. Mike Davis, "Stopwatch and the Wooden Shoe."
26. For a superb study of why and how the AFL succeeded and the IWW failed, see Howard Kimmeldorf, *Battling for American Labor: Wobblies, Craft Workers, and the Making of the Union Movement*.
27. For an analysis of the contrasting political strategies of exit and voice, see Albert O. Hirschman, Exit, *Voice and Loyalty* (Harvard University Press, 2nd edition, 2007).
28. For excellent treatment of labour as a dependent variable after the formation of the New Deal, see C. Wright Mills, *New Men of Power* (University of Illinois Press, 2001).
29. For a good history of the resurgence of neo-liberalism, see David Harvey, *A Brief History of Neo-liberalism* (Oxford, 2007).
30. For an analysis of Labour's position on the Vietnam War, see Levine *Labor and the New Left* (University of Illinois Press, 1994).

31. Lou Dobbs, *War on the Middle Class: How the Government, Big Business, and Special Interest Groups Are Waging War on the American Dream and How to Fight Back* (Viking Publishing, 2006), p. 2.
32. Ibid.
33. Ibid., pp. 206-207.
34. For a good history of the end of the shorter hours discourse in American politics, see Ben Hunnicutt's book, *Work Without End.*
35. Robert Reich, *The Work of Nations: Preparing Ourselves for 21st Century Capitalism* (First Vinatage Books, 1992), p. 304.
36. Ibid, p. 219.
37. Ibid, p. 245.
38. Ibid.
39. Ibid, p. 247.
40. Ibid.
41. Trumka's testimony can be found at http://www.aflcio.org/mediacenter/prsptm/pr06202007a.cfm.
42. See Mike Hall's article, "Days Before the Elections, Bush Announces New Job Training Program," at http://blog.aflcio.org/2006/10/27/days-before-the-elections-bush-announces-new-job-training-program/.

9

Global Media and the Social Construction of Unreality

P. Tom Semm

INTRODUCTION

Since the 1980s, large national media corporations located in the first world, mainly the United States, have been expanding globally. This expansion has been accomplished by their penetration of foreign domestic media markets and their purchase of partnerships in local and regional media companies. Both new technologies and global, regional, as well as bilateral trade agreements have made this expansion possible. Simultaneously, there has been an increasing concentration of ownership in these emerging multi-national media corporations. At the present, about ten media conglomerates dominate the global media market with several dozen smaller media corporations dominating regional markets.[1] Both expansion and concentration of ownership meet the demand of the profit imperative for these corporations and also demonstrate how globalization serves the interests of first world multi-national corporations.

However, in the case of multi-national media corporations, there is something more involved. These corporations are a central component of the globalization process itself through the production, distribution, and exhibition of their media content—entertainment, advertising, and carefully framed and targeted "news" shows. They are the main ideological institution of globalization. As Robert McChesney and Edward Herman say in their book, *The Global Media*:

> The global media system is an indispensable component of the globalizing market economy . . . communication and information provide a large and growing area of investment . . . (and). . . the global media also provide a vital forum for advertisers and the promotion of demand and consumerist values.[2]

The multi-nation media corporations will benefit from globalization economically but also through their entertainment and advertising content, they will create the "subjects" of the new global empire, consumers, and the "reality" that they will desire. The commercial "news" shows will reassure the new global "subject" that all is right with the world of desire and their pursuit of it. They will filter and frame information and ideas so that none will interfere with this "social construction of unreality". As McChesney and Herman say, "the global media system has fundamental structural flaws that limit its service to democracy".[3]

U.S. MEDIA AS THE MODEL FOR GLOBAL MEDIA

It is important to understand the structural flaws, but it is equally important to understand the specific methods and techniques that will be used by these media corporations to accomplish this social construction of unreality. In order to develop strategies of resistance to these methods and techniques, it is most enlightening to look at the United States, the country where the social construction of unreality has been most successful. In the United States, the broadcast media was given to commercial interests almost immediately upon the recognition by commercial interests of the efficacy of the newly developed technologies, radio and then television, as media for advertising. Advertisers referred to radio as the technology that "conquered living space" and advertisers referred to television as the "dream machine".

This gift of the broadcast media to commercial interest had impacts on the news and entertainment in the United States. A small public space for non-commercial broadcast news and entertainment was allowed to exist through the Public Broadcasting Act of 1967. This act created the Corporation for Public Broadcasting and ultimately the Public Broadcasting System (PBS), public television, and National Public Radio (NPR) public radio. However, these non-commercial media were never adequately funded, and Congress controlled what public funding there was. Even the inadequate public funding has declined under pressure from conservative legislators, ideologues, and the commercial media. As a consequence PBS and NPR, which occupy only a single space on the broadcast spectrum in each community, have become dependent on fund raising directed at their largely upper middle class viewers, charitable foundations, and corporate sponsorship (not called advertising in the world of U.S. public media). It is obvious that this might be the model for globalized public media, both news and entertainment, that would be acceptable to global commercial interests. It exists but is limited by funding and ideological constraints, therefore it provides no competition, and no alternative points of view.

Reproducing the media landscape of the United States globally is the obvious goal of commercial global media. And that landscape is what Ben Bagdikian calls a media monopoly; it is a fait accompli with only the final boundaries yet to be drawn. As this article is being written, the new Chairman of the Federal Communications Commission, Kevin Martin, is pushing for further deregulation. The result of this would be the creation of media monopolies in municipalities. Under the proposed new regulations, cross-ownership of media within a city would be allowed. A city could become a Time-Turner-Warner or a Newscorp city with the media conglomerate controlling radio, television, and newspaper media outlets. It would be a twenty-first century example of the company town.[4]

In an early edition of his book *Media Monopoly*, Bagdikian says that fifty U.S. media corporations controlled almost all of U.S. media. In a more recent edition, he says that eight media corporations control almost all of U.S. media. This concentration of ownership also exists in all mass media in the United States. Television, film, radio, book publishing, music, and newspaper ownership are more concentrated than ever before and the trend is for increasing concentration of ownership. For example, six corporations control film production, all "Hollywood"-based corporations. Five corporations dominate television production, distribution, and exhibition. Radio is dominated by Clear Channel, which owns more than twelve hundred stations and by Viacom (one of the corporations that dominate the film and television industry). Book publishing and music are dominated by only a few media corporations. And eighty per cent of newspapers in the United States are owned by corporations (immediately after World War II, 80 per cent of newspapers were privately owned), and only one per cent of news papers have competition.[5] Just recently, the Tribune Company, a giant, but second tier, media conglomerate, purchased the *Los Angeles Times* and now owns the *Chicago Tribune*, *Hartford Courant*, and the *Orlando Sentinel*, along with a dozen smaller newspapers. Cable and satellite delivery systems are dominated by the same media conglomerates that dominate the production and distribution of content in other media, either through ownership or share ownership.[6]

Although monopolies have been illegal in the U.S. since the Sherman Antitrust Act of 1890, shared monopolies, four or fewer corporations controlling over half of an economic market, exist in most U.S. media. These shared monopolies are not illegal but function much the way that monopolies do. And the same media conglomerates are most often the same partners in shared monopolies in other areas of media. An example is Time-Turner-Warner-AOL. It is part of both the television and film shared monopolies, part of the music recording and book publishing-shared monopolies, and it owns three of the magazines with the largest circulation in the United State. These media conglomerates are integrated both vertically and horizontally. An example is Disney. It is part of the television and film-shared monopolies and it owns theme parks, retail stores, and sports franchises. Each of these venues can be a means for expanding marketing strategies and increasing sales for Disney's television and film content.[7]

The profit imperative demands expansion, so that media

content can both reach a wider audience of consumers and also be distributed throughout the conglomerate's media outlets (synergy). And the profit imperative demands increasing concentration of ownership; the top three largest media corporations are significantly more profitable than the next three corporations.[8] While the profit imperative drives the media conglomerates, the political system in the U.S. has created the legal and regulatory environment that allows them to do so.

The public policies that were most decisive for creating the environment for a media monopoly in the U.S. were enacted during the Reagan Administration. The Reagan administration professed an ideological commitment to the principles of the free market. Its policies, though, were only consistent with its principles in regard to the poor, labour organizations, and to deregulation. One industry that the Reagan administration deregulated was the film industry. The Reagan Justice Department vacated the consent decree gained from the movie industry. The decree was derived from an anti-trust suit brought by the U.S. government against the film industry in the late 1940s (originally brought in the late 1930s). The suit was US v Paramount Pictures, et al. In the suit the Truman Justice Department argued that the film industry dominated by five Hollywood film companies (called "the studio system") was engaging in predatory monopolistic practices with its policies of blind and block booking of films. This was a policy that made movie exhibiters accept movies that they had not viewed, blind booking, and accept a group of films, some of which the exhibiters may have not wanted, block booking. In the consent decree the movie industry agreed to stop the practices and also to give up ownership of its own movie theatres. The result of the suit and the decree was not only to end the practices of blind and block booking but the break up of the vertical integration of the studio system. The result of the Reagan Justice Department's vacating the consent decree was the reverse; it allowed the movie industry to be integrated again into a shared monopoly of production, distribution, and exhibition.[9]

While the above policy of deregulation affected entertainment media and ultimately its content,[10] another

Reagan policy had an affect on "news" in the U.S. This was the administration's elimination of the Fairness Doctrine. The doctrine had been adopted as a formal rule in 1949 by the FCC and then in 1959 Congress made it a law. It reads: "A broadcast licensee shall afford reasonable opportunity for discussion of conflicting views on matters of public importance." The U.S. Supreme Court upheld the doctrine in 1969 in Red Lion Broadcasting Co. v. FCC, 1960. The Court decision was based on the First Amendment and the fundamental right of the people to have access to an "uninhibited marketplace of ideas". As Steve Randall at Fairness and Accuracy in Reporting has pointed, the two requirements of the doctrine were that broadcasters devote some air time to discussing controversial matters of public concern and that the broadcaster air contrasting views regarding those controversial matters.[11] The elimination of the Fairness Doctrine has had significant negative consequences for democracy in the United States, but it has had significant positive consequences for commercial "news" and broadcast "journalism" in the United States. The emergence and domination of commercial radio frequencies by very profitable right-wing talk radio has been one consequence. The other consequence has been the complementary emergence of six twenty-four-hour news channels governed by no fairness rules.

The most significant legislation for deregulating media however was passed during the administration of a Democratic president, Bill Clinton. The Telecommunications Act of 1996 was presented to the public as a necessary revision of the 1934 Communications Act. Advocates claimed that it would allow for more competition and create the environment for the development and dissemination of new technologies. In reality, the Act restructured the media landscape for the benefit of commercial media interests, broadcasters, cable companies, and telecommunication companies.[12]

Along with legislative deregulation, there has been the transformation of the Federal Communications Commission's regulatory function, or at least a re-emphasis. The FCC, originally the Federal Radio Commission, was created as part of the Radio Act of 1927. Its mandate was to regulate the airwaves in the public interest and create an environment for commercial interests to be profitable. Michael Powell, the first Chairman appointed by George Bush, emphasized the latter function of the agency. An example of the FCC under Powell's Chairmanship is the FCC ruling in 2003, which, despite overwhelming public protest, further deregulated the industry.[13] The new Chairman of the FCC, George Bush's second appointee, Kevin Martin, as mentioned earlier, is pushing the policy of deregulation even further.

ADVERTISING: THE SOCIAL CONSTRUCTION OF UNREALITY

The commercial media in the United States is highly concentrated, dominates all media, and is arguably free of regulatory constraints. This makes it free to pursue the profit imperative. The customer of the commercial media is not the viewer, or the reader, but the advertiser. A consequence of profit, concentration, expansion, domination, and no regulation of commercial media has been the saturation of cultural space in the United States with advertising. The goal of commercial media is to provide the audience for advertisers, therefore commercial media, entertainment and news, are primarily a means of distributing advertising. Over one-fourth of television and radio time is appropriated for advertising. Newspaper and magazine space is over one-fourth advertising. At the movies, advertising now precedes the showing of movies, as does a seemingly endless stream of promotions, called previews, for future movies. The technique of product placement allows products to be advertised in the movies themselves; and a mention of the desirable characteristics of the product may be written into the screenplay. Advertising is on buses, taxis, billboards, stadiums, blimps, and it is pulled by airplanes; logos are placed on private vehicles; slogans are written in the sky; commercials are the subject of conversation. It is in schools, hospitals, and public buildings. It is everywhere, and it is accepted, or more accurately experienced, as a natural phenomenon, rather than a humanly constructed one. This is the sign that victory is complete; the "ism" that won the century has consolidated its victory by making itself visible to all who can see, and making itself heard to all who listen. The "ism" is consumerism, and it is necessary for consumerism to conquer global cultural space the same way that it has conquered cultural space in the United States for globalization to realize its goals.

Consumerism is more than consumers buying things and advertising does more than sell things; it is the main institution for creating "subjects" and the "reality" that they desire. The "subjects" and their "reality" are opposite sides of the same coin. Together, they constitute a totalizing world view, a way of life that marginalizes or eliminates other possibilities. This way of life is organized in such a way that high level and continuous consumption is the dominant norm, and as the dominant norm, it is the activity around which all of life is arranged. Therefore the primary social role is that of consumer; the role of worker and wage earner is a subordinate but necessary role in that it, along with debt, allow the subject to keep consuming. And freedom is the dominant value in this world view, but redefined as the freedom to consume.

The social construction of consumerism actually began in the United States in the 1920s when the economic and political elite realized that the newly developed process of mass production, Fordism, demanded the mass production of consumers. The result of this realization was an organized plan to transform the domestic population into consumers; this was called the Gospel of Mass Consumption.[14] A political ideology based on the same assumptions complemented this plan. Walter Lippman, the pre-eminent political theorist of the time, argued that a technical elite made up of social scientists needed to govern the American democracy, because the public was incapable of the rationality required to govern itself. He characterized the public as the "bewildered herd". The emphasis on the social construction of consumerism would prove beneficial to both economic and political elites. American society, from this point of view, would henceforth be made up of consumers whose lives would be organized around the continuous consumption of things while a technocratic elite made their political decisions for them.[15]

During this time, new techniques for creating consumers and shaping their desires were developed. Early advertising had assumed that people were rational and that they could make rational decisions about their needs. Advertisements appealed to this, albeit not without deception. The new techniques that were developed by advertisers were based upon new assumptions. Some were derived from the newly emerging field of psychoanalysis and some were derived from the field of collective behaviour. The new assumptions were that people were motivated by the unconscious and that appeals to the unconscious were the best way to sell products but also the best way to transform the public of mass societies into consumers. Increasingly, commercial interests used emotionally charged and value-laden images in its advertisements to create the world of desire.

The new techniques of advertising combined with the emergence of television, the dream machine, in the 1950s expanded the possibilities and scope of consumerism. Television assumed a central place in the home of most Americans by the mid-1950s; as it did, advertising became one of the most important institutions in American society. The number of television sets in the United States grew astronomically once their commercial value was discovered, and the amount of television advertising in time and investment increased tenfold.[16]

There has been a significant change in the social construction of consumerism in the last three decades. The world of desire has changed. In the 1950s the world portrayed on entertainment television and in television commercials was the middle class world of the new suburbs. Fifty million white middle class and upper middle class Americans fled the urban area to the suburbs in order to become "neighbours" with the families of the prime time domestic situation comedies. The world of desire was a middle class world, a ranch home, two new cars, a lawn, a black kettle barbeque in the backyard, and in some instances a small swimming pool with a diving board. The "Joneses" – middle class families in middle class suburban neighbourhoods - were the objects of desire. "Keeping up with the Joneses" was the demand that this world of desire placed on the new consumers.

The world of desire is quite different at the turn of the century; it consists of what Juliet Schor calls the "new Joneses"; these new Joneses are not living in a middle class suburban community. When one looks closely, one finds that they are living in an exclusive community that is more likely gated than integrated by race or class, or they are more likely living in even more exclusive urban environment. This new world of desire is upper middle class, and quite often upper class. Schor has tracked this new world of desire in her book *The Overspent American*. It still includes backyard barbeques and swimming pools, but they only partially resemble those objects of desire in the 1950s. According to Schor, the social construction of consumerism has created a psyche that while it sleeps, dreams about things that it wants to buy, always has something in mind that it wants to buy, and has a wish list so exotic that only a small per cent of the population could ever acquire what was on it.[17] This "desiring American" is the perfect subject for commercial interests, eternally desiring, but never finding fulfilment, and experiencing itself as free. This is the dream of globalization and the necessity; three billion "subjects" dreaming the dreams of the advertising industry and calling it freedom. But to make sure reality, visions of the victims of globalization, the hungry, the sick, the cluster bombed, do not interrupt, the commercial media must control the "news". Again, the United States can serve as the model for global commercial interests.

U.S. "NEWS" AND "JOURNALISM": A GLOBAL MODEL

The commercial media is the dominant providers of news in the U.S. And under U.S. law public corporations have an obligation to maximize profit for shareholders. The result of corporations driven by the profit imperative and dominating the news has transformed the news and journalistic practices in the United States. The results of the transformation have been the blurring of the line between entertainment and news as commercial news seeks to attract viewers for their customers, the advertisers. It also involves the presentation of news that targets a "quality audience" (consumers) and creates a congenial environment for that audience's viewing of the advertisements. And it involves the adoption of cost-cutting measures. These measures include firing reporters and support staff, closing news bureaus, and limiting the amount of time that can be spent on stories. Simultaneously, there has been an expansion of television news shows; there are now five 24-hour commercial news channels. Under this structure, commercial "news" in the U.S has become "infotainment"; it has become dependent on access to elite sources and material from both the government and private interests; and it has adopted a journalistic practice of disinformation, called "balance".

"Infotainment" has been the product of this blurring of the line between news and entertainment and the result are news shows that emphasize violence, natural disasters, and celebrities. Television news directors admit to following an imperative, "If it bleeds it leads". This leads to an emphasis on the coverage of violent crime, or street crime. These crimes include murder, rape, "home invasions" (formally burglary, the preference is obvious). Excluded from coverage is the violence of war, or the violence of corporate crime. In his book *Culture of Fear*, Barry Glassner points out that media coverage of violent street crime may increase as crime itself actually declines.[18]

Studies have shown that this emphasis on violent crime has a negative impact on American society. Heavy television viewers develop a psychology in relation to the media created fear of violence. They tend to be anxious, angry, and afraid. They are more likely to buy a gun, turn their house into a fort, buy an alarm system, and buy a guard dog. This "unreality" of violence also has anti-democratic consequences as fearful and uninformed citizens are more likely to support harsher punishments, fewer constraints on police, and more money for the criminal justice system.[19] Because it is not as "entertaining", and because it would require time (cost), the commercial media excludes from its coverage of crime such important issues as long-term trends in crime. It fails to explore correlations between poverty, lack of education, unemployment and street crime. The commercial media also does not cover the increasing cost of the criminal justice system and how it impacts the funding of education. Beyond the boundaries of the commercial media's coverage of crime, for obvious reasons, is any examination of the systemic nature of corporate crime, and its violence towards individuals and whole communities.

The commercial media further "infotains" its viewers with coverage of natural disasters, tornadoes, earthquakes, and floods. However, the natural disaster that lends itself to infotainment coverage the best is the hurricane. This is because an entire televised drama can be built around the hurricane. The commercial media can use its increasingly sophisticated technology to identify a "developing" storm somewhere in an ocean. As the storm becomes more intense and its course can be identified, "journalists" are sent to targeted areas to assess the pre-disaster situation. When the hurricane approaches, the "journalists" stay long enough to "infotain" the American viewers with such "newsworthy" insights as how windy a hurricane is. After the hurricane passes, the "journalists" return to the devastated area seeking personal interest stories.

Just how dangerous infotainment coverage can be was revealed in the commercial media's coverage of *Hurricane Katrina* and the subsequent humanitarian disaster. The commercial media covered the catastrophic event as if the most important news was the "wide-spread collective violence". In order to cover the disaster in this way, the media had to accept totally unverified claims and ignore eyewitness accounts by their own "on the spot journalists". But the media did not just repeat unsupported claims; it used its outlets as an echo chamber. An example was Matt Lauer, persisting in the questioning of the commander of the National Guard about "rules of engagement". The fact is that none of the claims about violence wase true, but this is only one part of the problem of infotainment, the other part, pointed out previously, is that the infotainment has consequences. With *Hurricane Katrina*, the social construction of unreality was one of the factors that kept help from reaching stranded victims of the disaster.[20]

News as infotainment reaches its nadir, though, with the coverage of celebrities.

One study claimed that after the death of Anna Nicole Smith, over one half of live television news coverage was focused on the "event".[21] The fickleness of this practice of celebrity as "news" was revealed when the "story" of Anna Nicole was bumped unceremoniously by the important story of Paris Hilton's arrest, conviction, and sentencing for a reckless driving. Hilton's re-arrest and reincarceration for violating her probation was covered extensively, as was the day of her release, including what she had for dinner. Hilton was subsequently banished from the headlines by Lindsey Lohan, but only temporarily. "Journalists" had discovered that Hilton had been wearing a fashionable item from the new Paris Hilton collection when she "walked" from jail, so the commercial news media repeatedly played the "walk". Some might say that Americans are getting what they want, but that assumes a concept of freedom that is so diminished that it is without meaning. The question might be: how can those living in a media-saturated environment dominated by large commercial media corporations which themselves are dominated by even larger advertisers be said to be choosing anything?

Another consequence of the news being dominated by the commercial media is the dependent relationship the commercial has with those persons in power. That which becomes essential for commercial news within this structure of dependency is access to those persons, but also the commercial news media has become dependent on press releases, news conferences, and public relations material (VNRs). Those in power have been aware of this dependency since the Reagan administration and take advantage of it in a variety of ways, ways the shape the delivery of what is called "hard" or "political" news in the United States.

Broadcast journalists do not report; they interview or moderate. To do either, they need what is called access to those in power. A certain set of rules follows - do not be hostile to the guest, or even too aggressive, do not be prepared, and do not ask the "wrong" questions. If a journalist violates any of these rules, further access to this person and others may be denied. This system of reciprocity, access and dependency, makes commercial news a congenial environment for those in power to present their agenda.

A perfect example of this was Dick Cheney's frequent visits to Tim Russert's Meet the Press, NBC News flagship "hard" news show. During the trial of Scooter Libby, former Cheney Chief of Staff, for obstruction of justice a memo was released. It revealed that Cheney liked to be a guest on Russert's show because as the memo put it, Cheney usually got his point across.

As mentioned earlier, administrations and powerful interest groups have been aware of this dependent relationship since the Reagan administration and have learned to take advantage of it in other ways than controlling access. One way is the careful framing of "talking points" and then the transmission of those talking points via news conferences and press releases. The "talking points" then become the news as they are reproduced as headlines and leads. Subsequently, they determine the interviews and panel discussions that make up the majority of non-advertising time on the 24-hour news channels. Studies by Fairness and Accuracy in Reporting have shown that guests/experts on television news, panels, including public broadcasting, are predominately from administrations, corporations, and the military.[22]

Private corporations also understand this dependency relationship, and hire public relations firms to create what are called video news releases, or VNRs. Then the public relations firms submit these "fake" news stories to commercial news outlets who then use them as if they were real news. In *Corporate Media and the Threat to Democracy*, Robert McChesney says that anywhere between 40% to 70% of news is from press releases and public relations material.[23]

There are occasions when the commercial news cannot avoid examining an important and controversial issue. For these occasions it has developed a new journalistic called "balance". The proponents of balance, including many broadcast "journalists", claim that the practice of balance is the best way to be objective. The practice of balance involves the journalist assuming the role of moderator and inviting guests from both sides of an issue to be on the news show and to present their position. The function of the journalist/moderator within this practice is to follow the above rules so that each side gets to speak. A critique of this practice was depicted on the Peabody Award-winning *Daily Show*, a comedy show that is a satire of commercial television news shows. John Stewart, the fake anchor, asks his fake reporter, Rob Corddry, why there is a debate in the media over John Kerry's war record. Stewart says that it is in the official documents and it is based on incontrovertible facts. Corddry replies that those incontrovertible facts are one side of the debate. Stewart replies that those are the facts, that's the end of the debate, what do you think? Corddry replies that as a journalist, it is not his place to get in the way of the people talking and the people listening.

The practice of balance conforms to a narrow concept of objectivity, does not lead to any illumination about the truth, and gives credibility to positions that may not deserve them. An example is the coverage by the commercial media in the United States of the serious problems that humanity faces as a result of global warming. The commercial media does not deal with either the problems or possible solutions but treats the reality of global warming as if it were questionable, a subject for debate. Individuals and groups with serious conflicts of interest and no scientific standing are invited to present their side (usually Exxon Mobil's) on both commercial and public broadcast news shows. In fact, in peer-reviewed scientific studies there is no debate about the reality or causes of global warming.[24] And beyond the bounds of corporate defined balance is any debate about the connection between consumerism and global warming, or the connection of consumerism to other environmental problems.

The "success" of these techniques and structural determinates and their efficacy as a model of "news" for global economic interests can be seen in their coverage of the United States war against Iraq. The commercial media's dependence on access, its dependence on press releases and news conferences for "war news", and its presentation of war as infotainment have been successful in creating an unreality for the American public.[25] Knowledge-based surveys showed that by as late as December 2006, almost half of the public that was surveyed believed that Saddam Hussein was directly responsible for the September 11, 2001 attack on the World Trade Centers in New York, and an almost equal per cent believed that weapons of mass destruction had been found in Iraq by the U. S. military. Neither claim is true.

CONCLUSION: STRATEGIES OF RESISTANCE

Two philosophical assumptions must underlie any attempt to formulate strategies of resistance. The first assumption involves the concept of power. Power has historically been conceived of as being coercive. This concept of power assumes that force (violence) and propaganda (lies) are necessary to control autonomous subjects. As Michelle Foucault has argued, a modern concept of power must take into account the new technologies of power and the power to create compliant subjects. The mass media uses propaganda, but it is not simply the power to lie that it possesses; it is the power to create subjects who do not need to be lied too, and to create the reality that they desire. These "subjects" experience their desire as natural, and understand freedom as their pursuit of that desire. Consequently, they are easily lied to.

The second assumption involves the concept of a democracy. A democracy can only function as a democracy, self-government by the people, if the people have the information and broad range of ideas necessary to make informed decisions. The media is essential to this end, and to this end the airways must belong to the people.

Given these two assumptions, progressive movements and newly emerging popular governments must have as a central policy the creation of a viable, vital, and independent public broadcast media. In order to do so, it must find ways to make the public media self-sustaining, relevant, and immune from ideological and commercial constraints. A system of adequate and consistent funding must be developed so that journalistic practices relevant to the functioning of democratic societies can be maintained. The system of funding must also be adequate and consistent for the production of non-commercial entertainment. The development of low-watt radio stations should be an integral part of any public media. Low-watt radio stations have a limited range but low start-up costs. This means that local groups such as churches, universities, and civic organizations could produce media content relevant for their neighbourhoods.

Second, each country should establish a regulatory agency that has the power and resources to enforce media regulations in the public interest. The regulatory agency in the United States, the FCC, serves as a counter example. The five members of the commission are appointed by the President of the United States, three are from the party of the administration including the Chairman. They are political appointees who serve the interests of their political patrons. Also, the budget of the FCC is determined by Congress on an annual basis. And the power of enforcement is limited by legislative threat to the budget, ideological constraints, and inadequate regulatory statutes.

It seems clear that a regulatory agency has to be autonomous, that is not constrained by funding, politics, or ideology. It also has to have the majority of its members from public interest organizations; it has to have a budget adequate for regulation and enforcement; and it has to have a clear mandate regarding its function. The mandate cannot include the contradictory function of creating a congenial profit-taking environment for commercial interests.

Advertising needs to be contained; it is already expanding globally. Still, a twofold approach needs to be undertaken. The first approach would be limiting advertising that targets children. Targeting children is the primary way that commercial interests produce subjects; advertisers use sociologists, psychologists, and anthropologists to learn how to transform the "inquisitive child into an acquisitive adult". As Eric Schlosser points out, advertisers have discovered that children can be branded as young as the age of two.[26] The second approach would be to introduce media literacy into the educational system. Children are spending more and more time with all forms of media, and are well informed about how to use it, what Aristotle called "techne" and the form of knowledge that he gave the lowest place to in his hierarchy of knowledge. Children and adolescents, however, remain uninformed about the social, political and economic implications of the expanding media culture.

The commercial media has already responded to efforts to protect children. Some of the toughest anti-child advertising regulations have been overturned because they were determined by global trade regulatory institutions to have violated international trade agreements. As a consequence, the affected governments chose to eliminate the regulations rather than face economic penalties in the form of fines or sanctions. Commercial interests in the United States have taken a different approach; they claim that any constraints on advertising are constraints on the corporate right of free speech. In the United States, corporations have gained the status of legal persons, mainly by legal rulings based on the Equal Protection Clause of the Fourteenth Amendment to the Constitution. This Amendment was ratified to protect black Americans from states denying them their right to life, liberty, and property; however, it has been used many more times to guarantee corporations their right of profit. These legal decisions have established corporations as persons. Because corporations are persons within the meaning of the law, they can claim that limits on advertising are limit on free speech. It is obvious that corporations are not persons and advertising is not speech. Legislation codifying the obvious might be a possible strategy of resistance.

The author is somewhat doubtful, but hopeful, that these strategies of resistance might prove helpful in the battle against globalization. However, there are several other possibilities that might allow for some hope. The global media may meet challenges in the global construction of reality that it did not meet in the United States. For example, the educational system in the United States functions in an almost complementary way to the commercial media. From corporate-sponsored educational supplements for grade schools to Channel One for high schools to the branding of universities, advertising has penetrated the educational system in the United States. An educational system does not have to allow this to happen and in many countries it does not.

Also, Americans as a public, may be more susceptible to lies because of a cultural phenomenon called "Americanism". Americanism involves the acceptance of conventional wisdoms about the nature of American society that are never questioned by the majority of the population and as such they provide a kind of protection against "reality". And last, in the United States, television was in almost every American home by the end of the 1950s. This made every family vulnerable to advertising and to commercial "news". This will never be the case globally; because of the nature of globalization, its structural inequality, there will always be several billion people, expendable, non-consumers, beyond the reach of the global media. Perhaps these people are the real hope.

NOTES

1. Robert W. McChesney, *Rich Media, Poor Democracy: Communication Policy in Dubious Times* (New Press: New York, 2000).
2. Edward Herman and Robert W. McChesney, *The Global Media: The New Missionaries of Global Capitalism* (London: Cassell, 1999), p. 189.
3. Ibid.
4. Story on new deregulation FCC.
5. Ben Bagdikian, *The New Media Monopoly* (Boston: Beacon Press, 2004).
6. Ibid.
7. Stanley D. Eitzen and Maxine Baca Zinn, *Social Problems*, (Boston: Allyn and Bacon, 10th edition, 2006).
8. Bagdikian, *The New Media Monopoly.*
9. Arthur Knight, *The Liveliest Art: A Panoramic History of the Movies*, (New York: McMillan Publishing Co., Revised edition, 1978).
10. Leonard Quart and Albert Auster, *American Film and Society Since 1945* (Westport, CT: Praeger, 1991).
11. Steve Randall, "The Fairness Doctrine", is available at www.fair.org, (Feb 12, 2005).
12. Telecommunications Act of 1996.
13. FCC regulations.
14. Jeremy Rifkin, *The End of Work* (New York: G. P. Putnam's Sons,

1995).

15. Noam Chomsky, *Media Control: The Spectacular Achievements of Propaganda* (New York: Seven Stories Press, 2nd edition, 2002).
16. David Halberstam, *The Fifties* (New York: Fawcett Columbine, 1993).
17. Juliet B. Schor, *The Overspent American: WhywWe wantwWhatwWe don't Need* (New York: Harper Perennial, 1999).
18. Barry Glassner, *Culture of Fear: Why Americans are Afraid of the Wrong Things* (New York: Basic Books, 2000).
19. Cultural Indicators Project.
20. "Demonizing the Victims of Katrina", *EXTRA* (November/ December 2005).
21. Project for Excellence in Journalism.
22. "Who's On the News?" *EXTRA* (June 2002).
23. Robert W. McChesney, *Corporate Media and the Threat to Democracy* (New York: Seven Stories Press), p.16.
24. Al Gore, *An Inconvenient Truth: The Crisis of Global Warming* (London: Penguin, 2006).
25. Program on International Policy Attitudes, can be found at www.pipa.org.
26. Eric Schlosser, *Fast Food Nation* (New York: Houghton Mifflin 2001).

10

The Global Network of Players

Eric Kramer and Taesik Kim

INTRODUCTION

In this paper we discuss the role of the "player" and the globalization of the player ideology and mindset. Globalization is characterized by widespread standardization of beliefs and behaviours. As this occurs, the difference based on temporal and spatial separation is declining; space and time, as philosophers like to say, is "collapsing", while economists argue that a single market is expanding, at the same time that political scientists argue that this involves the internationalization of domestic politics and the inevitable growth of democratization, and critical cultural studies people observe the diffusion of consumerism across the globe. As space and time collapse civilizations are thrust together, clashing, fusing, interpenetrating, sharing an increasingly common space. For the player, his playground is expanding.

All such descriptions are correct in their own ways. The diversity of perspectives points towards a gathering sameness of not merely machine functionality, of "universal pragmatics"[1] of "how to" (even talk), but also and much more important, a reduction to a small repertoire of credible ambitions and dreams linked to a realism and rationality based on positivistic pecuniary ambitions.[2] From banking to agriculture to manufacturing to pedagogy, even the pragmatics of "how to" involves a convergence on common modes of functionality and common tasks done in increasingly systematized and routinized "efficient" and "competent" ways. But there is also a convergence on a shrinking repertoire of common fantasy themes.[3] One of them is to be a player. According to this ideology every sane, normal, honest, realistic person should want to be a player, a wheeler-dealer who practises the "art of the deal". The profiteer is the new saint.

One of the dominant models of appropriate behaviour and mindset operant in this shrinking repertoire of realisms, we argue herein, is that of the player. Entire fields of applied social scientific methods such as marketing and public relations are now deployed in industrial strength to enhance ("spin") the image of the player. Campaigns of dis- and misinformation are expertly crafted and positioned. This is the age of mass advertising and public relations. This[4] is the age of the Third Sophistic where lying has been elevated to an art form and professional liars form an entire industry backed by academic units training behavioural and cognitive experts for hire.[5]

THE NATURE OF THE PLAYER

In his short essay, "Crap Shoot", Garret Keizer dichotomizes people in terms of those who deal in information and those who serve their needs.[6] The former are called "players" and the latter are called "workers". Keizer defines play as something different from ordinary life, and thus this difference is crucial to understand the concept of a player. Consequently, he analyzes what "player" means by looking at the possible antonyms of the concept, such as "spectator". However, Keizer also argues that in order to find the best antonym for "player", one should trace the identification back to its linguistic root, "play". The opposite of play is "work", and thus the opposite of a player is a worker. We argue herein that the old dichotomy of bourgeoisie and proletariat is obsolete. Today the proletariat believes and wants to be a player. He does not have contrary dreams and ambitions. And today the player, unlike the modern capitalist bourgeoisie, is not at all conservative or even patriotic. The player does not desire to be admired, to be a pillar of his community, a leader, a saviour, a hero. The player wants no such obligations that come with being part of a leader within a community.

For instance, all traditional societies had versions of God/kings such as the emperor of China, the Inca, the king of the Aztec, the Egyptian pharaoh, and so forth. All such social structures were highly structured and hierarchical so that even the emperor had to follow very carefully the dictates of heaven. Royals had profound obligations. Royals in such societies had to follow very strict doctrines of formality and etiquette and then of course their subjects had to obey them just as they obeyed heaven. Even the sex of their offspring had to conform, putting great pressure on female royals as evinced in recent years with the stress Princess Masako in Japan suffered (including a miscarriage and the birth of a girl, Aiko) until she produced a male heir. Royals were identified utterly with their land, their country. The Confucian hierarchy is typical. But the player obeys no one. The post-modern player has no allegiance to any country, creed, religion, or ideology. The player is the ultimate, hypertrophic ego but with a floating identity.

Keizer elaborates upon the concept of the two groups, two "races" of humans, players and workers, so identified by John Ruskin. Ruskin says that workers cultivate and manufacture.[7] The worker provides the necessities of life while the player is "proudly idle, and continually therefore needing recreation, in which they use the productive and laborious orders partly as their cattle, and partly as their puppets or pieces in the game of death".[8] The player "has it made". To Ruskin, business and its curriculum is a "bastard science", "the 'science' for getting rich".[9]

Keizer argues, "The first true player as the first person to successfully ride a horse...[in so doing he] entered a zone of being almost instantly faster, higher, and stronger than anyone on foot."[10] In ancient Rome the Plutocratic class was named the "equestrian order". Consequently, a player tries mightily never to be pedestrian. Paris Hilton is a good example of a player. According to Keizer, "There are players and the people who wish to be players", Paris' pathetic fans for instance.[11] The player has an insatiable need to be exceptional and transcendent, and they thrive on exhibitionism and voyeurism. Keizer includes the technocrat as a player. The hacker he calls a subspecies of player as he has your password, invades your computer and points and clicks at your "private parts" while he is out of his body and "out of your league".[12]

Keizer identifies the greatest difference between the player and the worker by analyzing their respective attitudes toward each other. According to him, the definition of the player itself implies "exclusion". "If everyone is a player, then no one is a player, [and] when everybody comes onto 'the field,' it is no longer a field, [but] it is a park."[13] On the other hand, the worker wants more participation for lessening his or her burden. In this sense, Keizer expects that change in American society will come only "when people who work, who love work, whose conception of the world is of a work in progress, come to realize they have no choice but to fight".[14]

This is not the same as Marx's concept of class struggle in nineteenth-century capitalism, because the working class described by Marx was still looking for the liberation from the name "worker". However, Keizer's worker will still be a worker even after losing his or her chain.

This essay borrows the concept of the player and the worker to analyze globalization, and the dominance of the network of global players. Although it is common to regard the nation-state as a unit of analysis of global capitalism in social science as well as in everyday life, this essay posits that the nation-state is less and less significant in the globalized world. Our unit of analysis is the player. Modern players control local and global institutions including mass media and reside in urban centres and remote rural luxury retreats. This essay does not posit the nation-state as a unit competing to be a player in the globalized world, even though we recognize that competition between modern nation-states does generate a pattern whereby some nation-states are players while others are excluded. Instead, the focus is on the background stabilization of the new super-players' playground which is the globalizing network of economy and culture; the emergent player monoculture.[15]

The player sees the game, reality, as contingent, the rules

flexible; so flexible as to be practically nonexistent. This claim is important. It is essential to understanding our take on what is happening. The game, its rules and parameters are itself gamed, not merely played by players. If all participants adhere to the rules of a game equally, then it is a much more sporting, a much more equitable competition. But a player is not a predictable participant in a social system in the way a speaker is in a Wittgensteinian language-game. The player is a rapper. A player disregards the rules, the grammar; the received structure. The player is an opportunist. The player is adaptable and innovative. The player often crosses the line of criminality and sees himself as a robust buccaneer. A good recent example is Jack Abramoff, the lobbyist at the centre of much wheeling and dealing during President George H.W. Bush's administration.

Players proclaim the sanctity of laws and rules only when it is advantageous to them. Though they often claim the moniker, they are not conservative. The claim to be conservative is only the first in a long line of lies. Another is the bloodthirsty Christian who supports war, no matter how many innocents are killed. The identity-claim to be conservative does however ingratiate the player to real conservative supporters, those who want and need faith, giving the player a political power-base. But the player plays them just like she plays the rules. They are duped by the confidence game. For instance, during the 2001 parade of inaugural balls held to celebrate Bush and Dick Cheney's victory, a *Washington Post* reporter inquired of two Bush aids whether either Bush or Cheney were likely to show up at a particular party. The aids basically laughed and said it was highly unlikely that either would bother with a ball filled with car dealers, even though that group formed an almost monolithic and very generous bloc of support for their election. Economic and Christian conservatives have also felt duped by Bush, the Neocons, and Carl Rove.[16]

The most basic criminal quality of the players is their disregard for rules and laws. They are hypocrites and they are so transcendent, so dissociated from the obligations of games that they don't care. Hypocrisy is not a sin to them. We might say that they have no shame; a profoundly "thick face". Be it in the conduct of human or natural physical and psychological behaviours, a law that is not universal is not, by definition, a law. This is a basic fact of set theory. A law that does not apply to the person who proclaims it is not a law. Players presume privilege, and this privilege involves not having to play by the laws, mores, and rules that they expect others to play by. They claim exceptionalism for themselves. The first exception is the power to purvey others, to collect all sorts of information about others but to remain invisible to them. This violates the major tenet of genuine, "authentic" communication, which is reciprocity. Players are not friends. They do not allow reciprocity. They do not communicate but strategically "leak". Though they claim to function on a quid pro quo basis, they actually try to always maximize their personal profit and to minimize any liability (obligation). A good example is the insurance business. On the face of it, insurance looks like a community service, even a form of Marxism; "from each according to his ability to each according to his need". But in fact they work day and night to minimize "exposure", to be invisible to the vagaries of life, to avoid obligation, which to the player is risk. Their actuarial models are astoundingly complex and they endlessly keep their "valued customers" under surveillance, always gathering more data to "crunch" in their computations. Often players desire *not* to be understood for this aid in their effort to have their moves misread, at least until it is too late for the larger community to do anything about them. As authoritarian personalities they are, as John Dean calls them, "conservatives without conscience", but more accurately they are simply players; not in any meaningful sense conservative.[17]

The player is in it for personal profit. He lives by the social exchange modality of constant cost versus benefit analysis.[18] The baseline assumption, the ground of all reckoning is the self. All is reducible to intuitive calculus. Thus this is hardly rational unless one sees absolute egoistic interest as the bases of reason. This is the economic animal, *Homo economicus* par excellence.[19] John Stewart Mill presents this ideology in its first full expression in 1848, "[Political economy] does not treat the whole of man's nature as modified by the social state, nor of the whole conduct of man in society. It is concerned with him solely as a being who desires to possess wealth, and who is capable of judging the comparative efficacy of means for obtaining that end."[20] The player takes to heart the point of not taking the "whole of man's nature...nor the whole conduct of man in society", for the player dissociates his actions from the actual to the virtual system of accounting. This is what a group of French economics students in their manifesto calls "autistic economics", a science so abstract that it loses the human element entirely in pure econometrics. This manifesto, this written protest against how economics is perceived and taught, has led to a small but vocal movement among economists such as Edward Fullbrook and Anne Mayhew. In Ivy League economics departments a small movement called "post-autistic economics" (PAE) has begun and its central tenet is the principle of intersubjectivity. PAE argues that economics must begin by recognizing the social quality of economics and the economic actor. They are trying to change the discourse, moving it away from the autistic economic model that sees the economic actor in neoclassical theory as a function within a "dazzling" array of "calculations of utility maximization despite being entirely unable to communicate with this fellow man".[21]

In pure hypocritical style, the player, maximizing his own subjective wants and needs, embraces the neoclassical autistic version of other people as mere functions – tools to be used for his own personal satisfaction. And this utterly subjective perspective is elevated to the status of pure "rationality". The player is the embodiment of utilitarian pragmatism. The player sees everything in her life, including other people, as merely base resource. Her mission, her desire is to find a way to exploit everything to its maximum potential. She is an efficiency expert when it comes to achieving personal wants and needs. Life is a grand balance sheet, a competition for who can accumulate the most profit by the time they die. And so time too becomes money. All is competitive gaming, which is the nice way to refer to the complete fruition of Machiavellianism. But even competition involves some interest, some caring about how the other is doing. It presumes some form of communication and community right. No. Data gathering and surveillance is not communication; it is informatics. And the player despises competition even as he sings the praises of it and other social Darwinian principles. The pure player really does not care about how others are doing unless their fortunes affect his. He has no "bleeding heart" and expects no such sympathy in return, but as an opportunist will exploit such compassion if it comes his way.

To the player nothing is sacred except his own freedom to play at will. That which proves to be more of a cost than a profit is thrown overboard. In this sense the player is truly "objective" but hardly disinterested. The player is intently interested, observing as closely as possible and plotting demographics and psychographics down to the smallest possible variance. He longs for the power of prophecy/prediction. This obsession indicates calculation, intelligence; in a word agency. But to avoid responsibility, the player likes to say all is natural, causally determined by natural law. Yet at the same time the player likes to gloat over his superior decisions, his abilities to manipulate the system and thereby win. He believes in free will and inherent "talent".

This old Spencerian ideology, including its internal contradiction of law governed fatalism coexisting with individual agency, has recently and curiously worked backwards from social behaviour to biology as some economists are now arguing that the very existence of human beings is a consequence of natural economics.[22] We are told that economic decisions led to the success of *Homo Sapiens*. Wealth, life, and evolution are thus collapsed into a single process, which is the purest form of economic reductionism. Not unlike the linguistic turn, the economic turn argues that humans did not invent economy but instead that economy led to humans.

For the player, self-interest is identified with rationality. *Homo economicus* bases his choices on a consideration of his own personal "utility function". Economic man is amoral. He ignores all social values unless he gains personally from adhering to them, but such a coincidence is practically accidental. What is a rational course of action is the course that most enhances the accomplishment of his desires. Thus reason becomes utterly subjective while the player appears completely objective or disinterested in values and the interests of others. This is ego-hypertrophy leading to pure relativism. Perspectives multiply with the number of egos. There are as many realities, as many moralities and truths, as there are individuals.

A Case Study of Playing and Replaying

Consider the accounting practices of Silverado Savings and Loan, Broward Savings and Loan, Enron, Sally Mae, and Long Term Capital. Their accounting practices were created specifically to confuse and misdirect whatever oversight by law enforcement there might be. During Ronald Reagan's charge to eliminate oversight altogether, especially in the financial industry, we saw the results. "Conservatives" demanded lawlessness. The results of the Reagan era are now being repeated with foreclosures soaring to rates not seen since the mid-1980s (according to FBI and U.S. Census Bureau data, not surprisingly homelessness, poverty, and violent crime are also on the rise again). There should be no surprise that this debacle is being repeated because it is the same people, the same players replayed.

For instance, the Federal Deposit Insurance Corporation (FDIC) recognized as criminal the "land flipping" that led to the failure of many financial institutions including Empire Savings of Mesquite, Texas in April 1984. A month after Empire Savings failed, the Bank Board and the FDIC, seeing the looming financial disaster, tried to eliminate insurance coverage for speculative, brokered lending, but a federal court blocked the move. The result was that the taxpayer was forced to back the players.[23] Fast-forward to 2001. W. Bush, no longer a failed oil man but now President of the U.S., convinced his first Federal Reserve Chairman (and ardent admirer of Ayn Rand) Alan Greenspan to cut the prime interest rate to historic lows so that Americans would stop saving and start buying and borrowing. Bush also wanted to force all retirement funds including social security into private markets so that financiers, brokers, and speculators could get access to them. Forget that many older Americans saw their limited livelihoods linked to their certificates of deposit collapse.

The player's psychology, often expressed in fraternity rituals, is classically Freudian as they conflate sex, money, and death in the irresponsible pursuit of thrills and power. Even conservative liberals often admire and envy their chutzpah. What real conservatives consider irresponsible is the essence of the player's attitude and lifestyle. The player, like a child, also has lots of energy. They are movers and shakers, not bookworms or lazy types.

Savings in the U.S. is at an-all time low and it is lower than any other industrial nation. This is not a good sign, as most economists believe that "Economic growth occurs from high personal savings rates and increased labor force participation, and from technological change".[24] The imminent wave of baby-boomer retirement population has little to live on. Most experts agree that the "conservative" players' policies are leading to a burgeoning and massive population of elderly poor in America.

As of the summer of 2007, the current and precipitous escalation in foreclosures across the nation is, as Yogi Berra famously said, *déjà vu* all over again, for in the 1980s the entire Bush family was involved in a gigantic savings and loan scandal which, according to the FDIC cost the American taxpayer an estimated $1.4 trillion (with a "T"). At the time this amounted to nearly one quarter of the U.S. national debt. Each of the three Bush brothers and their father, George Sr. profited hugely by taking out massive loans and also granting huge loans to friends and business associates who then defaulted on them, leaving the U.S. taxpayer to pick up the tab. It is said that if you owe a bank $500,000 and you cannot pay, you are in big trouble. But if you owe a bank $500 million and you can't pay, the bank is in big trouble. This is true but it is not the executives of the bank, the players who are caught in the breach but instead the institution and the federal government that backs the financial infrastructure of private loans. It is taxpayers who have to bail themselves out. Meanwhile, the players in the "private sector" do their profit taking and run.

In the 1980s the Bushes got control of financial institutions. For instance, Neil Bush at the ripe old age of 30 became Director of Silverado Savings and Loans. They then began promoting predatory lending practices through unwise home ownership and real-estate acquisitions. They created a massive bubble that then burst. Today (2008) it is happening again only this time, the borrower has far less recourse to legal protection because the Bush's learned an important trick during the first fiasco, eliminate the ability of borrowers to file for bankruptcy protection. This in effect puts the borrower in the position of indentured servitude, and the government sponsors the entire private affair.

THE END OF BOUNDARIES/OBSTACLES, IDENTITIES

Around the world, poor people are disregarding nation-state boundaries as well as ethnic and racial boundaries. People are moving into societies that are predominantly different from themselves, to subject themselves to being a minority. They are flocking toward perceived relative economic opportunities with profound consequences for major cities everywhere.[25] Meanwhile, globalizing systems of exploitation are reaching into more and more remote communities. Development, progress, we are positively promised, is on the march.

The player is not an ethnic or tribal leader/hero. The player displays profound, late-modern, perhaps even post-modern dissociation. The player is an independent operator who can switch allegiances at will. The player's passion is for his own satisfaction. He does not share. The interest of the player is contrary to the interest of those played.

For instance, while 6 of the 10 cities in the United States struggling with the highest rates of real estate foreclosures are in California, at the same time and in the same state, even the same cities, the number of super mansion sales is soaring.[26] Each hollowed-out American city now has a suburb or two that is filled with huge single-family homes, tracts of status mimicry that have inspired the apt moniker "Vulgaria". At the same time manufacturing jobs, the backbone of the U.S. middle class, are vanishing. Players have allegiance to no one and no place and therefore they have allegiance to everyone everywhere. Players are like capital; truly global. They are willing to exploit any opportunity, anywhere, without prejudice. They are, according to some economists, saintly. Capitalism, it is argued, will overcome all forms of bigotry. All labour is equally one-dimensional, equally rolled flat under this transcendent god.[27] Thus jobs are fleeing high wage regions for repressed wage regions.

THE GOLDEN MEAN: THE SACRED MIDDLE

From the heights of the player's view, workers have no human dimension. From this perspective they are, as Herbert Marcuse put it, one-dimensional *Homo Laborans*.[28] The new form of control is for everyone to want, to long, to strive with all their might to enter Vulgaria, while those living it, the players, have always already harnessed that straining effort to their own ends. They are the ones who provide the frame for directing such desire. Either things work or they do not. It is therefore very important to advertise the gap between rich and poor, to "rub their noses in it". It is a calculated risk that players take for this could spark revolt, but the system allows for just enough mobility to defuse such an actuality. That is the function of the middle class.

The middle, between the rich and the poor is a buffer zone. Moving from poverty to middle-income levels is much easier than moving from middle to elite economic status. The limited mobility functions to defuse potentially destabilizing stresses among populations. It is not an illusion that if a person works extremely hard and invests, for instance, in their education, they can better their lot. But it is an illusion to believe that one can move to the top of the heap. This limited mobility "proves" that the system is a meritocracy, that it is fair and just. But that justice is as limited as the mobility enabled by the structural characteristics of the political economy.

Showing off the goods seduces the masses to want, to strive, to work. Providing cheap mimic or knockoff products to take the place of expensive original products proves profitable and also effective in satisfying "what the customer/worker wants". But in this process what the human being wants, namely equality and dignity, is replaced with commodities which are not only more easily acquired but, and this is vital, also reinforce indignity and inequality. The modern status struggle is one of social status but it has been transformed into one of commodity consumption.[29] The social and psychological dimensions of being for the inhabitant of the modern industrial, increasingly global world are rapidly being reduced to and defined by the political economy of consumerism.[30] No longer do traditional ritual and ceremony function. The magic and mythic dimensions of life are being exterminated as irrational. Only economic decisions are rational.

The "middle" class is the grand buffer, the modulator that keeps the system running. It is moderate: the moderator that the player class uses to keep the system of structural inequality stable. Allowing for a middle class was the most brilliant move the player class ever conceived. The middle class presents the truest of the true believers because they are supplied with products and services that mimic the world of the players on a smaller scale. They cannot afford a Ferrari but they can, if they work hard and are patient, late in life, perhaps, manage to acquire a Corvette. They cannot afford a yacht but they can take a cruise and be "treated like royalty". They cannot afford a true ranch or estate but they can be proud of their McMansion on half an acre, which itself requires massive debit burden. This burden keeps the ox-like worker moving "forward".

The greatest enemy of the lower classes is not the elite but the middle class who believes and strives. To attack the middle class dream and the Protestant work ethic, which became the core virtue, the sacred ideology and leverage the bourgeois players used not only against the clergy and nobles, but also workers as well — is to take away their motive for striving. The workers are their own worst enemy as they identify falsely with a mobile (progressive—liberal) "middle class" rather than their fixed "working class" reality. The Protestant work ethic and its internalization, is hardly a protest against unfair labour practices. It is the doctrine one small group, the bourgeoisie, used against other small groups, the clergy and nobles, in their struggle for supremacy. Meanwhile, the workers did not change their power position or status. If they work, they are not flawed or broken and therefore destined for the trash heap. If they do not work, they must be "fixed"; perhaps sent to a "correctional" facility.

The rewards of labour, as Max Weber noted, are said to be supernatural.[31] The rationalization of Christian-based capitalist asceticism is thus understood. But this is only partially correct. The real genius of the current system is that it gives actual, real, material consolation prizes to those who are most ardent defenders of the faith. This is why the current "prosperity theology" is actually playing with fire, because the faithful may come to realize the myth of the story, as preached, for unlike the traditional theology that stressed supernatural rewards, prosperity theology can be empirically tested. Otherwise, the true believer internalizes the belief that their failure to achieve upward economic mobility is their own private, personal fault; not a consequence of systematic, structural obstacles.

The market is portrayed as a mathematical miracle.[32] When markets are good for the player they are bad for those played. No longer do generals lead charges, captains go down with their ships, or CEOs lose when their decisions run a company into the ground. Beginning with the highly corrupt deals cut to build the transcontinental railroad in the United States during the 1860s, a new dissociation of the player from the game was instituted called "limited liability". The modern player came to hover over, to transcend the game, which he played. With limited liability, a company could be ruined while its management and/or owners took their personal profits and remained financially insulated from the outcome. Unlike the worker, whose work cannot be dissociated from industry, the player can take profits and leave. No longer is the player part of the system but rather the player games the system abandoning it if the chips are down.

OBSOLETE BUT USEFUL MODERNIST HEROISM AND REALISM

The fallacy of the grand ideology is the myth that those who sacrifice most gain the most. If one dies in service to the cause, reward must be had in the afterlife, a widely held belief that motivates millions not from reason but from emotion, indeed repressed instinctual drive from which are born "good" and "evil" as such, a strange motivator which prompted Friedrich Nietzsche to observe the obvious absurdity of the promise of "life *after* death".[33] How does a soldier or flyer justify to himself the fact that he destroys scores of innocents in places such as Dresden or Hiroshima or Baghdad? He does so by insisting that he is doing his job and not letting his mates within his clique down (for the ultimate clique is the platoon).[34] For young males pumping with testosterone, the more violent the dance, the chant, the communal activity, the "job": the greater the commitment to the group. Risk is the source of peril and so the greater the risk, the more emotional the bonding process. The menace must be defeated for the sake of all. The threat to "our way of life" equates with civilization itself in the most ethnocentric of narrow definitions. The true believer identifies with his job and those who help him get it done. Preservation of the system, not progress, is the goal. Thus, 17th-century positivism is revealed as an imperialistic apologetic, a myth based on emotion far more than reason. What counts as "progress" is the advancement of techniques and systems that defend and preserve the order; the "bigger bang for the buck" is the essence of efficiency.

As Sigmund Freud noted in his classic *The Future of an Illusion* irrational religious and nationalistic belief systems, and we add, down to the level of street gang membership and identification, is so closely associated with wishful thinking that it is never likely to disappear.[35] Wishful thinking, dreaming, is both escapism and also the catalyst for efforts to make reality perfect. Narcissism is at the core of all utopian wishful daydreaming. The hero, the central figure in control achieves eternal life, immortality. But he does so only by doing his job, even if that includes dying and murdering.[36] Such is the morality of ascetic self-contradiction. It is idealistic. The player is no idealist. He is a "realist", which is to say, an opportunist. For the modern hero-idealist, to die heroically becomes the goal of life. It is narcissism as social construct, self-love reflected by the adoration of others who need salvation. To be a hero, one must have a crisis and a weak constituency. Most glorious histories are motivational stories for the sake of this absurd ideal. Such is the dream of having tales and song written about and memorializing one's sacrifice. But the post-modern hypertrophically egoistic player wants his cake and to eat it too. He wants glory, *if it plays to his advantage*, without the need for self-sacrifice. In step the public relations experts. So too comes the proliferation of fake diplomas and fake military service medals to generate images without the need to actually embody it.

This is the age of simulacra, where image and symbolism is more real than obsolete spatial materialism.[37] But this world of symbolic force is something essentially different from mere representationalism. It is the "hyperreal", which is an endless, "always already" reproduction without an original or authenticity. The player feeds on the fact that there is no reference behind his reference letters, that there is no truth that could expose his lie, that he cannot be accused of lying at all because one cannot lie if there is no truth. The player is a player; not a liar or cheat. Such old identifiers are obsolete, hopelessly wedded to the notion that there is a reality independent of claim. In this world of pure discourse, hypocrisy and falsehoods are impossible. The will of the player is to be self-made, without referent, a true free radical. Such is the hypertrophy of militant individualism. Everything is available for acquisition and even spouses are contingent trophies, symbols to be displayed on one's arm at parties and galas as "mine" *for now*, the current Mrs. X. But this is a myth. The shepherd, the player is nothing without a flock and his loyal dogs. At some point, the person being most fooled by the slight-of-hand, by the cosmetic surgery of life itself, is the magician himself. As the street philosophy states, aging is not for sissies. Certain truths are inescapable, no matter how hard we wish. Donald Trump's hair becomes a joke.[38]

The basis of the carnival is the stark contrast between the pompous image and reality. Critical assessment is epistemological (as opposed to political) positivism in the service of justice. The fundamental break from mythological/religious hegemony comes when someone is brave enough to speak, to say publicly that in fact, in reality, the Holy tyrant, the demigod, has no clothes on. The nakedness is not of his well-fed paunch but of his well-fed narcissistic self-delusion. Insofar as this image is sustained as a social construct, when the herd begins to turn, the image evaporates. The hope of justice is that eventually, the magician ends up fooling only himself, and that others are freed from the delusion. For Socrates, the final straw is when the magician realizes this about himself. Saying it is so does not make it so.

The modern capitalist exploits others, giving them "value", in terms of his own agenda. The modern capitalist is often eager to lead the charge, to be the alpha male. By contrast, the player demurely allows others to lead the charges. The modern player prefers to profit from war without risk by, as the Du Pont family did, selling arms to both sides of conflicts while floating above such human, all too human, struggles.[39]

As a consequence of systematic distortion of communication, the buyer of products and political agendas, including wars, cannot tell what a "fair price" is, as based on costs, and therefore cannot bargain in good faith but only compare among profit takers. What is the true cost of going to war or not going to war? Presuming that people could make a rational choice if they had all the facts ("rational" being increasingly abbreviated by modern Machiavellianism as simply following one's own personal best interests), players, who often have very different interests from the majority such as trying to get as much labour out of workers as cheaply as possible, try mightily to obfuscate and distort facts. Just a few examples of this appear below.

The marketplace of products and ideas is distorted. And insofar as it is, it is antidemocratic, anti-justice. One ubiquitous example is the curious dual class structure within transactions between the wholesale universe and the retail universe.

While is may seem quaint today, many modern capitalists actually believed that their enterprise was spiritually motivated and that they were achieving progressive goals for society at large, elevating civilization, even if their methods were sometimes brutal. The player has no such motivations or delusions. He transcends religious and moral ideology. He is "beyond good and evil". The player is a narcissist and he does not care what others think of it.

THE SUPER-PLAYER

Now we turn to discuss the globalization of playing and gaming, the outreach by means of secret societies and communication between various government leaders and their intelligence, military, and trade agencies as they craft strategies and tactics to assure the success of their personal agendas. Much "international cooperation" is based on personal ties, as for instance the Bush family's intimate relationship with the Saudi royal family. While interlocks among royal families may seem to be a thing of the past, a secular version now reigns.

The super-player manifests an essentially post-modern, Western attitude and identity. He sees himself liberated from all religious and nationalistic associations, all obligations and limitations be they of investors, workers, colleagues, or law. As Karl Marx noted, capital knows no boundaries, no limits; morally, geographically, culturally, or ethnically. The super-player is an equal opportunity exploiter who, for instance, cares little for local traditions taking many wives and trophy women, men, companies, and toys such as mega-yachts, mansions, airplanes, et cetera. Arguably the first wide scale outbreak of the super-player mentality was during the gilded age. But today's super-player egomaniac makes the old guard look positively conservative by comparison.

The super-player, unlike the modern capitalist, cares little for being a national hero, a pillar of any community. The super-player is dissociated not only from place and tradition but from the lives of the vast majority. For instance, from 2001-2004 the jobless rate in the United States rose to over 6 per cent despite the surge in defence spending (which keeps the U.S. rate lower than most European nations), and the earning power of the working class has steadily declined for the past 30 years. At the same time everything has become "super" and "mega" with new terms emerging such as "superyacht" and "megafortunes" being coined just to try to describe the new post-national, global lifestyle of the super-player.

SUPER-PLAYERS AND THEIR SUPERYACHT ENVY

For instance, while jobless rates rose in the U.S. supersales of super luxury yachts 120 feet or longer jumped by 10 per cent every year from 2001 to 2004. The keels being laid are growing in size dramatically along with their price tags.[40] Players are fighting for the longest boat. Paul Allen, co-founder of Microsoft, has three superyachts including the 301-foot *Tatoosh* and the 198-foot *Madusa*. Until 2005, the longest was his new 416-foot yacht. Most of the details about *Octopus*, as it is called, and perhaps appropriately as the moniker conjures up images of Allen's vast diversification of business interests, are a tightly held secret. It is known that *Octopus* has state-of-the-art communications capabilities, multiple helipads, is manned by a crew of over 60, including former Navy Seals, and has its own 12-man submarine that deploys from the bottom of the hull.[41]

The real story of interest here is the player's mindset. A case in point is super yacht envy, whereby super rich players compete with each other to own the longest yacht in the world. What might have seemed unseemly flaunting of riches by previous capitalists, holds no reservations for today's super-player.

Super rich players become dissociated from money and its value. Money takes on a meaning for them, which is quite different from what money means to the vast majority of human beings. In this case it is expressed as the competition between Allen and Oracle founder Larry Ellison. The magazine *Power & Motor Yacht* now covers the explosion in super yacht construction like a race because the genteel pastime of yachting has been overtaken by the player mentality. The rivalry between Allen and Ellison has become legendary. Ellison's boat was under construction about the same time as Allen's. Ellison's original design was for a boat a few feet shorter than Allen's, but mysteriously Ellison's yacht ended up being a few dozen feet longer. The result is Ellison's 452-foot *Rising Sun*. *Rising Sun* is actually only one ship in a flotilla. *Rising Sun* is part of a 200+ million dollar fleet which includes the super yacht itself and three smaller boats, known as tenders, each more than 40 feet in length, that accompany it. *Rising Sun* has 5 storeys of 82 rooms. It has 86,000 square feet of living space, which is roughly the size of an average Wal-Mart. It has a gym, a basketball court, a private cinema, and an extensive wine cellar.

This may seem the final word in super yacht envy but Ellison's boat was soon surpassed by a 525-foot super yacht built for the crown prince of Dubai. Others in the global game of who has the biggest super yacht include Russian oilman Roman Abromavich, with his 354-foot *Le Grand Bleu* (in addition to at least two other super yachts), Leslie Wexner, whose 315-foot *Limitless*, which is a play on the clothing company that made him rich, Limited Brands. Others in the game of show me how long it is are Peter Lewis, former CEO of the insurance company Progressive Corp., who has the expedition-style 255-foot *Lone Ranger*. One observer of the super yacht scene has noted that converting deep-sea tugs into a pleasure craft such as the *Lone Ranger* is very expensive and rare. "This is much more than a Hummer. It's as if someone bought themselves an M1 tank and decided to drive through the Jack In The Box with it."[42]

MODERN CAPITALISTS VERSUS POST-MODERN PLAYERS

The size of personal fortunes started expanding dramatically concurrent with globalization beginning in earnest around 1980. Before this time there were players and the superrich to be sure, but the new breed is far less nationalistic, far less conservative, much more mobile and richer than the old denizens of the Gilded Age could have imagined.

While modern capitalists held family as sacred and patriarchal hierarchy as sacrosanct, the player does not care for any such obsolete notions and their socially imposed obligations. Today, players see themselves and their work as transcending the parochialism of communities, cultures, nations, languages, religions, and races. They play at the orders of things rather than defend them. They express a highly dissociated attitude which means that the player is "objective", careless, which is another way to say uncaring except for her own "bottom line".

Capitalists were yet associated with community, while players are utterly dissociated. Modern capitalists often thrived on investing other peoples' money and lives, but often their own too. The Kennedy brothers were quick to respond to the chance to fight in World War II. Similarly, Theodore Roosevelt was so eager not to miss participation in his generation's war that he resigned his prestigious position as Assistant Secretary of the Navy to enlist as a lowly Lt. Colonel in the Army forming the First U.S. Volunteer Cavalry Regiment out of a ragtag bunch that ranged from cowboys from the Western territories to Ivy Leaguers. It was a diverse group with little experience and who were poorly equipped. But they shared a common sense of nationalistic obligation and patriotism. Only Roosevelt had a horse in this "cavalry" regiment. But it is a fact that Roosevelt the romantic risk-taker did fight. Modern capitalists like to see themselves as adventurers-leaders. The player, by contrast, often "flies under the radar".

The real risks that capitalists take sometimes pay off, and sometimes end in disaster. In either case, nothing is left alone. Another example, another struggle junky, if not flat out war junky (at least in his youth) was Winston Churchill who, in 1895 secured a commission from the *Daily Graphic* newspaper (the name of which is itself is more than suggestive) to travel to Cuba and observe the fighting between Cuban guerrillas and the Spanish. Later, Churchill, the war correspondent, was disappointed that the Greco-Turkish war ended before he could join the fighting, but he got his chance to fight in India. One might think that his lust for action would abate but as First Lord of the Admiralty, his eagerness to engage the Turks at Gallipoli led to a disaster for the British troops who were slaughtered as they tried to fight up the beaches on the

Dardanelles during World War I. Churchill had personally fought in the Second Boer War and at the Battle of Omdurman, so he knew war, but not enough it seemed to become cautious of it.

Such is the character behind the Western notion of global conquest. Its ambition comes out of Western philosophy's dream of grasping universal understanding and control, first articulated in the person of Alexander the Great. A similar universalizing attitude is seen in the tyranny over mere mortals, anonymous soldiers, mere contingent people (later to be called general issue canon fodder) under the first emperor of China, ÇØÊ¼»Ê (Qin Shi Huang). This attitude, which has emerged in many cultures through time, found an efficient confluence with a new scientific and technological prowess in Renaissance Europe, a power that enabled reach across oceans to globalism. This confluence led through the development of the navigational chronometer, steam power, the telegraph, the radio, the airplane, the atomic bomb and up to today's genius for mass destruction and global reach from extraterrestrial orbital platforms. The desire of the player is to rise above the mundane, to ride a horse, to escape the mere pedestrian perspective, to make history, to make history as truly his personal story of exploits and conquests. The new super-player's ego is not interested in being a saviour of his nation. It is now global in scope.

Mobility is the player's goal and the game, reality, is mutable. Players don't play by the rules, they play the rules themselves; they "game" the system. To a player, rules are for dupes and pilgrims; innocent, harmless fools. The player seeks angles. Rules, harmonies are stolen, borrowed, manipulated, and disregarded at will. The player often sees himself as a Nietzschean *ubermensch*, as a person who "transvaluates" his own and the community's values. But this is false for the Nietzschean *ubermensch* famously has the courage not of his convictions but the courage to challenge his own convictions. The confident player never abandons his self-interest. He creates and manipulates the game at will, which, having such enormous power through lobbying and access to capital and armies of politicians, lawyers, and accountants who distort the intent if not the letter of the rules, makes community practically impossible.

CONCLUSION

Disregarding the Hobbesian warning, the great message of global capital is an assault on the obligations social contract put upon individuals. The mantra is that every person has not only the right but the duty to pursue his/her personal happiness, and in arenas of scarce resources this leads to Machiavellian tactics in the social Darwinian struggle of every man for himself. Under such conditions, to not be a Machiavellian is to be a dupe. Of all the phrases in the United States Constitution, the one that repeatedly is used in product and service advertising is the God-given right to pursue personal happiness.

Gaming the system and being a player are hypertrophic egocentric attitudes. They are not conservative. Conservative societies revere tradition, responsibility, obligation, social status as proper place, which is often regarded as an inherent, unchangeable quality of a person. Conservative societies change little. Late-modern/post-modern society changes rapidly. Fortunes are made and lost. Social and physical mobility are accelerating. Everyone wants to believe they are players, are in the game scrapping as a free agent to make their reality as they wish. But in traditional conservative societies, though equality exist and is even canonized, even the elite, the kings and emperors are forced to abide by sacred ritual and comportment lest the cosmos falter. There are countless examples of this. The ritual bloodletting ceremony of the Inca royals is an example. To maintain the cosmic status quo, the Inca regularly scarified their own genitalia so that their royal blood could be used in rituals to assure the continuance of the world. They had no choice in this and if one tried to rebel and avoid the pain, he was seen as an extremely dangerous disruptor of cosmic harmony and killed. In traditional, conservative cultures, the inherency of blood dictates the social station even for the royals so that privileges and obligations are dictated by sacred law.

Conservative cosmologies tend to be grounded in sacred, eternal beliefs that guide their motivations and behaviours.

The player is the ultimate expression of post-modern ego hypertrophy. He articulates a kind of militant liberality, an extreme fundamentalist expression of individualism. The player is a player precisely because she does not see herself bound by any traditional norms or mores. They do what they want. The law is more problematic but that too is part of the challenge of the game to the player. Now breaking norms and mores and "stretching" the law may be frowned upon by "normal" folk so secrecy is an important aspect of playing. Keeping one's moves hidden and controlling visibility are important powers the player seeks to enhance. Players sometimes crave visibility, to be celebrated, to flaunt their wealth and power. What good is being a player if you can never show off? But at the same time, they want to control the image and so they have public relations experts at their beckon call and lawyers ready to slap down unwanted publicity with threats of libel and slander lawsuits. Beyond this, as Ben Bagdikian has observed, players in utterly unrelated spheres of industry and influence discovered in the 1970s that it is easier and more controlling to buy-up the media than to constantly struggle with it.[43] Why threaten an inconvenient investigative reporter with slander when you can just fire her and kill the story altogether? Thus the moves, made by one "holding", say a financial "unit", can either be puffed or ignored by another media holding within a conglomerate. Boards of directors have become notoriously lax in oversight of corporate operations.

The player has no association with the product or service they produce or with community. Nothing has any essential meaning or quality to them. Everything is contingent. The player is totally liberated and mobile. Unlike the old "captains" of industry, who often actually invented their products and processes such as Goodyear, Edison, Ford, Carnegie, and who saw themselves, and were seen by most, as pillars of their communities, benefactors to the neighbourhoods bringing jobs, prosperity, and a free Christmas ham or turkey, the post-modern player has no interest in the community or even the product.

They are scientific. They have no passion, no associative attachment to the product or service. With the rise of management schools on university campuses and increasing emphasis on quantification and computational methods, the player today believes that she can move from business to business with no need to even know what the product or service for sale is and be successful. All that matters is the accounting, the bottom line. Whether it is shirts, automobiles, pest control, arms manufacturing, health care, even running a church, the job is the same, work the books, maximize profit for the shareholders. Manufacturing and selling pharmaceuticals is basically the same as manufacturing and selling bombs or pimping sex slaves. The street drug dealer is not lying when he says, "I'm just a business man. I just offer a service that is in demand. If I didn't service the market someone else would."

Consequences? Like the predatory loan shark who talks a young inexperienced and marginally literate couple into a mortgage they cannot afford, the excuse is the same. Whether it is buying street drugs or an often even more hazardous mortgage from a treacherous money pusher, everyone is free to make their own mistakes and their own fortunes. This mentality achieved global proportions in the 1980s when commercial banks, seeing profits galore in developing nations, bundled loans into "super loans", plunging many of the poorest countries deep into debt. The motto: Let the laws of Machiavellianism work, including exploiting, when convenient, the doctrine of social Darwinism. But while the player espouses risk-taking and decries government welfare for losers, she makes sure that the tax-supported bailouts are codified for her own risky business. Thus, if banking managers make horrible decisions, the Federal Deposit Insurance Corporation (FDIC), founded by the Glass-Seagall Act of 1933, and Federal Reserve are there to guarantee their investors' accounts.[44] Forgiving foreign debt is even seen as saintly. Hence the player's mantra. Never risk your own money, health, and well-being, always risk someone else's. I don't want my own to go to war, or down into the mines, or my own money to be invested. I'll just take a percentage if it succeeds.

Everything is subsumed under the new science and technology of the market. Its laws are written in the sacred discourse of accounting, which is often purposefully mystified along with associated jurisprudence; part of the secrecy of power. This is the new global religion and the player is the new high priest. But it is not conservative and the player/priest enjoys a power previous clerics could never have imagined. She does not fight to uphold the law but fights to skirt it and to escape the obligation and duty of community norms and mores.

The player is the most hypertrophic late-modern. In fact, the player is the deficient aspect of liberality which is bad faith and cynicism. The player is actually an expression fo deficient postmodernism. The player believes in nothing but herself. And she believes that reality is not fixed, certainly not sacred or eternal. Reality is what she can make of it, which means her ability to manipulate reality against other manipulators. Rules, certainly not eternal rules, such as the inalienable rights of humans as Denis Diderot called them, do not exist except as obstacles to self-fulfilment. Transcending law implies equality "under" its purview. Equality is, to the player, the most pernicious of liberal myths. The player sees nothing but opportunity. But the freedom to exploit is limited by other opportunists. This is the game. Rules are made to be broken. Taking risks is the gamer's drug. Thus, players use tools of manipulation to shape their reality such as advertising agents, public relations agents, army-sized legal departments, various managing techniques (some threatening, some appeasing), shrewd accountants that find loopholes and ways to hide income, private detective agents, and lobbyists.

Players "game" the system, which means to cheat or seek a semi-legal way to avoid the intent of policy and law. And when this is pointed out to them, the players' rebuttal is that they did not invent the game, they merely play by its rules. But of course, through lobbying they also help invent the rules. This is bad faith for they are denying their own freedom as a rhetorical move to be free of responsibility as a member of a community. They are willfully ignoring the consequences of both the system and their gaming of it. Hence the argument that "I did not invent the system, I just play by the rules", is the same as saying it is okay for me to pull the trigger because I did not invent firearms.

NOTES

1. Jurgen Habermas, *Communication and the Evolution of Society*, trans. T. McCarthy (Boston: Beacon, 1979).
2. Eric Kramer, "Cosmopoly: Occidentalism and the New World Order," in *The Emerging Monoculture: Assimilation and the "Model Minority,"* ed. E. Kramer (Wesrport, CT: Praeger, 2003), pp. 232-291.
3. F. Bales, *Personality and Interpersonal Behavior* (New York: Holt, Rinehart & Winston, 1970); R. Bormann, "The Force of Fantasy: Restoring the American Dream," in *Communication Theory* (New York: Holt, Rinehart & Winston, 1980), pp. 184-190.
4. Eric Kramer, *Modern/Postmodern: Off the Beaten Path of Antimodernism* (Westport, CT: Praeger, 1997).
5. See Vance Packard's 1958 classic *The Hidden Persuaders*, which chronicles the original marriage of social scientific psychographics with mass rhetoric to formulate messages of mass persuasion and image manipulation.
6. Garret Keizer, "Crap shoot: Everyone Loses When Politics is a Game," *Harper's*, February 2006, pp. 31-39.
7. John Ruskin, *Unto the Last and Other Writings* (New York: Penguin, 1986).
8. Ibid, p. 44.
9. These harsh criticisms appeared in two essays published in 1860 in the *Cornhill Magazine*, "Ad Valorem" and "The Veins of Wealth". The outcry by subscribers against the essays was so great that the publisher stopped publishing them after 4 months. Ruskin responded in 1862 by compiling his essays on economics and publishing them as a book titled *Unto the Last*.
10. Ruskin, *Unto the Last and Other Writings*, p. 32.
11. Ibid, pp. 32-33.
12. Ibid, p. 32.
13. Ibid, p. 35.
14. Ibid, p. 39.
15. Kramer, "Cosmopoly: Occidentalism and the New World Order," pp. 232-291.
16. V. Gold, *Invasion of the Party Snatchers: How the Holyrollers and Neo-cons Destroyed the GOP* (New York: Sourcebooks, 2007); R. Viguerie, "Bush's Base Betrayal," *Washington Post*, May 21, 2006, B01.

17. John Dean, *Conservatives Without Conscience* (New York: Viking Adult, 2006).
18. G. Homans, "Social Behavior as Exchange", *American Journal of Sociology* 63 (1958): pp. 597-606.
19. The phrase "economic man", first appears in the utilitarian John Stewart Mill's *The Principles of Political Economy: With Some of Their Applications to Social Philosophy* (1848).
20. John Stuart Mill, *The Principles of Political Economy* (Amherst, NY: Prometheus, 2004).
21. G. Bigelow, "Let There Be Markets: The Evangelical Roots of Economics", *Harper's*, May 2005, pp. 33-38.
22. See: R. Horan, E. Bulte, and J. Shogren, "How Trade Saved Humanity From Biological Exclusion: An Economic Theory of Neanderthal Extinction", *Journal of Economic Behavior & Organization* 58, no. 1 (2005): 1-29.
23. For a detailed timeline of the great S&L scandal of the 1980s see the FDIC website at http://www.fdic.gov/bank/historical/s&l/
24. J. Ritter, "Economic Growth and Equity Returns", *Pacific-Basin Finance Journal* 13, no. 5 (2005): 489-503.
25. Kramer, "Cosmopoly: Occidentalism and the New World Order".
26. CNN, "Report: 8-Figure Home Sales Soar", *CNN Money*, May 7, 2005.
27. W. Greider, *One World, Ready or Not: The Manic Logic of Global Capitalism* (New York: Simon & Schuster, 1997); T. Frank, *One Market Under God: Extreme Capitalism, Market Populism, and the End of Economic Democracy* (New York: Anchor, 2001).
28. Herbert Marcuse, *One-Dimensional Man* (Boston: Beacon, 1964).
29. D. Morris, *The Human Zoo* (New York: Kodansha, 1996).
30. The phrase" political economy" was originally the standard nomenclature for economic phenomena until the free market ideology enacted by true believers in the political realm, generated a series of human disasters such as the Irish potato famine. After such debacles, academic apologists sought to inoculate themselves from such realities by dropping the term "political" from "political economy". Thus we have the new science of economics that claims to have no political dimension. Such sophistry attempts to conceal (a typical player move) the fact that government policies effect economies and vice versa.
31. Max Weber, *The Protestant Ethic and the Spirit of Capitalism*, trans. Talcott Parsons and R. Tawney (Meneola, New York: Dover, 2003).
32. H. Cox, *The Secular City* (New York: Viking Adult, 1966).
33. Friedrich Nietzsche, *On the Genealogy of Morals*, trans. Walter

Kaufmann (New York: Vintage, 1967).

34. G. Dyer, *War: The Lethal Custom* (New York: Carroll and Graf, 2006).
35. Sigmund Freud, *The Future of an Illusion*, trans. J. Starchey and P. Gay (New York: W. W. Norton, 1989).
36. The totally divergent positions taken by Heidegger and Nietzsche here illustrate Walter Kaufmann's (1992) contention that Heidegger understood Nietzsche very little, though he wrote a three volume work ostensibly about Nietzsche. It was based on very little study of Nietzsche's workers and mostly on Elizabeth Nietzsche's ideas more than Friedrich's.
37. B. Baudrillard, *Simulations*, trans. P. Foss, P. Patton, and P. Beitchman (New York: Columbia University Press/Semiotext(e), 1983).
38. While writing this in 2007, a feud between a famous female comedian/troubadour, Rosie O'Donnell and the real estate tycoon, Donald Trump titillated the herd. A good example of the carnivalesque aspect of the feud is an amateurish video O'Donnell posted on her website showing her and her lesbian companion tipping longneck beers while mocking Trump and the fact that he announced to the world that his latest trophy wife would not dare fart in his presence.
39. P. Ndiaye, *Nylon and Bombs: Dupont and the March of Modern America*, trans. E. Foster (Baltimore, MD: Johns Hopkins University Press, 2006).
40. CNN, "Unemployment Hits Eight Year High", *Lou Dobbs Moneyline*, May 3, 2002.
41. CNN, "Superyachts of the CEOs: From Miniature Submarines to Multiple Helipads, Boats of the Business Elite Keep Getting Fancier", *CNN/Money*, July 29, 2005.
42. Ibid.
43. Ben Bagdikian, *The Media Monopoly* (Boston: Beacon Press, 2000).
44. Until February 2006, there were two separate FDIC funds; the Bank Insurance Fund (BIF) and the Saving Association Insurance Fund (SAIF). The latter, not coincidentally, was established after the huge savings and loan crisis of the 1980s, which the Bush family had a major part in. In February 2006, President George W. Bush signed The Federal Deposit Insurance Reform Act of 2005 (the Reform Act) into law. The FDIRA merged the Bank Insurance Fund (BIF) and the Savings Association Insurance Fund (SAIF) into a single new fund, the Deposit Insurance Fund (DIF), thus eliminating one backup system for depositors.

11

A Critical Education for a Critical Era: A Global Pedagogy

Steven L. Arxer and David L. Reznik

INTRODUCTION

Anyone who has gone through or is currently experiencing the process of obtaining an advanced degree can testify to the sense of excitement and anxiousness felt before beginning one's educational journey. The prospect of being in a classroom where a wide range of new and challenging ideas are discussed, each offering a different understanding of one's sense of self and the surrounding environment, can be quite exhilarating. Indeed, what can be more invigorating than having the ability to escape reality through imagination and investigate those aspects of life that are taken for granted? Even the etymology of education points to the basic promise to offer persons a way out of even the most difficult of predicaments. Education is meant to free and improve the lives of persons by providing alternative possibilities to an event, thus eliminating any form of servitude. In short, education is supposed to foster the type of illumination that leads to self-mastery.

Nevertheless, those of us who are students, teachers, or have been involved in the educational process for some time are likely to describe a very different scenario. The prevailing message conveyed nowadays is that education functions optimally for persons when conceived in a realistic, not idealistic, fashion.

Students, for example, are encouraged to be exceedingly pragmatic and use their education to better adapt to the dominant social, economic, political, and environmental conditions. Engaging in philosophical speculation about who they are or alternative ways of relating to one another and the world is too abstract and distant from daily needs. As the saying goes, utopian thinking may have well-founded intentions, but it should quickly be dismissed and discouraged as it is irrelevant and unproductive in the so-called "real" world.

A growing number of people are becoming familiar with the technical term used to describe today's "real" world—namely, globalization.[1] Through television broadcasts, newspapers, popular magazines, and (in)formal conversations, the public is regularly informed about the basic reality of globalization. Specifically, they are told the entire globe is facing dramatic changes to which everyone will have to adjust, if they wish to survive the current reconfiguration of life. Adjusting, in this case, means accepting and implementing the new norms, policies, and practices associated with making economies more efficient on a global scale with respect to managing the production, distribution, and consumption of goods and resources. Simply stated, the current mode of globalization refers to the international refinement and sedimentation of capitalism.[2] Moreover, these developments are said to be intimately tied to progress and thus should not be disrupted, as such interference would only cause societies to miss key opportunities for growth and consequently fall behind.

However, the question remains as to how these significant changes should proceed. After all, the present age is marked by a deep sense of disillusionment with political processes. The public's everyday experiences, and unfortunately too often those of young persons, breed distrust and skepticism for politicians or any platform. Why should the citizenry trust a political machine that seems increasingly more interested in garnering votes and political cache, instead of fulfilling the interests and needs of the larger community? If popular comedic television programmes, such as *The Daily Show* and *The Colbert Report*, signal anything it is that politics denotes manipulation, deception, and self-aggrandizement and thus should not be taken seriously.

It is important at this juncture to recognize the current interest in the market and its attendant values for filling the public's attitudinal vacuum while also accomplishing the demands of globalization. The market is being advertised as the best mechanism for regulating the process of globalization, an economic viewpoint popularly known as neoliberalism. More vital, however, is what the public hears about the market. Specifically, the market is touted to be free from bias and able to respond effectively to economic needs. So long as the market is not interfered with, neoliberals argue, the best possible outcome for the production, distribution, and consumption of goods and resources will be forthcoming. This comes as a relief for an already disenchanted public facing the challenges of globalization, for now the well being of society is guaranteed through the abandonment of politics altogether.

But how does education fit into this scenario? Education is largely viewed as a core strategy for taking advantage of key life chance opportunities.[3] This is not altogether a new theme. Education, after all, has for some time been associated with the improvement of one's standard of living. However, with the advent of globalization it is said that "education is more important than ever before".[4] The rationale behind this is that in a dynamic world that has a more competitive global economy, a greater necessity for cross-national communication, and constantly advancing information technologies, persons' survival depends more than ever on their ability to be flexible and stay up to speed with the rapid changes taking place at work, school, and other social arenas. Furthermore, because information is viewed as perhaps the most valuable commodity in the current high-tech globalized world, persons without an advanced degree or sophisticated job training will soon find themselves on the periphery of society.[5]

For both developed and underdeveloped countries, the message is thus the same. Receiving an education is closely tied to globalization as it promises to help persons manoeuvre around obstacles but also exploit the ever-expanding new possibilities available to them. Education provides individuals with the information that is highly-valued at the marketplace, along with the means for utilizing this knowledge.

It should therefore come as no surprise why more and more students are becoming adamant realists. For, rather than being critical or utopian, relevant/valid thinking in the current context means reflecting reality as closely as possible. Again, the idea is that those who desire economic enhancement within a complex world should first and foremost become fixated on how the world works. Questions related to the meaning of reality are assumed to be a liability. Critical thinking (i.e. not simply problem/puzzle solving but investigating underlying assumptions) is a distraction and contributes little to those living within the era of globalization. Questioning reality, after all, frustrates the simple absorption of the world.

As a result, the neoliberal perspective of globalization has led to the marginalization of philosophy and other humanities in education. This is accomplished by encouraging students to avoid critical thinking and spend time focusing on how the market functions and wealth is generated. Thus schools are becoming places of refuge, being flooded with students seeking a way to weather the storm of globalization. Their hope is that armed with the latest information and techniques, the deleterious effects of globalization will be tempered.

Nevertheless, there is some question if this educational approach will help students avoid the difficulties of a globalizing world. After all, an overemphasis on the market seems to support the ability of corporations and other business interest groups to operate freely in society without reservation. In this respect, the present class structure and its repression are reinforced and treated as if they are normal and inevitable. The marginalization of large portions of the population, for example, is attributed to personal flaws or motivational deficits, rather than how society has been organized. The amelioration of social problems, which was the purpose of education, now becomes difficult since efforts toward social change lack a supportive environment.

THE RISE OF MARKET EDUCATION: A BRIEF HISTORY

Before looking at some of the deleterious consequences of market-based education on student life, the theoretical legacy of this educational approach must first be examined. Reviewing this philosophical-historical context will improve our understanding of the rise and growing impact of the market in education. To begin with, market education should be recognized for its close association with the theoretical perspective known as functionalism, which dominated a wide-range of disciplines in the mid-20th century. While French sociologist Emile Durkheim is credited as its founder, Talcott Parsons gave this perspective serious momentum with his influential work, *The Social System*.

According to functionalism, society should be understood as a system. On the surface, this may seem a rather innocuous metaphor to describe the social world. After all, persons today regularly use a systems approach to understand an array of phenomena, such as blood circulation in the body, complex computer networking, and even social interactions. Nevertheless, the problematic implications of adopting a systems world-view, especially for education, can easily be missed without a deeper examination of its underlying assumptions.

A system is a complex whole whose parts emerge and develop specific functions to maintain the system's overall existence. In this way, systems are considered relatively autonomous and self-sufficient, since each element is neatly integrated with one another and their surroundings. This, in turn, creates a closed circuit effect within which survival takes place through the functioning of parts. For example, society is thought to naturally produce social roles and institutions that generate the prerequisite values, norms, and resources necessary for society to achieve a state of interdependence and equilibrium. The social world, therefore, should be thought of as a comprehensive, well-oiled machine that is devoid of fundamental conflict. Systems, after all, are supposed to be deeply interconnected, based on consensus, and thus harmonious.

This type of imagery suggests a very specific and clear purpose to institutions. Simply put, institutions exist because they provide the basic function of ensuring the survival of society.[6] Given Parsons' ongoing concern for order, this view of institutions makes sense. Parsons is well known for being obsessed with what he called the "Hobbesian Problem", or the idea that chaos is always looming because of the inherently greedy and self-interested human nature. What this meant for Parsons is that human action cannot be trusted to be the foundation of social order. Persons are overly subjective, rendering them inadequate to substantiate something as important as society. But by envisioning institutions as emerging naturally from the social system itself, organizational rules and directives are available that are allegedly divorced from human bias. In short, systems have objective needs and produce the proper mechanisms to fulfill them. Why then should society be thought of as any different?

Following this line of thought, Parsons argued that persons should be viewed as linked together structurally via their roles. In this case, roles possess the behavioural expectations (i.e. norms) set out by the larger social system and thus should be viewed as superior to other considerations. Roles are external to individuals, part of an "ultimate reality" according to Parsons, serving to orient persons by generating a consensus on the basic attitudes, values, and actions necessary for social cohesion. As he articulated in later works, elements high in energy are subordinate to those high in information.[7] The idea is that without the guidance supplied by information, energy would be directionless and tending toward chaos. Not surprisingly, Parsons viewed roles as housing the information, while human action simply contains untamed energy.

But what is the function of education within this outlook? Education is supposed to instill the information and proper motivation to foster the continued operation of society. Schools, simply put, are agents of socialization. In actual practice, schools are expected to transfer the values and technical skills people need to operate in society. The implications of this style of education are obvious. Students are grossly passive, primarily seeking assimilation into social values that have been universalized. As Freire noted, this constitutes the "banking method"[8] of education in that learning is uni-directional and largely a process of depositing, storing, and retrieving facts.

This scenario mirrors perfectly the way Parsons envisioned the operation of roles. Roles are linked by what Parsons called reciprocal expectations, or double contingency. Roles, in other words, are not isolated but complementary. For example, teacher and student fit together because of their respective functions, thus ensuring the preservation of the institution of education. Simply put, the "educator's role is to regulate the way the world 'enters into' students".[9] This relationship is thus asymmetrical, with students being placed in an inferior position respective to their teachers. Inferiorization is deemed necessary, since passivity allegedly makes it easier for the acceptance of higher order information—namely, scientific, technical, and de-contextualized knowledge. Students' subordinated status, however, is described as only temporary, lasting until the internalization of the curriculum has been achieved. But despite the promise of upward mobility, the validity of the dominant values being propagated by teachers, texts, and other authorities is never seriously critiqued or questioned. Hierarchical authority within education and society at large remains intact, since mobility refers to people being merely reshuffled within social structures. In this way, the main purpose of education is the "reproduction" of persons who function within current institutional arrangements and not the promotion of agents of social change.[10]

The dominance of functionalism began to wane during the 1960s and 1970s when many students and activists rebelled against this educational approach. They argued that functionalist theory encouraged passivity and support for a social and political status quo that was full of racism, sexism, and other forms of discrimination. Indeed, some functionalists even suggested that poverty was required by society in order to motivate people to work hard.[11] Nevertheless, a different view of education was surfacing, one that was influenced by the work of many critical and Marxists theorists, as well as social movements, calling for resistance and liberation. Most important, individuals were seen as active agents who "make history". Persons were understood as shaping their institutions through concrete actions, rather than simply being channeled by organizational structures. The idea was that because social order reflects the efforts and maintenance of human action, a framework is available for social change.

Change, however, was imagined in an overly narrow way, emphasizing individual liberation. For example, "consciousness raising" and "personal development" were popular topics in education, but they became easily interpreted in overly individualistic ways.[12] A liberal version of education was promoted, which assumed that personal growth would automatically equate with social improvement. The common good was viewed as the by-product of personal change. Certainly, personal development and an understanding of unjust structural conditions are essential, but what was missing was a serious focus on how to create the context for autonomous community organizing. A discussion of class conflict, for instance, does not necessarily include an articulation of the type of action needed to foster a collective, democratic life. In other words, when conceived within a liberal framework, emancipation does not automatically have a communal thrust. Ultimately then, the fact that questions related to social and economic justice were indirectly addressed limited the depth and relevance of these movements' critique of educational theory and practice.

This deficiency helped set the stage for the backlash that occurred during the 1980s, which saw even the most minimal changes rolled back by politicians like Ronald Reagan and other neoconservatives. While part of their message included the familiar rhetoric of a return to traditional values, something new was added that radically altered the nature of education to the present day. Specifically, it was stressed that the market, because of its neutrality, should guide social life by supplying the rationale behind every institution. In short, the preservation of society was linked to the promotion and expansion of market values into all social spheres. As might be expected, education was not exempt from this new proposal. According to Harvey Cox, this period was unique as it saw the rise and intermixing of a new religious and economic fundamentalism, as the market became God.[13]

A MARKET PREREQUISITE: THE COMMODIFICATION OF STUDENTS

As part of creating this "Total Market", as Serrano and Hinkelammert describe it, education was reconceptualized to more closely embody market values.[14] Schools were meant to turn students into functioning adults who are able to navigate through markets successfully.[15]

Similar to functionalist theory, the purpose of market education is also the social reproduction of the values, ideas, and practices that legitimize existing power relations. The primary difference is that the market seems immune from the type of criticism launched against functionalism. Functionalism, it should be noted, was severely criticized for mistaking the interests of the few and powerful as synonymous with the interests of all. The market does not make this error because it is portrayed as value-free and transparent. Thus if existing social structures are being replicated, it is not because of the political or economic interests of certain groups. After all, everyone, irrespective of background, is fairly judged and rewarded at the open marketplace. Market proponents, therefore, draw a distinction between the enforcement of market values and the propagation of class ideology.

While neoliberal rhetoric is quite enticing, the market-based education results in nothing short of transforming students into commodities. As part of this process, students are described as "human resources".[16] The idea is that schools are supposed to manage students in such a way as to make them valuable at the marketplace. The goal is to increase student's "human capital", so that when trying to secure employment they will have more leverage during the bidding process. Like the production cycle of a factory, students are viewed as raw materials that, once processed by the educational system, become high-priced products to be traded within the system of exchange.

As a result, an increasing number of teachers are trying to make their coursework more socially relevant and "grounded". What this means in reality is that all disciplines are in a desperate search for an economic niche to monopolize, so they can advertise themselves as offering marketable skills to students or other interested parties. For example, sociology students are trained to aid the criminal justice system in solving crimes, rather than questioning the social etiology and construction of criminality. Even philosophers frequent corporate news stations like CNN, as many have become advisors for businesses, addressing issues related to ethics.

However, all of this is not news to students today; they are quite used to hearing from faculty and fellow colleagues the importance of their "professional development". While the idea of professionalism can be quite admirable, in that it can mean bringing integrity and rigorousness to one's work because of its potential social impact, this is not exactly the message being conveyed. More often than not, a professional student is described as someone who anticipates market demands and chooses a line of study by projecting into the future which research will yield the greatest market returns. Now schools and universities whose mission was to foster the ideals of the humanities begin to act more like high-tech vocational programmes; their aim is to transfer the technical knowledge and skills required to perform marketable tasks. In this way students are made into commodities, since the acquisition of an education takes place in order to increase persons' saleability and purchase value.

At this juncture some may ask: Hasn't vocational training always had a place in the curriculum? Isn't being productive necessary for living and even part of the process of empowering persons? No one is arguing against developing a skill set, but rather how productivity is conceptualized within the market. What has changed, therefore, is the acute lack of competition among values. Specifically, student development is framed in economic terms, as the optimization of the ratio of input to output. Skills that increase students' performativity at the market are esteemed, while those that do not are deemed irrelevant and subordinated. Given this economistic backdrop, technical skills rather than reflexivity become most important, as the former offers immediate utility. But more troublesome is that with the emphasis on performativity, the aim of education is to improve persons' utility at the marketplace, rather than to raise questions regarding the nature of any enterprise. The scope of education is thus narrowed because market mentality dominates the scene, guiding the way discussion, conflict, and knowledge-production are conducted.

The popular slogan used today by many universities and technical schools—"education for the future"—describes this extremely conservative approach used to direct learning.[17] Schools are considered reservoirs of information and technical skills, which can be reorganized at any time to stay in tune with market conditions. Students are being told that success in the new global market requires that they be up-to-date with the most current data and techniques. For, without a dynamic and pliable workforce, the forecast appears quite grim: Those individuals and economies unable or unwilling to upgrade their technical skills are likely to lag behind as the rest of the world pushes forward into the future. Moreover, the fear associated with deviating from this course guarantees that students will accept the market system as the only rational line of action.

In this manner the support needed to foster alternative ideas is truncated once the market becomes the only possible and reasonable option. In some circles this scenario is known as the "hidden curriculum", wherein schools covertly socialize students to be flexible and compliant employees within the division of labour. These themes, however, seem to be the prominent principles of education, as many teachers and administrators now candidly and unabashedly state that education should serve this end.

Despite the reductionism of values, this sacrifice is viewed as worthwhile since market-based education is tied to persons' survivability. Educated persons, simply put, are more marketable and, in turn, can create the advantages necessary to attain a sense of power over their own lives. Faced with the challenges of a global economy, education is a primary strategy adopted to ensure economic freedom and mobility, not only for individuals but for society as a whole.

MARKET ONTOLOGY, DUALISM, AND STUDENT ALIENATION

As mentioned earlier, neoliberals believe that society will be improved with the introduction of the market into every aspect of social life. Economic performance will be enhanced with a good dose of the discipline instilled by the market, they argue. In particular, the unbridled competition found at the free marketplace is what allows this device to respond favorably to the best ideas and products, while eliminating any bad ones. Furthermore, society as a whole is improved because only the most effective and skilled traders emerge victorious.

A fundamental assumption that persons must make at this point is that the market rewards solely on the basis of merit. Failures, for example, must be looked at as individual shortcomings as opposed to institutional flaws or biases. Losses do not result from discrimination or select classes having more economic and political might. For, as neoliberals point out, life-outcomes determined by these factors would be irrational in the market system, as they would only restrict the maximization of profit. Instead, those who do not succeed at the marketplace are said to have failed because they did not take advantage of available opportunities and were not able to adapt to market demands. According to this logic, stratification "out there" (in society) is thought to mirror natural inequality "in here" (within individuals). Presently Americans are asked to adhere to this logic and believe President Bush when he says that "[o]ur society rewards hard work and honest ambition".[18]

For the market to accomplish this task, however, it must first be given a special ontological status. This mechanism must be viewed as autonomous and ahistorical, so that the familiar biases and prejudices of economic or any other human interaction can be removed.[19] Once this perception is in place, all outcomes from the market can be trusted to be fair and rational, given that politics has been purged from the economic process.

But what legitimizes the market's unique status? The universality of the market is attained through the belief in a fatuous philosophical position known as dualism. Dualism is the assumption that the human element can be removed from the pursuit of knowledge and order. In other words, the knower is separated from what is known. Once facts and values are sequestered in this fashion, objectivity is said to be available for ready use. Neoliberals argue that the market supplies this necessary dualism because it operates on the so-called objective principles of "calculation, preferences, costs, profits, prices, and utility".[20] And language that is more formalized and scientific is usually viewed to be less biased and offer a clearer depiction of reality than everyday speech.[21]

As a result of this dualism, the market is catapulted into a superior realm. Given the almost divine stature of the market, the value of everything is determined within the confines of its logic. Severed from the human condition, the market is presumed to be bereft of the personal and political problems that plague everyday living. It is no surprise why neoliberals are so excited about, and even fetishize, the market. For them the market simply represents a superior mode of trade that avoids the biased nature of prior economic forms, such as planned economies. As Smith reveals, the value and legitimacy of the market has always stemmed from its alleged ability to "escape or transcend economy altogether".[22]

Throughout the Western tradition, a variety of factors have been used as an ultimate referent. Be it God, the state, the crown, natural law, or human nature, the idea has been to provide an unadulterated standard people can follow to avoid disaster. In this respect, the market can be located within a well-known, but problematic philosophical tradition. Specifically, the market represents the latest model of power in a time when old-fashioned themes, such as mythology are viewed to be irrational, undemocratic, and passé. Absolutism therefore has not fallen by the wayside; rather, it has been reorganized and deployed anew. Today the market reigns supreme, standing as the premier method of social control in our times.

At this point, the central question for us becomes: How does the metaphysics of the market affect student life? How does the market, for example, shape how students perceive themselves, others, and the future? It should be remembered what proponents of the market say about their style of education. Specifically, education geared towards making students valuable at the marketplace will only increase persons' success in the face of globalization and their sense of personal freedom in an ever-complicated world. The irony, however, is that liberty is significantly undermined by the market. As with any dualistic proposal, individuals are made to confront and fall victim to institutions of their own making. The validity and status of the market would be irreparably damaged if human volition and intention were allowed to profoundly influence this mechanism. Subjectivity, in short, must be contained in order to avoid jeopardizing the objectivity and generalizability of market logic.

A variety of serious, but subtle, problems emerge that are associated with the supposed universality of the market which greatly minimize the freedom, control, and quality of persons' actions with respect to their present social conditions. Put differently, the market produces what Marx called alienation, wherein humans are estranged from, and controlled by, products of their own activity that falsely appear autonomous.[23] To illustrate this point, quotes have been gathered from undergraduate and graduate students, as well as professors, who attend and work at one of the largest state universities in the United States. They represent some of the thoughts, feelings, and experiences of students and teachers from various settings, such as the classroom, on-campus group meetings and events, as well as personal conversations. Three main themes emerge that reveal the effects of the market in education.

HISTORY AS AUTONOMOUS

The first problem associated with market education relates to the perspective of history it propagates. As is customary, neoliberal globalization is described as a trend that is inevitable and unavoidable. Persons are told that this process cannot be reversed, nor should it, since its economic outcomes are rational, progressive, and beneficial to the entire world. Advocates of globalization claim that once markets have become deeply integrated and their discipline instilled in traders across the globe, the resulting efficiency will create prosperity for everyone. Given this portrayal, why would any person or society seeking success resist this trend and not join the rest of the modern world?

In this respect, the market perspective on development is reminiscent of how history has largely been viewed within the Western tradition. Specifically, history is conceived as an autonomous process. For example, Plato, medieval thinkers, and Hegel saw history brought on through the efforts of an eternal form that reconciles and integrates conflicting positions over time. Materialists, such as Aristotle, Comte, and Spencer, attributed historical movement to evolutionary laws. In both cases, however, history is linear and guided by an ahistorical apparatus, whether it is in the form of spirit or matter. Staying with this evolutionary motif, change is conceptualized as slow, gradual, and incremental, rather than spontaneous, rapid, and multidirectional.

According to Lyotard, a dualist view of history eviscerates human action, as the meaning or purpose of an event is found by simply locating its place on the "itinerary of the Spirit".[24] The market's current position on the historical continuum therefore signals, if anything at all, its immediate relevance and inherent legitimacy. Because history is considered an immense project that transcends specific contingencies or disputes, it guarantees that the future always represents an improvement from the past. Introducing markets into every aspect of life, such as schools, is thus considered a progressive move that will only enrich and strengthen those sectors. The market, in short, is not simply one mode of regulating global affairs, but rather the epitome of economic and historical development

Fighting the process of modernization should therefore be seen as a useless battle, which indicates one's ignorance of the economic realities of the day; at least this is what critics of globalization are told. Disrupting the present trend will only cause individuals and societies to miss important economic windows. Those who criticize neoliberal globalization are presented as either ignorant or unable to adjust to the direction the world is taking. Given this context, should the fatalism and malaise to present conditions exhibited by students be any surprise? Students, after all, are faced with nothing other than what Fukuyama called the "End of History".[25] The course of history is already set, in that patterns are the result of an ahistorical mechanism working itself out. Human involvement is therefore ancillary because it is mainly reactive; persons simply *respond* to the autonomous movement of history. This viewpoint, moreover, reinforces the aim of market education to teach students how best to respond to and exploit the process of globalization.

REDUCTIONISM OF INTELLIGENCE: THE DOGMATISM OF COST-BENEFIT THINKING

In addition to its perspective of history, a market world view assumes a particular understanding of human intelligence. Because of the emphasis on the market in education, students begin to imagine themselves to be traders. And intelligent traders are, of course, those who can identify market signals and quickly devise a plan that will optimize profitability. To be a good trader, therefore, students should be vigilant to burgeoning market opportunities and exploit these growing niches. As was mentioned earlier, students should think of themselves and their research as valuable commodities to sell to the highest bidder.

In this context, the mind should not be distracted with theories or questions about human existence, but rather focused on the costs and benefits of any scenario. Students should work at becoming adept at calculating. At the marketplace, value is determined by whether or not a particular commodity yields greater returns than its competitor. The majority of students' energies are thus directed toward the ceaseless accumulation of facts and data that will provide the basis for making correct decisions. Gathering information and organizing it as quickly as possible is central, so that likely trading scenarios can be projected and advantageously executed.

No doubt, students working within this framework are very pragmatic and sober. Seasoned traders are not ones easily swayed by utopian ideals or rigid dogmas, but people fixed on the world and how it operates. The serious student, in this respect, should not be interested in philosophical arguments or questions, but follow the example of veteran traders who are primarily concerned with how to best position themselves on the market. Students are well advised to keep their feet on the ground and politics at the door, since their job is simply to gather, process, and make logical decisions.

However, this sort of intelligence is not necessarily critical or reflexive, since rational thinking is mathematized and logic perceived to be a unified system. Reason consists of simply drawing conclusions from premises and data. Consistent with dualism, this type of logic assumes that reason and judgments are disconnected. Reason, therefore, is decontextualized and activated in a vacuum, in which the presuppositions built into cost-benefit analysis or any methodological technique go unscrutinized.

This is precisely how market mentality introduces its own dogmatism, as it uses its own logic for self-justification and removes from inquiry the conceptual, historical, and other situational considerations that gave rise to this form of thought. Such a manoeuvre is accomplished in actual practice through slight of hand: technical competence simply avoids anything that is not related to procedural issues. As is common to hear in classes, questions that critique the foundation of positivistic projects are said to be off topic and eschewed from discussions. Cost-benefit logic is now presented as universal, rather than reflecting the power arrangements and social commitments made to the particular assumptions that underlie this style of reason. Intelligence is thus reduced to mere calculation, while other ways of experiencing the world are discredited for being irrational or indicative of emotionalism.

The absolutism of market logic has serious implications for student life. First, with the emphasis on gaining marketable skills, alternative ideas and experiences are lost. Students are repeatedly cautioned against working in "unmarketable" areas, as this would only create a disadvantage vis-à-vis other competitors. For example, languages, practices, and ways of thinking that are part of students' culture, but are not translatable into market mentality, must be removed from the learning process. In this case, students go to great lengths to make themselves acceptable to employers and thus alter their physical and interpersonal being. Reminiscent of Marcuse, students are made to reflect a "one-dimensional" market culture.[26]

A second consequence is the elimination of philosophy and the underdevelopment of critical thinking. Philosophy has little to contribute to the market, unless it is reduced to calculation and puzzle solving. For at the centre of philosophy is wonder, or what the Greeks called *thaumazein*. Philosophers are supposed to examine the underbelly of reality, or those dimensions of life that are taken for granted. Moreover, through critical self-reflection the philosopher can be released from the implied necessity of reality. Thinking based on wonder blurs the boundaries between the necessary and the possible. Critical thinking, in other words, shows the limits of the current world and thus frees persons from the legitimacy of reality. This intersection of the necessary and possible creates what Walter Benjamin called a "disruptive moment", which is the precondition for social change. In short, a new condition is always possible, since critical philosophy can aid to "salvage relative truths from the wreckage of false ultimates".[27]

Students entrenched in market logic, however, find this model of philosophy deeply problematic. It is customary to see students roll their eyes whenever the teacher mentions that philosophy will play an important role in the class. Never mind that many of these students who continue on to graduate school will be receiving a Ph.D. and become *doctors of philosophy*. Yet it must be understood that the thrust of students' whole raison d'être may be undermined with the introduction of critical philosophy into the classroom setting. To be sure, this type of inquiry may help break the universality of capitalism and other social arrangements, since interpretation and reality are allowed to intermingle. With nothing short than their identity at stake, it is no surprise why students are increasingly becoming more adamant realists and defenders of the status quo than their professors.

Nevertheless, educational processes that do nothing more than help students adapt to the market impede the development of democratic institutions. For example, students are instructed to avoid and be suspicious of divergent ideas. Creativity becomes something that should be fostered only within the confines of the market. Artistic or other skills should be used to improve products, help businesses advertise, and create larger profit margins, since these applications of one's talents are market-centred and productive.

But teaching students to be acceptable to employers encourages a monological relationship with institutions. Students are groomed to be nicely inserted into the division of labour, rather than to challenge corporate employers and their practices. In this respect, globalization becomes passively accepted, as students have been primarily instructed to reinforce institutional mandates. Democracy, however, is severely weakened in the process, for people do not know how to think and act critically with respect to institutions. Any critique that may lead to fundamentally questioning the assumptions of the current order are labeled troublesome, self-destructive, and a waste of time and resources. With such a weak-minded citizenry, however, what kind of democratic society is possible?

ZERO-SUM GAME AND LOSING THE SOCIAL BOND

Perhaps the most unsettling implication, though, is that the imagery and values that support the market destroy the social bond and any sense of community solidarity. A characteristic trait of market theory is that education is mostly an individual affair. According to the liberal mantra, the improvement of society results from the pursuit of personal gain; personal enhancement is viewed as the panacea for all social problems. To this end, persons should not intervene to purposely alleviate structural inequities, as this activity would only disrupt and distort market operations. Instead, students should be narrowly focused on enhancing their own position, rather than dedicated to ending poverty, sexism, or other social problems.

If these social issues are on students' agenda, they are overwhelmingly conceptualized within market logic. Poverty, for example, is solved by further expanding the market to include others, so that they too can increase their human capital and saleability. Furthermore, the subordination of women and other minorities is rectified by placing them in higher-level positions within the market economy, ignoring all the while the inherently exploitive nature of capitalism. As one female military general explained to an auditorium filled with students, women have surely come a long way, for now they can also shoot the big guns.

In both cases, the common good is eventually cast aside, whether sooner or later, as students ultimately see themselves embroiled in a zero-sum game that they cannot escape. Because of the market's emphasis on individualism, other persons begin to be viewed as a threat to one's personal freedom. Simply put, repeated success in a competitive world means always having an advantage over one's opponent, which in turn ensures victory. Just like any other game, market participants know that their gains are balanced by the losses of another. Social ties become a liability, since they can begin to restrict persons' capacity to implement the most effective strategy for winning. For example, collaboration may reduce competitiveness among persons, likely inhibiting their aggressiveness and performance at the market. Developing bonds to a community may fortify one's concern and care for its members, thus making it difficult to act mercilessly, precisely when the market demands that businesses downsize, relocate, or implement other cutbacks to increase profits. Indeed, students are quite aware that some time in the near future, they may be competing for a job with the person sitting next to them in class. As a result, persons opt for strategies that enhance self-protection, rather than build ties that may disadvantage them at the marketplace.

The point is that ethical or moral concerns are marginalized as a result of the social imagery forwarded by the market. The world is portrayed in an atomistic way, wherein persons are independent entities simply pursuing their own preferences without serious regard for others. For in the end, everyone is a potential adversary and obstacle to achieving success. Even family bonds become a hazard, limiting one's physical movement and ability to follow market trends. Thus all relationships begin to lose their fundamental human connection, or what Marx called their "species-being", since collective action and sharing are debilitating ventures for those who seek to maintain their competitive edge.

Given this scenario, who then will address and work toward ending the fragmentation, war, and violence witnessed daily in the world? Many may still cry out, "Our students, they've done it before. Their idealism and hope will save us!" Our students, however, may be ill-equipped to take on this challenge, given the heavy dose of realism to which they have been exposed. Thus, a new ethos is needed to guide education, one that allows students to respond critically and collectively to the world.

A NEW STUDENT FOR A NEW WORLD

According to many critics, the market is not the appropriate metaphor to use to organize education in a democracy.[28] For these critics, a democratic society is forged when a diverse set of autonomous and cooperating bases can express their ideas while community members work toward putting them into action. Simply put, pluralism, egalitarianism, and a deep commitment to social justice are the hallmark characteristics of a free society, rather than ideological absolutism, inherent hierarchy, and indifference to one's fellow human being. The idea is that in fostering diversity, all institutions will begin to embody and reflect the multiple perspectives, histories, and practices that constitute the citizenry. This is the true meaning of representation.

Yet market-based education undermines this process by fostering assimilation and alienation. Because education is overly pragmatic and constructed to support the demands given by the capitalist order, marginalized positions are expected to adopt a similar viewpoint on pertinent issues, such as the superiority of the market. Rather than the preservation of the

Other, the market presents a ruthless ultimatum to persons: Adapt or Die!

For this reason, critics argue that at the heart of education should be a critical dimension, so that persons can become well equipped to devise alternative means of addressing personal and social problems. An education that simply aligns students with the market can very well produce good competitors, but it most certainly also fosters "low intensity" democracy.[29] Here students do not question the legitimacy, relevance, and social consequences of what is being taught, while fulfilling parliamentary procedures becomes their only means of ensuring a democratic society. It is important to note that this situation is forthcoming from an educational system that trains students primarily to become technicians. Technicians, after all, are not critical but only know how to respond to procedural requirements and instructions.

A popular idea found in Latin America may serve as an alternative to market education. Many there are calling for an educational process that originates "from below". The point here is that education should not be in the business of supporting market values and its associated class interests. It should not be doing business at all! Instead, education should live out the spirit of democracy and emerge from the masses. The purpose of education, in short, is not social reproduction, but the democratization of social life, whereby ideas and actions are fashioned and directed from all segments of society. Only after this radical de-centring of knowledge and power occurs can education be removed from the control of corporations, investors, managers, and other capitalist henchmen, and placed in the hands of the people.

The message here is simple: Control over one's life is not attained by learning how to placate those in power. Assimilating the values of the elite and portraying them as universal does not foment the independence necessary for persons to become self-governing. Education will serve the people only when it can sufficiently critique and offer an alternative to the belief that history and the current order are inevitable and require the polity's submission. Unless participation is accompanied by appropriate social imagery, this activity can be simply another, more insidious, name for instituting and nurturing economic and cultural homogeneity.

At the core of introducing this new democratic imagery is the basic rejection of dualism and its myriad of manifestations. Specifically, the proposition that the human presence can be sequestered from the search and production of knowledge and order should not be given any credibility. Reminiscent of Lyotard's idea of the post-modern condition, persons should express "incredulity toward metanarratives", or a disbelief of anything that claims to be ahistorical.[30] Simply put, a more democratic vision is one that views all phenomena as intricately related to human action and thus contingent. The validity of knowledge, in this case, is tied to interpretation and human creativity, also known as *praxis*.

To gain an appreciation of what this means, a central issue must be grasped at this juncture. Specifically, the influence of language (i.e. interpretation) cannot be avoided. That is to say, at no time can persons escape making assumptions, or "language games", to organize social reality. Knowledge and order originate from the linguistically constituted assumptions made about this phenomenon. History, therefore, is simply the story of which assumptions (views) were acted out, invested, and maintained as opposed to others, while also recounting the lived consequences of these actions. In more modern parlance, an established order is truly nothing more than a *social construction*. The point is that rather than ahistorical, reality is deeply interpretive but no less consequential. From a myriad of possible constructions of the present, any one can be highlighted, but any final rendition of reality is "agreed on by its players and subject to eventual cancellation".[31]

Democratic theory, therefore, is necessarily critical, as freedom is constituted negatively—through a recognition of the limits of assumptions, alternative positions gain significance and emerge as realistic avenues for action. Democratically speaking, only after the subject-object divide has been bridged and nothing distances the polity from their social order, can a society be forged that is truly "of and by the people".

A new world for the betterment of the human condition must be the aim of education today, while its purpose should be to fashion students who turn this promise into a reality. While there are many facets to engendering this new model for education,the following suggestions may serve to guide this process:

1. ***Students are not blank slates and passive receivers of information.*** Empiricists are incorrect that persons simply record and respond to the impact of sense impressions. Subsequent to the demise of dualism, the mind cannot be granted such an ancillary role in the production of knowledge. Students, instead, represent beings of *praxis* who give the world meaning and modify this phenomenon through interpretation. Students actively engage in, negotiate, and generate knowledge. The problem up to now has been the deadening of this capacity through the reification of a specific style of learning and form of knowledge. Contrary to functionalists and market proponents, education should not be the uni-directional transmission of information, but should be "co-intentional".[32] Here teachers and students work together to chart a path of self- and social critique meant to produce a better world for everyone. All ideas are subject to examination, criticism, and even revision so that the most conducive context for the establishment of democracy and social justice is in place. Students should not be reprimanded for being utopian or idealistic, bur rather pushed to make dreams come true. By encouraging creativity, innovation, and social reflexivity, students can overcome the "narrow minded empiricism"[33] and cost-benefit logic of the market and enter into a commitment to improve the world by becoming, as Ellacuría says, "agents of change".[34]
2. ***The classroom is not a static place of reproductive socialization, but rather a space for liberation.***[35] In this context, teachers interrupt the everyday rhythm of life so that students can be wanderers who freely entertain a diverse set of proposals and experiences for organizing

social existence. The key is that the prevailing reality does not determine how the past and future are viewed, and students are free to critique the status quo so that new worlds can gain sensibility and be experimented. Moreover, the breadth of this process is defined only by the limits of our students' imagination. Schools, therefore, should encourage a critical defiance to social injustices, promote self-determination, and give rise to collective action. In other words, schools should exhibit an "aggressive disposition" and confront any impediment to developing a more humane world.[36] To be clear, academia and education in general are never neutral, but constitute thoroughly political endeavours. The reason for this is simple: given the rupture of dualism, all epistemological claims are intimately tied to value judgments in the form of interpretation and are thus *interested positions*. Politics, as Stanley Fish notes, is not simply what happens in government, but represents the inescapable process of elevating in importance particular proposals that cause other views to be obscured.[37] The current model of education is certainly political in this sense, since it reifies the market while eclipsing (if not decimating) alternative positions. Schools must openly recognize the political thrust of education and purposely elevate those positions that seek the humanization of the world and not its alienation.

3. ***The market and the present form of globalization are not inevitable***. Through an anti-dualist stance, the market and globalization can no longer be viewed to be autonomous forces that demand automatic recognition. Rather, these two phenomena are an outgrowth of a particular historical practice and commitment to certain ideals. In this regard, the realism and fatalism associated with market globalization must be eliminated. Capitalism, in short, represents nothing more than a convention that has simply been more deeply reinforced and invested than other models. This formation is just one among many ways to envision and organize social

life, although it is one that does not promote the interest and well-being of the majority of persons. Students, therefore, should view history as *immanent*, in that events are closely linked to human action. The stability of the current world, therefore, represents the historical and present efforts of particular persons or groups, and not the result of an ahistorical trend. Accordingly, alternative plans are not indicative of irrationality and unworthy of serious investment.[38] Because history is the product of *praxis*, globalization can be rethought and redirected to better represent the needs of the world's population, including humans and the environment at large. In short, a post-capitalist logic is possible and should constitute an essential element of any educational process that aims for democratic, and not simply economic or "sustainable", growth.

4. ***Students are not commodities***. Students should not be conceived as material objects to be improved for the marketplace. As Kant noted some time ago, persons are not things and should be treated as ends in themselves. The rationale behind this claim is that because humans give value to the world, they become worthy of being valued. However, the valuing that takes place at the market reduces moral beings to the level of price. In capitalism, as Marx argued, everything is appreciated for its "exchange" rather than its "use" value. People are worthy because they *have* much, rather than because they *are* much.[39] Thus commodities, human capital, and human resources are the wrong metaphors to use to guide the educational process, since they only serve to dehumanize students. Good schooling should not be equated with success at the market, but should include the development of moral beings. In this case, students should study, critique, and develop their intentional capacity so that their humanity is further refined.
5. ***Education should serve the common good***. Education should embody the democratic ethos and strive to improve life on this planet. Schools, therefore, are

ethically responsible for the well-being of others and should be a "voice for those who have no voice".[40] This requires the elimination of the atomistic world view characteristic of the market. Persons are not isolated atoms and threats to one another; instead, existence unfolds intersubjectively with the Other.[41] Simply put, a community exists before persons begin to feel like discrete beings, since an "I" is presupposed by an "Other". Because life is fundamentally communal in/with nature, questions should pertain to how best to articulate and plan this communion. Education is not an exception and should have at its core a basic obligation to attack those ways of thinking and acting that debilitate the strength of a global community. The structural inequality and alienation endemic to capitalism, for example, must be vehemently fought and replaced by projects that promote social solidarity. Accordingly, students should be encouraged to aid in the emancipation of local and global communities by articulating ways to get the goods, services, ideas, and support necessary to achieve this goal. In all, education should have an ethical thrust by promoting a "community pedagogy".[42]

CONCLUSION: LOVE IN EDUCATION

For globalization to offer dignity, and not just survivability, to all life across the globe, it must attain a more human face. Yet the construction of global markets will not necessarily foster this end, since this endeavour only finds increasingly innovative ways to dehumanize those who participate. At a scale never before seen, persons are reduced to the level of objects, bought and sold at the global marketplace, and their sense of community deeply eroded. Because these considerations comprise the underlying philosophy of neoliberal globalization, it seems unlikely that this approach will lead the world to a new and better future.

The world therefore will only benefit from globalization when resistance to capitalism's expansion is given support everywhere. A belief in a different world must be encouraged, so that a logic beyond capitalism is given legitimacy and further developed. Education can certainly help generate this new world view by reconceptualizing how persons view and treat themselves, others, and the earth. To borrow from Patricia Hill Collins, only when love becomes the purpose behind all human endeavours, will the world be a *home* to persons.[43] The construction of this home will no doubt require a significant amount of work and innovation, as the elimination or rethinking of old arrangements may be needed.

Nevertheless, with a new educational strategy available, students will be ready to deploy reality in multiple ways and thus recognize viable alternatives to the market version of globalization. Persons will no longer feel estranged and fearful of their world, since now what is necessary is defined and what was possible is made real. Through community pedagogy, a new world can be forged together and for one another. Rather than reflecting its end, education will teach of the "liberation of history".[44] Here praxis meets the world intimately, authentically and ethically in order to remove any mechanism of enslavement. A critical education can be a testimonial to this by illustrating that freedom can be secured so long as alternative worlds can be imagined. So, let's allow our students to dream!

NOTES

1. Anthony Giddens and Will Hutton, eds. *Global Capitalism* (New York: New Press, 2000).
2. Saskia Sassen, *Globalization and Its Discontent* (New York: New Press, 1998).
3. Nelly P. Stromquist, *Education in a Globalized World* (New York: Rowman & Littlefeild Publishers, 2002), p. 28.
4. Marcelo M. Suárez-Orozco and Desirée Baolian Qin-Hillard, eds., *Globalization: Culture and Education in the New Millennium* (Berkeley: University of California Press, 2004), p. 16.
5. David E. Bloom, "Globalization and Education: An Economic Perspective", in *Globalization: Culture and Education in the New Millennium*, eds. M. M. Suárez-Orozco and D. S. Qin-Hillard (Berkeley: University of California Press, 2004).
6. Talcott Parsons, *The Social System* (New York: The Free Press,

1951), pp. 36-45.

7. Talcott Parsons, *Societies: Evolutionary and Comparative Perspectives* (Englewood Cliffs, NJ: Prentice Hall, 1966).
8. Paulo Freire, *Pedagogy of the Oppressed* (New York: Continuum, 1992).
9. Ibid, p. 62.
10. Pierre Bourdieu and Jean-Claude Passeron, *Reproduction in Education, Society, and Culture* (London: Sage, 1977).
11. Kinsey Davis and Wilbert E. Moore, "Some Principles of Stratification," in *Social Stratification: Class, Race and Gender in Sociological Perspective*, 2nd ed., ed. D. B. Grusky (Boulder, Colorado: Westview Press, 2001).
12. Freire, *Pedagogy of the Oppressed*.
13. Harvey Cox, "The Market as God", *The Atlantic Monthly*, March, 1999.
14. Alejandro Serrano Caldera, *Los Dilemas de la Democracia* (Managua: Hispamer, 1995); Franz J. Hinkelammert, *Critica de la Razón Utópica* (Bilbao: Editorial Desolée de Brouwer, 2002).
15. Stanley W. Rothstein, *Schools and Society* (Englewood Cliffs, NJ: Prentice Hall, 1996), pp. 34-36.
16. Stromquist, *Education in a Globalized World*, pp. 29-31.
17. ITT Technical Institute, "Education for the Future", Retrieved June 24, 2006 (http://www.itt-tech.edu/).
18. Bush, George W. 2002. "Bush Announces New Initiatives for Corporate Reform". *BushCountry.org*, July 9. Retrieved November 3, 2000 (http://www.bushcountry.org/bush_speeches/president_bush_speech_071002.htm).
19. Franz J. Hinkelammert, "La Economía en el Processo Actual de Globalización y los Derechos Humanos", in *El Huracán de la Globalización*, ed. F. J. Hinkelammert (San José: DEI, 1999), pp. 239-249.
20. Barbara Herrnstein Smith, *Contingencies of Value: Alternative Perspectives for Critical Theory* (Cambridge, MA: Harvard University Press, 1988), p. 127.
21. Frederick J. Newmeyer, *The Politics of Linguistics* (Chicago: University of Chicago Press, 1986), pp. 31-62.
22. Smith, *Contingencies of Value*, p. 126.
23. Karl Marx, *Economic and Philosophical Manuscripts of 1844* (Amherst, NY: Prometheus Books, 1988), pp. 74-79.
24. Jean-François Lyotard *The Postmodern Condition: A Report on Knowledge* (Minneapolis: University of Minnesota Press, 1984), p. 35.

25. Francis Fukuyama, *The End of History and the Last Man* (New York: The Free Press, 1992).
26. Herbert Marcuse, *One-Dimensional Man* (Boston: Beacon Press, 1964).
27. Max Horkheimer, *Eclipse of Reason* (London: Continuum, 2004), p. 124.
28. C. Mendoza and Villarreal Montoya, *Democracia Multiculturalidad y Educacion* (Guatemala City, Guatemala: Ministerio de Educacion, 2001).
29. Alejandro Serrano Caldera, *Los Dilemmas de la Democracia* (Managua: Editorial Hispamer, 1995), pp. 103-104.
30. Lyotard, *The Postmodern Condition*, p. xxiv.
31. Ibid, p. 66.
32. Freire, *Pedagogy of the Oppressed*, p. 56.
33. Ernst Bloch, "The Conscious Known Activity within the Not-Yet-Conscious, the Utopian Function", in *The Utopian Function in Art and Literature*, trans. J. Zipes and F. Mecklenburg (Cambridge, MA: MIT Press, 1988), p. 106.
34. Ignacio Ellaucuría, *Escritos Universitarios* (San Salvador: UCA Editores), p. 199.
35. Ellaucuría, "Is a Different Kind of University Possible?" in *Towards a Society that Serves its People*, eds. J. Hassett and H. Lacey (Washington, DC: Georgetown University Press, 1991), p. 127.
36. Ibid, p. 184.
37. Stanley Fish, *Doing What Comes Naturally* (Durham: Duke University Press, 1989).
38. Francis Houtart, "Las Alternativas al Modelo Neo-liberal", *El otro Davos*, eds., F. Houtart y F. Polet (México, DF: Plaza y Váldes, 2000), pp. 66-85.
39. Erich Fromm, *To Have or To Be?* (New York: Continuum, 1976).
40. Ellaucuría, "The Task of the Christian University", in *Companions of Jesus*, eds., J Sobrino, I. Ellaucuría, et al. (Maryknoll, NY: Orbis Books, 1990), p. 150.
41. Emmanuel Lévinas, *Totality and Infinity* (Pittsburgh: Duquesne University Press, 1961).
42. Ellaucuría, *Freedom made Flesh* (Maryknoll, NY: Robis Books, 1976), p. 243.
43. Patricia Hill Collins, *Black Feminist Thought: Knowledge, Consciousness, and the Politics of Empowerment* (Boston: Unwin Hyman, 1990).
44. Ellaucuría, "Is a Different Kind of University Possible?", p. 205.

12

Globalizing Metaphysics of the Will

Algis Mickunas

In his work "The Gordian Knot", Ernst Junger attempts to solve the glaring East-West tension in terms of the history of Orient and Occident.[1] According to him, the confrontation of east and west is the ultimate issue, since the winner will determine the kind of global world we shall inhabit: despotism or democracy. From the outset, the difference between them was decisive. One was completely autocratic, Persian, Byzantine, despotic, lending itself solely to an interpretation of "imperative ordering" by the autocrat. While it is possible for an autocrat to be benevolent toward the population, his benevolence depends purely on his momentary dispositions, and the latter can coincide with the power of the laws the autocrat prescribes. It would not add much to our investigation to digress toward the psychological dispositions of the power holders. Our concern is more with its nature and "logic".

For Junger, freedom is the West, while despotism is East; we hear the chains from Siberia, the cries of holy wars from the Middle East, and Middle Ages, the torture cries from the dungeons of the autocratic papacy, the threats of total destruction by the reborn and their second coming - and all armed with the latest means of power. The division into the East and West is not geographic but composed of cultural topography. Hence the West has imported, or accepted an exportation of a Judeo-Christian-Islamic tradition stemming from, and completely correlated to the Persian autocratic mode of exercising power. This is well reflected in one, among numerous others, structural designs: imperial Persia and the divinities signifying such a structure. To understand this correlation we must revert briefly to the previous discussion of legitimation.

The ambiguity of legitimation can be dispelled mainly with respect to mythological legitimation. The mythological region is peopled by figures that are structurally isomorphic with the power inhabiting the "solar palaces". There is the celestial Lord-King, his Queen, their retinue, their subservient supplicants and worshippers, each with a sign of appointed and anointed rank, and hierarchical position. This is precisely the imperial regality, and in the final analysis the mythological composition coincides with the ruling composition. This is to say, there is no legitimation here, since the mythical does not justify the imperial deeds but is identical with them. The emperor can claim without a fear of contradiction that "we are divine". Thus we find that the Persian imperial morphology and the Judeo-Christian-Islamic composition also coincide. The ruling emperor is the law-giver and the law, and there should be neither deviations nor questions concerning the power of such law. The language here is one of edicts and imperatives. All that lives and exists must obey and be subordinate to the edicts, indeed must act in ways that would constitute a support and enhancement of the edicts. No one can question the imperial force of the law, specifically when the law coincides with the "making of the world". The imperial powers make the world by their commands, and their divinities make the world by uttering appropriate words. At this level, we are faced with an understanding of verbal power that becomes coextensive with making, and indeed with an indistinction between word and event. The power holder's every uttered wish becomes coextensive with deed and reality.

It is to be noted that the emergence of the imperial powers can be correlated to nomadic means, and, according to Bronowski, such means was the horse.[2] It is a "technology" that corresponds to other "domesticated" technologies, except for the difference in power and speed. The horse is mobile and fast and allows the nomad a wide range of rulership. This is to say, the horse can be a means by which one is capable of wasting one settled community and then going to the next for conquest and subsistence until this too is exhausted. Hence Bronowski adds the economy of settled peoples, i.e. agrarian and domestic, as an attraction for conquest by the mobile nomadic peoples who become the robbers yet with a claim to "superiority" in power and "birth". They are the leisure class, i.e. unconcerned with the production of the means of subsistence, but very much concerned with the "art of ruling". Bronowski's division into "settled" and "nomadic" is extended by him into the division between warlike and peaceful, power seeking and ruling and the ruled. Bronowski not only treats such ruling in the nomadic power of the horse rider-warrior, but equates such power to modern warfare of powerful and mobile machinery of war: tanks, ships, aeroplanes, rockets. This corresponds to Junger's concept of East and West as cultural topographies that include Persian, Byzantine, Mongolian, Christian, Russian and Islamic Empires that extend the conception of autocratic-absolutist power, correlating to an autocratic mythological structure, and in opposition to these, the Hellenic *demos* backed by discursive, interrogative and alterable mode of life that correlates to the *logos* of nature to which the human belongs. What is "natural" is what constitutes appropriate power. Thus it is natural for humans to use fire and it is inappropriate for someone to use power to deprive them of fire. There is a possibility to strike bargains, to change them, contest them in the public arena. Greek mythology, for example, reflects this way of natural bargaining. The understanding of power must be adjudicated discursively and not imposed by edicts. According to Junger, this "freedom" is what characterizes the West and at the same time what deflects the imperative absolutes of the East.

The logocentric conception of *demos* is what leads to the subsequent conception of "natural equality" of all persons. Of course, within such an equality there were marked differences between abilities and developments of potential, as was evident from Platonic and Aristotelian writings, leading to the Platonic call for a *polis* ruled by the "best".[3] This was, of course, the answer to the "inadequacies" of the rule by the many. In fact such a rule would be partially justified by the logocentric conception of the world where *episteme* was deemed to be in a position to decipher and hence correspond to, and indeed be capable of ruling in accordance with the "all ruling" *logos*. Thus those in possession of *episteme* should rule by virtue of their knowledge. What is to be understood is that knowledge could not be regarded as a power "to make". Knowledge of what is, by nature, is knowledge how one should act. This sort of rulership does not use power against a person or nature, but is capable discursively to show the mistakes the person might make with respect to the nature of the cosmos and its *logos*. If a person is made to understand what is natural, he/she will act in accordance with such understanding. If one knows what is beneficial to one's health and what is not, then one will certainly do the beneficial thing. No imperative from emperors or gods could alter the cosmic *logos*. To the contrary, emperors and gods come and pass with the sway of the cosmos.

APPEARANCE OF REFLECTIVE THOUGHT

The cosmic *logos* is not to be understood as power, but as enduring and elastic strength that yields but cannot be defeated. Those who live in accordance with its sway are also the enduring, the ones who bend with the storms but remain unbroken. The difference between strength of *logos* and power is that *logos* is ever present and never vanishes, while power has its rise and fall. It can be absent, withheld, and in the withholding can become awesome, more terrible than its direct exercise. Yet it could be said with justification that like the horsemen, it is nomadic. It cannot be continuously exercised without becoming exhausted. It seems plausible to suggest that emperors do not use power on every occasion, but only when necessary to inflict direct terror and then draw the power back in order to hold it in abeyance and thus maintain its awesome threat in withholding. The holding in abeyance does not exhaust the power and yet it makes it seem all pervasive and inescapable.[4] In addition, it is also plausible that legitimation of power appears as one effort to conserve power. No ruler could continuously use power; hence legitimation is a maintenance of power by other means. Such a maintenance does not abolish direct power; rather, power becomes concentrated for "exemplary" use not only to terrorize some segments of the population, but also to demonstrate that in its withheld state it remains awesome and vigilant. Legitimation is thus a means to conserve and yet to maintain the "all pervasive", although withheld presence of power.

Obviously, even legitimated and maintained power need not be eternal; it can be conquered, dissipated, abolished, or decadent. In this sense it is distinct from the strength of *logos* that is not nomadic, it does not come and pass, even if it is never at rest. At least this thought was pervasive among the "settled" peoples who endured the shifting, clashing, and transient powers of their nomadic "masters". Perhaps the very mobility of the masters, their relative indifference to the places they ruled, lent them a peculiar "transcendence", a position that was regarded as higher, prouder, nobler, perhaps even purer and less soiled than that of the eternal peasant, the proletarian, and the plebian who were steeped in the soil of labour, and bent to perform the "lower" tasks.[5] These are not yet the so-called "class distinctions" of the later age, but rather ontological dimensions constituting two different modes of comporting in the world: the enduring strength of *logos* and the transcendent, transient powers. The ontological distinction does not signify a spatial and temporal difference. The two dimensions are inseparable, and neither would appear without the other.

The movement toward transcendence and the pre-eminence of the ruler's *will* over nature on which he is not only dependent, but which could not be completely submitted - not even the peasant could be completely abolished - to his will and law, acquires the most pre-eminent expression with the myths of creation, and later with the conceptions of a supreme-transcendent being. The former lends credence to the ruler's edicts stemming from his will in the sense that nature is not an independent domain with its own strength, but that rather it is a product of a will, a created realm. After all, the initial depiction of creation is imperative and verbal: by speaking the highest mythical figures make things happen, thus indicating that the word is the law and deed at the same time. The word could have been spoken differently and the world could be different. This abolishes the necessity in the *logos*, and relocates it in the imperative power of the will. The latter point, reaching its culmination in the medieval West, intimates a transcendence which is imitated by nature and is superior over nature.[6] It is a "thought" that is purified from the imperfections of nature and the latter is an *imago* of it. Nature is an image of and depends on thought that can turn into reality by the act of *will*, such that even thought can become a result of the command of the *will*. In principle, this priority of the imperative power of the will appears in the prerogative of the supreme *will* to perform "miracles" and thus to disregard the order of *logos*. While this is mythology of *will*, subsequently it will appear as the metaphysics of the *will*, specifically in its modern Western guise that becomes the ground of post modernity.

THE REFLEXIVE DOMAIN

With the appearance of thought as transcendent over nature, and indeed being the determining factor of nature, there opens up a reflexive region that lends nature not only a secondary status, but above all a being that is dependent on thought. Thus in order to discover this dependence, one must turn to the composition of thought and how nature must correspond to, and become subsumed under thought and, in the final analysis, under projects of *will*. This calls for thought to reflect upon its own activities and content and to decipher its own standards by which nature becomes "determinable". The last term is selected to suggest that thought being prior to nature is not determined by anything and hence can determine nature in many ways, dependent upon the *will*. This is to say, if thought is the starting principle irrespective of the "height" of its transcendence, the nature is determinable in more ways than one.

There appears a peculiar reversal: the *logos*, with its enduring strength against which all powers were temporary and contingent now is forced to be contingent and unnecessary, a being dependent on the transcending thought and the ruling *will* which is deemed to be necessary and incontestable. The latter is the stable power that can determine by its *will* the way that nature will be and will remain dependent. Here the emperor and its nomadic power, i.e. a *will* that needs not respect the logos, returns in a new guise, except now as a supreme ruler. Within this reflexive context the human finds himself in a position of transcendence over nature, in a position of being a source of all the law that, while not yet in total command of nature, is in a position to establish such a command. This is to say, nature can be regarded as dependent upon thought, not in some ontological sense, but perhaps more fundamentally, in a practical sense, i.e., in a sense of being "made" in human image.

A fascinating syndrome appears that usually remains if not hidden, at least unexpressed: the very way that the human thinks first appears not as its own thinking and understanding, but as something cosmic and encompassing. The same could be said of the human positing of its own reflection as more fundamental than the *logos* of nature: the primacy of reflective thought is first attributed to a thought of a cosmic being and only subsequently is there an admittance of the thought that turns back upon itself. Thus the discovery by modernity of the ego that thinks its own thoughts, and knowledge as identical to power, is a discovery of a composition that was already invented and, so to speak, waiting in the wings to be recognized and appropriated. The structure of the priority of reflective thought and the power of the creative will was accomplished before the human would accept and recognize this structure as his own.

The priority of an already taken for granted primacy of thought as the creative power also permits the priority of will as that which can choose what sort of creation occurs. Thus the once necessary nature, with its own *logos*, has to be subsumed under a power that is in principle capable of dominating and altering nature and in principle making nature contingent. This is to say, the necessity shifts to the *will* and its creative power leaving nature exposed to arbitrary rule. Indeed, for all modern Western understanding, without an imposition of an order by the will nature would be without reason and form, without value and goodness. The composition here permits a direct translation into the domain where thought and will can have a direct influence and control; by now is well known that practical-technical transformation of the environment is the sole interest of modern philosophies, sciences, and moralities. Knowledge and *will* are taken to be prior and transcendent to nature and hence capable of imposing an order on an otherwise irrational material nature. What comes along with this structure from the cosmic assumption of the absolute power and its creation of nature is the shift of power toward thought and *will* over nature. Thought and *will*, logic and valuation, become the necessary conditions for the being of the world for man, while nature becomes, to borrow from Kant, blind phenomena.

The first result is the appearance of the initial syndrome of arbitrary power with respect to nature, except now in the guise of the subject who is "everyman", i.e., any individual is in a position to be the maker and master of his own destiny by his own thought, *will* and ability to make the surroundings into his own "image". He neither has a nature, nor a nature to settle; he can become, with respect to the environment, "nomadic". This is to say, he is "free" from any place and can remake nature in his own image anywhere he decides to settle - an image of the rape of Gaia has here become a reality. Yet here Junger's thesis of the difference between the despotic East and the democratic West finds a reversal: the West is the nomadic power of the unchained rule over nature, appearing both in the guises of capitalism and Marxism. The land of the peasant, the endurer of seasons and of natural rhythms, and the peasant attuned to them, are now exposed to become raw material and labour power for the technological edicts controlled by unknown emperors. Although the latter are interesting insofar as they seem to possess what the current designation would call "economic power", the more interesting factor is this reversal. It has broken down the traditional legitimation of power by birthright and demanded legitimation by "the people". But the latter are either "labour power" to be constructed in accordance with the needs of production, or are mobile individuals capable of settling where there are not yet exploited "raw materials" for production.

The appearance of the individual and his assumed right to be the master of his destiny, the ruling power, the government, whose inevitable centralization was triggered by equality under the law, led to what could be called "post-modernity".[7] One major issue that had to be resolved was *legitimation*. The reason that this issue did not appear with modernity rests on the assumption that the democratic revolution will lead to the conception of power concentrated in the hands of the people. The dream of a completion of democratization by the second history, i.e., by the establishment of a material power over nature and thus by the freeing of the human from any chains of established authority, turned out to be unattainable. And specifically it was due to the very scientific technologization of all processes in the social arena. As already noted by many people, the technologization led to the establishment of vast bureaucratic machinery of experts comprising a privileged elitism. No doubt, the establishment is not something that was forced on the populations. In most cases it was accepted in the all-pervasive ideology of scientific power to fulfill human wants in the material domain and thus to fill the gap of insecurity, to offer guarantees of well being that could not be otherwise attained. But as was seen in the case of mass opinion, the material incrementation of well being, demands, in its own right, a submission of the population under the control of bureaucratic technocracies. The management of complexities created by the efforts to attain power over nature creates its own material power that cannot be dislodged by political edicts. This is to say, the population's demand for material fulfilment, leads to a greater concentration of bureaucratic-technical power and hence a continuous diminishment of the importance of the once autonomous and free individual as a law giver. Thus we reach a material paradox: the more the individual strives to secure his material well being *vis-a-vis* the appointed or self-appointed social powers, the more he surrenders his power to have any say in the increasingly centralized fabric of bureaucracies. At this juncture we seem to stress the principle of "equality" for all individuals in the material domain with a complete disregard for freedom. The meaning here is quite clear. As noted by Weber, an aim at democratic laws that would be equal to all members of a society tends to centralize the appointed law makers charged with establishing and maintaining laws deemed equal for all.[8] This same tendency could well be present in the efforts to equalize material well being; centralized bureaucracy functioning under the guise of technical expertise is the way of securing equal fulfilment of well being. But the price must be paid: the experts are to rule by virtue of their scientific and technical sophistication. Although we are not contending that this is necessary or inevitable; rather, the very conception of scientific-technical expertise in modernity carries with it the view that it is in a position to "make" progress for the material benefit of the population, and the population takes for granted the mystique of science as a power capable of more or less divine intervention in all material affairs for the good of the human.

At first glance it might be possible to argue that some of the forms of the acquisition of material well being through the modern establishment of power allow the individual almost unrestricted freedom of choice without abolishing the principle of equality. One such form is offered by capitalism. Granting the most implausible proposition that capitalism somehow promotes freedom of choice, it makes no sense here to speak of freedom as autonomous. Freedom of choice, compelled by the material forces, i.e., by the constant pressure to maintain one's material edge, is reduced to the struggle for the management of instrumental means in order to secure one's constantly vanishing position. Indeed, the more one engages in this "freedom of choice" material domain, the more one is exposed to the determinations of its necessities, and the more one neglects the public arena due to "lack of time" for irrelevancies in face of "real concerns". In this sense the very notion of freedom is subverted and is paraded merely as an ideology to attract the unsuspecting and the innocent as a way of achieving power over them.

The ideological solicitation of the individual to "freedom" is quite transparent with power. The public opinion is not only shaped, but has already taken for granted that "other freedoms follow" from the "freedom" of materialism, specifically in its economic form. Two consequences seem to follow from this state of affairs. First, the public arena is neglected unless one's own material interests are at stake. And second, the collapse of the public and the social into the material sphere of interests, making the public arena of freedom exposed to the possessors of greater material power, i.e., economic, technical, and scientific.

This collapse has been always a danger, as is evidenced by the discourse of the Athenians concerning the case of Mytilene, where Kleon pronounces that the simple and good citizen is content to follow the law and not mix in the affairs of the state, allowing the state to pursue its power interests. Anyone challenging the "leaders" versed in power politics is an intellectual without any resolve and should be regarded as an enemy of the simple people. If we shift this to modernity, we notice that the public opinion is in favor of the material well being, stressing its securities and guarantees, and resultantly demanding that the public arena be reduced to concerns of material fulfilment. In this sense, if one is so bold as to call for freedoms in the public arena that are not concerned with the material well being, one is seen as a disruptor of order, a threat to job security or the hope of improving one's material lot. As Luhmann so aptly states, the modern public arena is reduced to a common denominator: material interest.[9] Capitalism and communism become coextensive. Thus the "battle" between the two "systems" at this level cannot focus on the maintenance of freedoms and the public arena, but a battle concerning as to who will maintain or possess the controls over the material processes. There is very little consolation for the population to discover that it is subservient to a "party" that determines the wages, the production, the health, or working for a corporation that sets efficiency quotas, prices and wages. Both function under the necessities of materially created forces and hence any talk of freedom on either side has only a soliciting attraction, i.e., an effort to win the minds of the population for one or the other side. One would have to be a more or less blind person to accept the view that once the material necessities are fulfilled, we shall somehow achieve freedom.

Capitalism and communism, after all, believe that the only moving force of history is material and in principle, any other view, such as the autonomy of the individual, makes no sense in such a belief. In this sense both would have to maintain that any worthwhile future is a continuous material fulfilment. Thus neither of these systems are compatible with the political enlightenments conception of autonomy, although this conception was a catalyst that unchained the material mastery of nature and in turn got lost in this very "labour" through history toward self-liberation from the material power, a self-liberation that set up the conditions for the opposite: self-enslavement through the incrementation of material power and thus the reduction of the very arena that would guarantee one's self-liberation to the pervasive forces of material needs. The result of this peculiar paradox is the resurgence of man ruling over man and not of laws posited by freedom and freely accepted by the very creators of the laws.

The issue here is somewhat complex. The so-called material forces of history are regarded as conditions, causes, necessities to which one must adhere, submit, and even use as basis for the construction of "objective" theories of socio-economic and political life. In turn, such forces are structured in accord with human designs and rules of functioning, and hence possess a "subjective" base. Moreover, with political enlightenment, there were posited principles for adjudication in the material sphere and the possibility of realignment of this sphere for the benefit of a consensual public. Although one might argue that numerous "founding" fathers of various modern national entities were most concerned with the maintenance of property discriminations and perhaps even the security of material wealth among the possessors of such a wealth, this very concern indicates that there was no longer any necessity to regard material force as preeminent. It appeared in its vulnerability and in principle required political adjudication. Hence all the arguments between those who stressed democracy, and those who opted for a republic present a disrupted necessity. It is possible to adjudicate the material domain by the public by raising the question of rational legitimation of the appearance of material power in the hands of some against other members of society. This is to say, if laws are to rule, then any inequitable distribution of material power, leading to a rule of the human over the human, is a contradiction. Such a misdistribution precludes the free positing and following of laws and introduces necessities in the arena of inter-human relations. As noted already, the only viable *polis* is rational and free, and hence the introduction of material-irrational component is counter to the concept of a political society. No doubt, one may offer rational justifications for the inequities, but it should be noted that such justifications are either efforts to legitimate an established inequity by positing an irrational factor in human life, or means to explain human activities by constructing reasons for such activities, reasons that do not coincide with the activities. Such justifications, in principle, accept irrationality as the base of political life; given such a base, one then becomes "free" to justify one's actions by any arbitrarily constructed reason in the guise of ideology.

At any rate, the legitimation of the production of increased material power through science-technology conjunction is offered by the lure that such a power is for human benefit. More things, more benefits, more enjoyment, more health, more... more.... One could even say that this power incrementation becomes self-legitimating in face of the public's demand for more securities in the material sphere. But this raises an immediate question concerning the legitimation of the *polis*. What must constitute its "arena"? The free discourse for the public benefit is not an issue; the issue is material well being - private. Hence, the public domain, in order to be legitimate, must be reduced to the sum of private material interests. The political parties must shift their operations toward the fulfilment of material wants. But once this shift is made, there is no turning back, since in order to be legitimate, the political parties must fulfill the material promises. Failing this, they cease to be regarded legitimate. This is what constitutes the legitimation crisis of the political domain in modernity. In order for the political parties to maintain themselves in "power", they must possess material power capable of satisfying the demands of the masses. If not in practice, at least in mass propaganda, the two systems vying for "the minds of the masses" offer their lines of wares in terms of material fulfilment. Both econologize every facet of socio-cultural and political life. The populations, in turn, take the economicalization for granted and exert pressure on the systems to "produce" visible results. Failing such results, one can justifiably argue that the system has no legitimation. The system responds by either military power to keep the populations working, or by promises of future improvements, or finally, by political theatre in various forms, inclusive of rituals and above all, ideological incantations. As Ricoeur suggests, there is a credibility gap between political rule and its legitimation.[10] Since the gap cannot be filled by material means, i.e., neither system can fulfill its promises of material well being, it must fill the credibility gap. Ideology is one pre-eminent mode of filling this gap and, at the same time, of providing an inexpensive way of obtaining legitimation.

It is important to note that the filling of the gap is not offered by some purely conscious structure, like ideality, which would be distinct from materiality. Rather, the promises are of direct material fulfilment in the multi-levelled modern sense. The first principle that rules such a fulfilment is the final "ideal" of modernity: man is the maker of himself. The second principle is: man is on the way toward fulfilling this state of affairs. Thus ideological incantations and theatre constantly stress human self-realization, fulfilment, material security, in an everyday language. The ideal self is already taken for granted by the modern man: material power to enhance oneself and to make of oneself what one wills. And the "ideals" of the ideological structure of consciousness are directly perceptual, sensuous, bodily, offering everyone the means to achieve those ideals in any corner drug-store, beauty parlour, grocery outlet, and exercise places. Moreover, there is a skin-deep equalization in numerous domains lending the appearance of increasing material equality. Everyone can have similar foods, spices, drinks, even similar looking clothing - despite differences in quality - and hence the promises seem to be approximated. While there might remain vast differences in social class distinctions, economic and political power inequities, at the surface level there seems to be an apparent equitable fulfilment. Everyone is "enjoying" an apparent equality in terms of the socially proliferated ideals and looks. "She looks like a million" and this despite the fact that she is working on an assembly line and is not the manager of production or an owner of the means of production. This seems to be an ideology of the ruling class inscribed in the commodities for the subservient class's consumption, lending the appearance that the working class is fully participating in the "style of life" of the ruling class. The saturation of all domains with the images, tastes, sounds, conceptualities of the good life, the working class is completely submitted to the power of ideology in "flesh". Semiotically speaking, this constitutes the trick of codification of the lower classes with the signs of the power of the upper, ruling class.

If ideology is to function at all, it cannot directly display power. Rather, it translates power into significance, and makes it "rational". We can no longer think of ideology in terms of the 19th century when it was deemed that ideology expresses the interests of a dominant economic class. Semiotics has dispelled this view by pointing out that economic power is not for the sake of economy, but for the sake of numerous socially coded important positions. This is to say, ideology prescribes signs of prestige and significance and, with the material power of transforming all events into a humanly designed image, it also imposes the coded bodily "look" both "on the skin" and as attire. Images of an ideal female, ideal male, ideal body, from toenails to hair, are proliferated for the "consumer".[11] This is to say, ideology is no longer a matter of consciousness reflecting the material-economic or technical conditions, but is an inscription in the body, in the images, the passions and desires appearing through the images and on the body. The idealities of the ideologies in the late capitalism and state-corporate systems are coextensive with the daily discourse, daily imagery, mass-media, sounds and tastes, architecture, popular arts carried by vast systems of circulation thus making any art-form accessible and "popular", and mimetic activities of the *subjects* in Foucault's sense.[12] Subjects in his sense have become "subject" to the codes.

The question must now be raised concerning the "credibility" of the political incantations, the verbal depictions of the good life, the material fulfilment and equality. It seems that the political promises, which would be merely depiction of conscious ideals reflecting the position of the ruling class, should have very little impact on the population. Yet it is to be recalled that the modern magic of language is one of power, an ability to transform words directly into deeds, indeed words having become deeds and material facts; hence there is a credibility of speech in all "educated" domains. And it is to be recalled that the political incantations are not dealing with such high and noble principles as autonomy, rights, dignity, liberality of the human but in a language of materiality, interest, incomes, shoes, cars, washing machines, crops, and "decent" incomes. And it is precisely this sort of discourse that is taken for granted by the public opinion as capable of "producing". Add to this sort of discourse some hints, veiled suggestions of utopian imagery, and the result will be a believing public. After all, the stress on materiality is already granted by the public opinion.

We are now in a position to connect the public opinion and its assumed wish for material fulfilment with the appearance of modern bureaucracy. According to Weber, the power of bureaucracy claims legitimation on the basis of its rationality.[13] The ground of this claim is not offered by Weber, and must be sought in the construction of modernity. It was already noted that the sources of power in the modern age rest on the arbitrariness of thought and *will* with respect to the environment. Thus this very source leads to a demand that in principle everything should be makeable, producible and the production of the human into an ideal image. This source of productivity is, in brief, irrational. Given a complex social fabric composed of irrational wants and their fulfilment, there must emerge a social class in the service of the state and capable of adjudicating the material resources of a society in a "rational way". No doubt, this rationality is not to be confused with any presumed "natural" reason, with logos, but simply with a calculative distribution of states resources in accordance with ideologically designated rules. What is unique about a bureaucracy is that it is capable of adjudicating such a distribution by interpreting the rules in accordance with specific situations and unique settings. In this sense the bureaucracy is given a direct power over the distribution and hence over the material well being of the population. In turn, the same bureaucracy is instrumental in writing the rules, since it is staffed by "experts" on whom the inexperienced political figures are completely dependent. Hence bureaucracy guarantees for itself a position and, with increasing material complexities, it also demands for increasing staffing and expansion of power.

What this means is that the arbitrary demands of the modern man must be rationalized, and with the increased demands, greater and more extensive rationalization must be instituted. In this sense bureaucracy enters the same logic of modernity: increased material power, controls, reshaping of the environment for human "consumption" is coextensive with the increased demands for the bureaucratic controls of distribution, effects, side effects, and interrelationships among the materially achieved results. Scientific and political technocracies, stressing the increased fulfilment of human want rush to produce numerous "miracles" and the latter bear with them numerous and unforeseen effects. The more demands the population places on the scientific-technological production and on the political establishments to guarantee for everyone an access to the products, the greater risks will arise with respect to increasing effects. Hence the bureaucratic management of the results calls for a greater concentration of power and functional incrementation of bureaucracies. After all, the populations not only want material welfare, but are incapable of dealing with the results and side effects, and hence places demands on the political domain to guarantee the control of results. This pressure inevitably leads the political arena to be dominated by bureaucratic power. Hence bureaucracy performs two opposing functions: first, it is structured to enhance the expansion of material power and the distribution of its products, and second, it is called upon to control the effects of such production.

It is irrelevant whether the societies are nominally "free enterprise" or "state enterprise", basically their modern direction of increasing material power and controls demands the appearance of vast bureaucracies as a faceless government that cannot be held responsible, although they have a direct power of adjudicating the political edicts. Bureaucracy could be called "material hermeneutics" since its interpretation of the political edicts is coextensive with an application of material means and material power. It is a hand that can give or withhold, liberate or suppers, and thus determine directly the levels of survival of a given social group. Bureaucracy is forced into a material interpretation of social events, and by accepting this necessity, it inevitably acquires increasing material power. It is by now well noted that the efforts to "liberalize" society in Russia are running into a solid wall of bureaucratic power. In the West, the willful productions of the "free" enterprise system call for the increased controls of its results and effects and, coupled with the popular opinion that the political institutions should enter the arena of offering material fulfilment, bureaucracies are an unavoidable medium.

Although the economic power was mentioned in passing, we should consider the economic "explanations" leading to the views that the human is a *homo economicus*. No doubt, since the dawn of the 19th century, there appeared numerous theses making a claim to an economic explanation of all socio-historical and even cultural phenomena. This view is so pervasive that to challenge it would be equal to waging war on all the prejudgments of the last two centuries with regard to the *basis* of all human sciences and engagements. Hence our task is not to oppose each economic explanation separately, but to decipher in principle the reason and the source of such explanation.

CONCLUSION

While discussing modernity, we have noted that priority is given to reflection. The reflective domain has been unbound from any natural constraints and has been set up to be the source of any criteria and justification. But this means that any effort at explanation, specifically the prevalent economic explanation of social life, is not a discovery but a design. In the future, to understand this state of affairs, we should offer a strict investigation of the constitution of economy and its relationship to power.

First, the economic reading of the socio-political fabric claims to be "scientific". Science, by its own insistence, must give a "true" account of facts. Hence each domain of scientific discourse must obtain univocity. Yet what we find in the domain of economic explanations by the 19th century are three theories of economic facts, each distinct from the other, and yet each claiming to be the sole "objective" reading of the economic data. This leads us to pose the Nietzschean question: if we have not discovered *the* theory, if we have a diversity of contrasting and even contradictory theories, then it is plausible that the theories do not reflect "reality" but are designed for some other purpose, and that the economic mode of explanations serves other than economic interests.[14] Such interests are an incrementation of power by way of economy.

Second, we have already noted that the very composition of modern ontology lends itself to a constant intervention in and incrementation of power over nature. Thus power is assumed at the outset as given. Resultantly, every function, including the economic, is a means in the struggle for power. Indeed, while it is argued that economy fuels the drive of technical inventions and scientific "breakthroughs", it can be countered that both technology and economy are inevitable tools for power. In this sense power is a more fundamental domain and can be regarded as an explanatory hypothesis of the functions of other domains.

Third, the economic explanation does not constitute a total explanatory hypothesis, specifically with respect to the proponents of this hypothesis. It is claimed that the reflective domain is a mirror of the economic forces and interests; hence all thought, all theories and models, are reflections of these forces. But this would mean that the very theses presumed to be explanations of all events, should be included in the explanation and should constitute the mirroring of the precise economic setting of a given time. But this would have to mean that there should be either one economic thesis mirroring the given period, or there should be various equally valid theses during a given period. The latter case could be argued to mean that since there are precise economic conditions for precisely delimited groups or individuals, then there should be numerous valid thesis. But in this sense, no thesis should be counted as *the* all encompassing one.

Fourth, the various economic theses also suggest a reflective domain that is free to design and hence transcend any economic determinants and hence to escape the economic hypothesis and explanation. This is obvious from the numerous revolutions, each promising a grand plan to solve the "economic" problems, and each providing "experts" that constitute a reflective domain, leading back to the previously discussed problems of political technocracy.

NOTES

1. Ernst Junger, "Der Gordische Knoten", *Sämtliche Werke* Vol. 7 (1953): 375–473.
2. Jacob Bronowski, *The Ascent of Man* (Boston: Little Brown & Company, 1976).
3. Plato, *Republic*, translated by Allan Bloom (New York: Basic Books, 1968)
4. Michel Foucault, *Discipline and Punish: The Birth of the Prison* (New York: Vintage Books, 1995).
5. Plato, *Republic*.
6. Lester Ward, *Applied Sociology : A Treatise on the Conscious Improvement of Society by Society* (Boston: Ginn and Company, 1906).
7. Fredric Jameson, *Postmodernism, or, The Cultural Logic of Late Capitalism* (Durham: Duke University Press, 1991).
8. Max Weber, *Economy and Society: An Outline of Interpretive Sociology* (Berkeley: University of California Press, 1978).
9. Niklas Luhmann, *Observations on Modernity* (Stanford, CA: Stanford University Press, 1998).
10. Paul Ricoeur, *Lectures on Ideology and Utopia* (New York: Columbia University Press, 1986).
11. George Ritzer, *The McDonaldization of Society* (Thousand Oaks,

CA: Pine Forge Press, 2004).

12. Michel Foucault, *The History of Sexuality* (New York: Pantheon Books, 1978).
13. Weber, *Economy and Society*.
14. Friedrich Nietzsche, *Beyond Good and Evil*: Prelude to a Philosophy of the Future (Oxford: Oxford University Press, 1998).

13

Scenario Planning as a Method of Responsive Social Planning

Vicente Berdayes

INTRODUCTION

The pursuit of social justice requires developing practices that allow people to encounter each other as reflexive collaborators in directing the scope and nature of social development. When oriented in this manner, human *praxis* can guide globalization in light of a deliberatively formulated ideal that recognizes people as participants in the effort to transform their societies. In contrast to the insular forces that now direct globalization, such practices would bring diverse social actors together to deliberate on ways to channel social change along democratic lines that nurture socially responsive institutions. A social order oriented by such practices would be global in scale and cosmopolitan in character, because its institutions would be based on a respect for difference and self-determination. In recent years, "scenario planning" has emerged as a plausible methodology for guiding this type of responsive social planning.

MODERNITY AND SOCIAL PLANNING

The Enlightenment first gave rise to the ideal of using human reason to understand and guide the interrelated dynamics, or "social forces" that comprise the social whole. Social planning emerged as a component of modernity as human beings became conscious of the variety of social and natural processes that shape their lives and to which they themselves contribute through their daily activities. For example, as people became aware of demographic regularities such as birth rates and pattern of migration, it became possible to anticipate the need for extensive social infrastructures and services and to plan for them in advance. Although often realized only in piecemeal ways or even botched completely, the contemporary social environment has been thoroughly shaped by this planning ideal, and modern life could not be sustained without the wide range of planning activities constantly carried on by both governmental and business organizations.

Fundamental to this planning ideal is the assumption that the forces which human beings have become aware of as shaping their lives are themselves amenable to conscious manipulation. To return to the topic of demography, in the 19th- and 20th-century people began to foresee the ominous results of unrestricted population growth and were able to chart a range of viable interventions – economic, educational, technical, and medical – to reduce this growth to sustainable levels. This nascent ability to direct the course of social development initiated a process of conscious self-conditioning in which human beings intervene in the creation of other human beings and, through planning, endeavour to shape the social environment in which they mature. Planning thus reflects the entry of reflexive human agency, or *praxis,* into the entire field of life and indicates not just a growing awareness of the processes that shape the social and physical environment but also confidence in the capacity of reason to control and direct such processes toward explicitly human ends.[1] Social planning is an expression of the Enlightenment goal of gaining mastery over the world in order to pursue an unrestricted project of collective self-creation.

However, efforts to plan for social existence have been marred by the narrowing of the definition of reason that occurred over the modern era and that moved the human element to the margins of this project of world-construction.[2] The resulting efforts to plan social existence have been directed by a managerial ethos that administers life in accord with the needs of the capitalist world order. From this perspective, human needs appear as only one factor within the narrower problem of how to propagate economic growth.[3] This administrative orientation validates repressive interventions into people's lives as part of programmatic efforts to "develop" other societies, and they thereby generate alienating institutions and social environments. Planning experts do not consciously pursue these repressive goals. On the contrary, the ideology of planning is oriented toward the opposite goal of knowledgeably bettering life. But because planning efforts are guided by theories that misrecognize or distort the nature of human agency, these negative social outcomes occur nevertheless. The contours of globalization have consequently been defined by unreflexively applied theories that justify autocratic intrusions into people's lives.

The three key variants of these theories are: sociological models of development, technological models of diffusion of innovations, and neo-liberal economic policies. The conventional sociological version of planning is an extension of positivist social theory. This tradition, which can be traced through Comte and Durkheim to the structural-functionalism of Talcott Parsons, portrays society as a structurally integrated whole that exists independently of human actors and which evolves through a gradual process of structural differentiation akin to biological evolution. This portrayal of society as a sui generis "system" marginalizes human agency because the overall scope, direction, and character of social development is thought to be predetermined. Consequently, in the most "advanced" societies, planning is reduced to a series of technocratic interventions designed only to regulate autonomous processes of growth and integration that produced the modern welfare state.[4]

This formulation of social order allows societies to be compared in terms of the degree to which they have developed a centralized state and communication infrastructures as well as institutions like the market that integrate social actors' increasingly differentiated activities. Entire societies can therefore be portrayed as evolutionary aberrations because they have failed to follow the supposed natural teleology of Western industrialized societies. These social settings then become the objects of "modernization" programmes designed to rend the social environment and bring about "the passing of traditional society". Modernization programmes of this sort, moreover, cannot be organized in a participatory manner, because members of other societies are handicapped by the pre-modern forms of rationality that correspond to their type of social system. Consequently, only Western experts and agents under their tutelage are capable of directing modernization efforts. The goal of modernization is to jump-start the process of social development in a form that quickly recapitulates Western history and carries along indigenous populations in a process of autonomous development.[5]

The technological variant of planning shares the goal of modernizing societies, but the emphasis in this model is on the piecemeal transmission of the fruits of technological rationality rather than conceptualizing societal development as a whole. Technological social planning is an expression of the narrowing and reification of scientific reason. According to this view, technology is the material expression of value-neutral scientific knowledge. Technology is an essentially rational, unequivocal good that increases human mastery over the environment. Planning efforts should thus focus on ways to transfer technology to less developed regions in an effort to increase productivity and standards of living. As this occurs, modern innovations will tend to throw into disrepute traditional knowledge and patterns of authority thereby leading to a broader process of societal change.[6]

Technological diffusionism limits planning to questions involving the application of technique. The approach is justified by a narrow conception of rationality that obscures both the value-laden character of technology and the fundamental ways in which technological expertise redefines the goals of social planning. Not surprisingly, technological diffusionism has produced socially and ecologically pernicious outcomes by treating the world as a realm of inert matter that can be reorganized at the whim of narrow instrumental goals. Such projects have a Faustian character in which regions of the world are subjected to resource exploitation or otherwise transformed with little regard for the concerns of indigenous populations or questions of sustainability. Moreover, because technology is considered a direct expression of objective scientific rationality, there is no point outside of scientific reason from which this approach to planning can be critiqued. A diffusionist project can be judged a failure only from the point of view of purely instrumental measures of technological performativity. By contrast, any other type of criticism is seen as forwarding essentially subjective and invalid concerns. The elaboration of diffusionist projects therefore occurs within a closed circle of rationality where it is impossible to oppose instrumental demands by reference to either local needs or broader ethical concerns.[7] As with the ideal of modernization, technological diffusionism invariably transforms human beings into objects rather than participants in the process of societal planning.

Neoliberal policies are in some ways diametrically opposed to the two forms of planning already discussed, but intersect with them in important ways. Unlike modernization efforts, neoliberalism is not based on a theory of society but on a totalized theory of the market. According to neoliberal thought, all forms of human interaction can be reduced to the calculative rationality of the marketplace. In this view, human beings enter into social relationships solely in the course of pursuing individual acquisitive goals. Thus the forms of sociability that other schools take as a fundamental feature of human existence are here considered only specific instances of economic exchange in which people add up the costs and benefits of entering into relationships with one another. Neoliberals, in other words, decompose "society" into a field of acquisitive monads linked transiently by the market.

Furthermore, because of its ability to respond to consumers' shifting wants, the market, rather than the political or social realms, is seen as the key expression and guarantor of human freedom. Any attempt to restrict the operation of the market is therefore oppressive, which is to say that the market should be made inviolable to democratic intervention. The ideal condition that neoliberal policies aim at is the creation of a social environment in which political institutions have been pared down to the minimal functions needed to protect and expand markets and in which all social relationships are increasingly organized on an economic model.[8] At the core, this approach is diametrically opposed to modernization efforts that recognize a legitimate sphere of political activity and that aim to develop the state's regulative functions.

Yet both schools may pursue superficially similar policies. For instance, like technological diffusionists and proponents of modernization, neoliberals may champion projects designed to develop transportation and communication infrastructures, but the neoliberal version of such projects have only narrow economic ends. Their goals are to extend a "network society" that facilitates capital flows to and from nascent markets, to provide quick transport of raw materials and manufactured components, and to exploit differences in wage rates across nations. Under the aegis of "flexibility", neoliberals champion the dendritic advancement of capitalism into less developed regions of the globe with indifference or even in explicit antagonism to the ideals of participatory democracy. The World Bank and International Monetary Fund accordingly tie the funding of such projects to policies that prevent nations from developing strong regulatory regimes capable of interfering in the marketplace.[9] This third rendition of societal planning seeks only to integrate capitalist production on a global scale and would make all humanity subject to the autonomous demands of the marketplace. Like the other forms of planning already discussed, this economistic version of globalization is based on a reified and especially crude conception of human reason that turns human beings into spectators rather than participants in the process of social planning.

Globalization is thus an ambiguous expression of both human beings' increasing dominion over the planet and the limitations of self-understanding that prevent this phenomenon from attaining its full human significance. To the extent that globalization has been oriented by progressively conscious efforts to direct social development for human ends, this world-spanning activity is a limited expression of *praxis*. Large-scale social planning has successfully led to the creation of a planetary web of infrastructures, technologies, and institutions that allow human activity to be coordinated at the global scale and which sustain new forms of sociality. People have thus gained the ability to interact and shape their world in ways that would have seemed vacuously utopian a few generations ago. But these efforts have been directed by ideologies that estrange human beings from their own creations and that generate alienating social environments. The billions of people who live in poverty, environmental despoliation of global scale, pervasive economic instability, and the decay of democratic institutions all evidence the flawed ways in which social planning has been conceptualized. These sweeping social problems cannot be resolved by subordinating human beings more thoroughly either to the *deus ex machina* of technology or the putative teleology of society or the marketplace. Instead, the formation of a truly human world society requires superseding modern conceptions of social order and human reason. This process of self-critique can bring the ideal of social planning forward in an affirmatively post-modern form. Scenario planning exemplifies the type of philosophically grounded practices that can redirect planning efforts along socially responsive lines.

AN OVERVIEW OF SCENARIO PLANNING

Scenario Planning is a method for revealing the range of viable futures that can develop from a given a set of social conditions. It is not a predictive technique, but a dialogically-based practice that allows people to understand the range of planning options open to them at a given time and place. Governments and corporations have used scenario planning methods for strategic decision-making since the mid-20th century, and in recent years, the approach been used to generate models of sustainable development, as a tool of conflict resolution, and to develop responses to international health and environmental crises.[10] Lately, an effort has been made to formulate "normative scenario planning" as a tool for community-based social planning.[11] Beyond identifying a range of possible options for social development, normative scenario planning can help community members distinguish the *socially appropriate* courses of action open to them.

Several methodological summaries of the scenario planning process are available.[12] At its core, the method involves generating a set of narratives that describes the qualitatively distinct futures that can emerge from current conditions. These narratives grow out of an extended discussion among participants of a scenario planning group. Participants are chosen on the basis of qualities that go beyond the technical expertise associated with traditional models of forecasting and strategic decision-making. These factors include diversity, intuitive and artistic abilities, personal interests, familiarity with the problem at hand, and even the indistinct quality of being a "remarkable person". Scenario planning conversations involve both ongoing structured interviews and group-based discussions designed to reveal the often divergent presuppositions through which people make sense of the world. Persons trained in social-scientific methodologies will recognize aspects of standard qualitative methodologies in scenario planning procedures, including the use of extended interview and focus group techniques, the precepts of grounded theory and "naturalistic inquiry", and a guiding orientation toward *Verstehen* – the ideal of arriving at an understanding of the meanings through which people experience and act within varied social contexts. Several key features distinguish scenario planning from more traditional models of strategic decision making.

The practice of scenario planning is based on different conceptions of social and historical causality than traditional models of social planning. As suggested, traditional planning experts believe they have access to an unequivocal stratum of facticity that grounds their predictive models. This foundationalist assumption contains an implicit philosophy of history that allows the future to be extrapolated from present conditions using casual models of varying complexity. Neoliberal policies, for example, explain all significant human activity as an expression of a simple acquisitive rationality. These immutable psychological facts energize the economy and guarantee expanding material abundance for all participants in a fully realized marketplace. Positivist systemics, by contrast, are grounded on the apprehension of social rather than psychological facts. Here, the methodical excavation of social reality is believed to bring to light a causative nexus of facts that determine how social system grow and differentiate. In either case, the process of historical change is conceived as a linear recapitulation of the present. The same is true of technological diffusionism, which pins social development on the idea of increasing technological mastery of the material world. In this case, dualism sanctifies this technocratic approach by framing physical reality as inert matter, technology as the expression of objective scientific rationality, and localized knowledge as essentially subjective and inconsequential for guiding social development. Shortcomings in the predictive power of these traditional models are assumed to arise from limitations in the information available to planners. This assumption, in turn, perpetuates the search for technical refinements to the research process and transforms planning into an increasingly mechanical exercise dominated by experts.

Scenario planning, by contrast, is thoroughly informed by the contemporary break with determinism and linear models of development. This is in part due to the method's early ties with game theory and strategic decision-making.[13] Game theorists presume that there is no way in which an opponent's moves in a strategic situation can be predicted with certainty. Instead, given a situation in which opponents have a number of viable responses to each other's actions, the best that can be accomplished is to chart the range of paths along which a strategic situation might develop. Assuming that both parties share the same motivations, some courses of action may be more probable than others, but no amount of information will reduce the fundamental indeterminacy of the game – there always remains a number of qualitatively distinct paths along which a situation might develop. To this extent, the future cannot be predicted regardless of how much information one gathers. The best that can be done is to assign relative probabilities to each sequence of acts under the localized assumption that both parties want to "win" the game by pursuing courses of action that maximize their benefits. Lacking this assumption, the outcome of a game becomes wildly indeterminate, but even with this assumption an irreducible break has occurred with traditional determinism.[14]

Similarly, a key insight of complexity theory and related approaches is that a dynamic field of elements can shift unpredictably into qualitatively new arrangements and give rise of unforeseen "complex interactions".[15] Complex systems commonly exhibit discontinuities and indeterminacies that cannot be overcome by more precise modeling. Rather, gathering more information about such systems only brings to light addition ambiguities that increase the need for interpretation.[16] In other words, the search for a grounding level of facticity only reveals additional points at which an expert must commit to a particular rendition of reality. In this sense, descriptions of complex situations are always laden with the assumptions of its drafters.[17]

The complexity theory and game theory have contributed to undermining the presuppositions of the classical scientific worldview, which saw the world as a deterministic field of causally linked matter. In describing this clockwork conception of the universe, the mathematician Laplace argued that a creature with complete information about all the objects in the world and the forces acting on them would be able to apprehend with certainty the state of the universe at any point in time, past or future. In the first half of the 20th century, this understanding of the world, which is based on the presupposition of the univocality of matter, was undermined within science by Einsteinian relativism and quantum physics and independently in philosophy by the phenomenological critique of consciousness. Each of these movements led to the recognition that the world discloses incommensurable aspects of its being in correlation with the methodological activities of an incarnate observer who is linked practically and historically to others.[18] This insight undermined the possibility of conceiving of the world as a self-contained field of matter whose facticity can be apprehended unequivocally by an independent observer. The interpenetration of consciousness and world also means that the process of social development cannot be "sociologized" by ascribing society an independent existence in which humans function as parts in a larger machine or organism. This sociological object would then only reveal its characteristics and processes to social-scientific experts employing a universal scientific method. On the contrary, this naturalized social totality must be seen as the material correlative of a form of technocratic rationality that apprehends social reality through essentially administrative categories. The discourse of modernization and development is thereby revealed as inscribing only one possible project, one social *telos*, among others.

Scenario planners have been influenced to varying degrees by these theoretical developments and their method reflects a commitment to working out a non-deterministic model of social forecasting. It is not surprising that one of the key metaphors that scenario planners have used to portray the future is the image of "the rapids", because a cascade of water epitomizes the fundamental unpredictability of complex situations.[19] Scenario planners believe that the social environment undergoes constant dynamic change and that the character of these transformations cannot be predicted. The ability to competently guide a company or a government through these changes therefore required a new model of planning designed to cope with complexity. Scenario planners argue that technocratic planning based on progressively refined quantification and modeling must be supplanted by a methodology that primes one to "think the unthinkable". This practice eschews the ideal of deterministic "prediction" in favour of "forecasts" that can be derived by becoming reflexively sensitive to nascent possibilities within social world.[20] More than just a superficial shift in terminology, this break with the ideal of prediction dislodges the expert as the key player in the process of social planning. The specialized forms of knowledge that experts produce are not dismissed within the scenario planning process. To the contrary, information about such dynamics as long-term demographic trends, limits on natural resources, and the pace and nature of technological change are examples of information that only experts can supply and that have to be incorporated into forecasts to distinguish them from airy speculations.

But the types of processes that experts focus on are seen as only select influences, and not necessarily the most important ones, upon a social milieu. The development of valid scenarios requires supplementing these sources of expertise with knowledge from a broader set of participants in the research process. Persons who have situated knowledge of a social milieu, whether that setting is an organization or a society, are key participants in the scenario development process, because they have access to the taken-for-granted assumptions that motivate social actors. As noted, "remarkable people" also emerge as key players in the scenario planning process. Notable musicians, artists, and polymaths have contributed to the development of scenarios because their talents, as Ezra Pound noted, make them the "antennae of a culture". Remarkable people, in other words, are uniquely attuned to incipient possibilities in a social milieu. The cultivation of such idiosyncratic perspectives is a basic component of the scenario building process, as Ged Davis notes, "As a practice, scenario building today is synonymous with thinking broadly and freely about a problem, enlarging frames of reference and involving different worldviews, rather than seeing a situation from a single perspective".[21] The methodology of scenario planning, in short, rejects traditional dualisms between abstract and local knowledge, science and art, objectivity and subjectivity that define conventional research programmes, and this eclecticism is essential for recognizing future possibilities and articulating "fragments of several possible futures".[22]

Scenario planning consequently requires eliciting the views of a heterogeneous group of participants – some with knowledge of economic, social, or scientific developments, others with direct experience of a social setting, still others with aesthetic sensitivities – who are unlikely to take each other's presuppositions at face value. Thus another key aspect of scenario building is to engage in an extended process of interviewing and extended discussions that allow participants to recognize and articulate their taken-for-granted assumptions about the social world and the processes that influence social change. This practice has the effect of de-centring knowledge and increasing reflexivity to the point at which participants gain the ability to see the future as a manifold of potentialities rather than an arrangement emerging mechanically from present conditions. As this reflexive awareness develops, participants become capable of describing a range of different but plausible future "scenarios".[23] Again, it is important to understand that these scenarios are not deterministic predictions but discontinuous forecasts about possible future states of the world. Scenarios describe qualitatively distinct futures without presupposing a causative sequence that no amount of technical refinement is capable of establishing. Thus, while it incorporates traditional forms of expertise in its conversations, the scenario planning methodology recasts the process of social planning as a dialogue.

A dialogue is a special kind of communicative relationship in which participants make some aspect of the world an explicit theme of their conversation while also recognizing one another's ability to reflect upon what is being said. Dialogues link persons as interlocutors who turn toward each other as equal participants in a process of articulating differing perspectives on a state of affairs. Furthermore, the reflexive modality of the dialogue requires persons to bracket the everyday commitments that characterize their taken for granted attitude within the world and to compare and contrast these commitments with those articulated by others. In so doing, each person becomes conscious of his/her role as an originator of an address about the world – that is, as one who articulates a specific perspective on a state of affairs – but also of others as partners in the dialogue capable of reflexively articulating overlapping and conflicting discourses of their own.[24] The scenario building process develops as a week-long series of such dialogical encounters whose outcome is an irreducible set of narratives about the future. The methodology of scenario planning is thus participatory in the sense that people do not simply appear as objects of a technocratic monologue about the world but enter into the process of planning as speaking subjects capable of knowledgeably rendering an outlook that inscribes their hopes and expectations. This dialogical methodology is built on a respect for difference, first, in the sense that difference grounds the possibility of articulating contrasting worldviews, and, second, in the sense that the goal is not to force a reconciliation of these worldviews but through language to carefully reveal their presuppositions and details. Scenario planners value heteroglossia over monoglossia: in contrast to the meta-narratives articulated by traditional planning experts, which present one deterministic view of the path of social development, the aim of scenario planning exercises are to articulate multiple valid stories about the future. Scenario planning efforts replace the technocratic monologues of experts with a series of dialogues that generate multiple stories about the future.

These features of scenario planning point to another key aspect of the practice: its reliance of narrative rationality. As James Ogilvy notes, "Narrativity is essential to scenarios", and this basis in language places the method squarely within a post-modern paradigm.[25] Scenarios are stories about the future. However, these stories are not simply decorative trappings designed to make technical issues palatable to laypeople. Casting scenarios as stories is not an exercise in what has traditionally been called "mere rhetoric". Instead, narrative is understood to be a basic modality of human reason and one that is richer than technocratic discourse. As we have seen, other forms of social forecasting contain unquestioned meta-narratives about the process of social development, but although they orient the actions of large numbers of people, these narratives are rarely articulated and are relegated to a pre-scientific status in the background of social inquiry. The goal of such approaches is rather to transcend language and arrive at an unequivocal and thus predictive model of social processes.

The creation of narratives, by contrast, is the core of the scenario planning methodology and reflects the anti-foundationalist stance of the practice. In this view, no amount of technique can sidestep language and elude the need for interpretation. Even the ability to link facts together in an elementary way has been shown to presuppose linguistic devices, such as metaphor, that give the resulting models their cogency and implicate them within broader narrative scaffolding.[26] Social actors also employ narrative rationality to orient and coordinate their activities in light of a "definition of the situation" that makes a social context meaningful. This narrative dimension of everyday life makes itself felt in every human response to the world, so that forces that seem to act on social life as purely material constraints, as in the case of limits on natural resources, nevertheless appear as components of a meaningful world that people interpret and respond to in diverse ways. Thus, more than a presentational device, scenario planners believe that narratives provide the only way to adequately conceptualize details about life in the future as well as to move people to orient themselves toward specific possibilities brought to light in these stories. In this sense, scenario building should be understood as a protracted exercise in socially sensitive interpretive sociology that begins and ends with a focus on the meaningful context of social action.[27]

CONCLUSION: FUTURE DIRECTIONS FOR THE DEVELOPMENT OF SCENARIO PLANNING

Scenario building exercises have increasingly been used to guide planning efforts in line with the values of sustainability and democratic participation and, accordingly, hold promise as a tool for reconceptualizing globalization. The methodology incorporates key philosophical developments that allow planning efforts to be formulated in more participatory ways. Chief among these is the recognition of the linguistic turn in philosophy, which as a critique of foundationalism forces a basic re-evaluation of the role and scope of expert knowledge and technocratic decision making. This critique undermines the pursuit of objective social facts and the determinants of social change that has anchored traditional planning projects and opens the possibility of basing such efforts on the linguistic bonds that link human beings. The resulting method is founded on a dialogical encounter between persons who freely engage in an extended reflection on the range of possibilities immanent within the present. Rather than assuming the mechanical and unilinear conception of progress that came into prominence with the Enlightenment, the scenario methodology explodes the future into a spectrum of non-synchronous and qualitatively distinct worlds. Human agency is thus brought to the foreground of planning efforts, because rather than merely attending the unfolding of a universal process of historical change, the task is to choose and pursue one world among others.

As Ogilvy has discussed, this goal of using scenario methods to choose from among rather than merely describe possibilities requires developing a theory of "normative scenario planning".[28] This extension of the method would transform scenario practices into an instrument of critical inquiry that can help people judge the relative value of scenarios in light of a social ideal. Although scenarios have been used for socially progressive ends in the past, the method has most commonly been applied as a tool for insuring institutional continuity within a range of possible contexts. This use of scenarios is oriented only toward forewarning governmental and organizational administrators of possible changes in the environment within which their institutions operate, so that they can plan strategic responses to various possibilities. The goal here is not social transformation but rather institutional adaptation to any given context. In this mode, scenario practitioners' recent concern with sustainability and political change reflects what Georges Gurvitch described as the "pragmatism devoid of humanism" common among techno-bureaucratic administrators.[29] Scenario planning in this sense is an attempt to exert cybernetic control within a global capitalist environment characterized by increasing crises and social dislocations that overwhelm traditional planning techniques.

Ogilvy, by contrast, argues that scenario planning can be used to pursue emancipatory goals and should be considered the "fulfillment of critical theory".[30] The distinguishing characteristic of normative scenario planning is that it turns toward communities as the source of narratives and of values to judge their validity. For Ogilvy, the category of "community" allows planning to be linked to collective goals while providing a way to sidestep the reification of both society as a sui generis totality and of the individual as a self-sufficient egoistic monad. He also sees community as a way to avoid the charges of relativism often directed at post-modern theory, because communities can proffer an intersubjectively grounded ethics through which to judge the validity of knowledge claims.[31]

The further articulation of scenario planning will require each of these themes to be worked out in more detail. For instance, Ogilvy suggests that communities generate narratives. Yet it is also clear that communities are brought together by means of compelling narratives, so the relationship between language and the self-understanding and self-representation of communities seems more complex than what Ogilvy suggests and this point has important repercussions for the way social order is conceptualized. The social ontology of community must be worked out to better understand how communities can serve as a source of non-repressive normative claims. An imagery of community that places language, difference, and heterogeneity at the centre of social order is needed to avoid reifying the principle of community. Beyond this, a still broader ethics must be worked out to understand how one arbitrates the conflicting normative claims of multiple communities. Clearly, such an ethics would be needed to direct globalization toward emancipatory ends.

Finally, there is no doubt that scenario planning is a powerful tool for helping people reflect on the course of social development. This socially responsive method grounds such reflection on the lived-experiences of varied social actors, so that the resulting narratives incorporate diverse horizons of understanding and point to divergent possibilities. These "futures" can then be recognized as practical possibilities to be pursued or avoided by the knowledgeable intervention of human beings into the processes that shape their world. Scenario planning thus takes place within that space opened up by modernity, in which the future appeared as an object of human *praxis*, but brings this heritage forward in post-modern form. While scenario planning can clarify people's understanding of the possibilities open to them, the pursuit of such options is a practical problem that requires intervening in a world rife with violence and repression. Thus, any normative theory of scenario building must also suggest how people can intervene and bring about change in a world in which power does not simply melt away in light of a good story. The linking of theory and practice in ways can lead to broad structural changes in society remains the key challenge to any critical theory of society. Yet, insofar as human life is always oriented and justified through narratives, the creation of lucid and compelling stories about the future illustrates Marcuse's argument that "the recollection of what can authentically be becomes a power that shapes the future".[32]

NOTES

1. Michel Foucault, *The History of Sexuality: Vol. 1: An Introduction*, trans. Robert Hurley (New York: Vintage Books, 1978), pp. 135-159.
2. Max Horkheimer and Theodor W. Adorno, *Dialectic of Enlightenment*, trans. John Cumming (New York: Continuum, 1991), pp. 3-42.
3. Herbert Marcuse, *One-Dimensional Man* (Boston: Beacon Press, 1964).
4. Alvin Gouldner, *The Coming Crisis of Western Sociology* (New York: Basic Books, 1970).
5. Daniel Lerner, *The Passing of Traditional Society* (Glencoe, IL.: The Fress Press, 1958).
6. Everett M. Rogers. *The Diffusion of Innovations* (Glencoe, IL.: The Free Press, 1962).
7. Jürgen Habermas, *Theory and Practice*, trans. John Viertel (Boston: Beacon Press, 1973), pp. 253-282.
8. F.A. Hayek, *Law, Legislation and Liberty. Vol. 2: The Mirage of Social Justice* (Chicago: University of Chicago Press, 1976); F.A. Hayek, *The Road to Serfdom* (Chicago: University of Chicago Press, 1944); Milton Friedman, *Capitalism & Freedom* (Chicago: University of Chicago Press, 1962).
9. Richard J. Barnet and John Cavanagh, *Global Dreams: Imperial Corporations and the New World Order* (New York: Somon & Schuster, 1994), pp. 339-358.

10. World Business Council for Sustainable Development, WBCSD Global Scenarios 2000-2050: Exploring Sustainable Development. World Business Council for Sustainable Development, November, 1997, http://www.wbcsd.org/includes/getTarget.asp?type=d&id=ODk5MA; Global Business Network, The Mount Fleur Scenarios. *Deeper News* 7, no. 1 (August, 1992), http://www.gbn.com/ArticleDisplayServlet.srv?aid=455; Global Business Network, "Destino Colombia: A Scenario Planning Process for the New Millennium," *Deeper News* 9, no. 1 (July, 1998), http://www.gbn.com/ArticleDisplayServlet.srv?aid=215.
11. James A. Ogilvy, *Creating Better Futures: Scenario Planning as a Tool for a Better Future* (New York: Oxford University Press, 2002).
12. Peter Schwartz, *The Art of the Long View* (New York: Doubleday, 1991); Kees Van der Heijden, *Scenarios: The Art of Strategic Conversation* (New York: John Wiley & Sons, 1996); Shell International, *Scenarios: An Explorer's Guide* (London: Shell International Limited), p. 203.
13. Art Kleiner, *The Age of Heretics* (New York: Doubleday, 1996), pp. 181-217.
14. Morton A. Davis, *Game Theory: A Nontechnical Introduction* (New York: Dover Publications, 1997); J.D. Williams, *The Compleat Strategyst: Being a Primer on the Theory of Games of Strategy* (New York: Dover Publications, 1986).
15. Charles Perrow, *Normal Accidents* (New York: Basic Books, 1984), pp. 62-100.
16. Kees Van der Heijden et al., *The Sixth Sense* (New York, NY: John Wiley and Sons, 2002), pp. 138-139.
17. James Gleick, *Chaos: Making a New Science* (New York: Penguin Books, 1988).
18. Ludwig Landgrebe, *Major Problems in Contemporary European Philosophy*, trans. Kurt F. Reinhardt (New York: Frederick Ungar Publishing Company, 1966), pp. 83-101.
19. Pierre Wack, "Scenarios: Shooting the Rapids", *Harvard Business Review*, November-December, 1985, pp. 139-150.
20. Van der Heijden et al., *The Sixth Sense: Accelerating Organizational Learning with Scenarios*, pp. 117-146; World Business Council for Sustainable Development, WBCSD Global Scenarios 2000-2050: Exploring Sustainable Development, p. 4.
21. Ged Davis, "Scenarios as a Tool for the 21st Century", Probing the Future Conference, Strathclyde University, July 12th, 2002.
22. Ogilvy, *Creating Better Futures*. p. 133.

23. Van der Heijden et al., *The Sixth Sense: Accelerating Organizational Learning with Scenarios*, pp. 162-171, 255-257; Schwartz, *The Art oft the Long View*, pp. 228-239.
24. Joseph J. Pilotta and Algis Mickunas, *Science of Communication: Its Phenomenological Foundation* (Hillsdale, New Jersey: Lawrence Earlbaum Associates, 1990), pp. 46-82.
25. Ogilvy, *Creating Better Futures*, pp. 140-141.
26. Kenneth Burke, *Permanence and Change: An Anatomy of Purpose* (New York: New Republic, 1936).
27. Schwartz, *The Art of the Long View*, pp. 37-43.
28. Ogilvy, *Creating Better Futures*.
29. Georges Gurvitch, *The Social Frameworks of* Knowledge, trans. Margaret A. Thompson and Kenneth A. Thompson (New York: Harper & Row, 1971), pp. 113, 199-212.
30. James Ogilvy, "Scenario Planning as the Fulfillment of Critical Theory." *Futures Research Quarterly* 12, no. 2 (1996): 5-33.
31. Ogilvy, *Creating Better Futures*.
32. Herbert Marcuse, "The Concept of Essence", in *Negations* (Boston: Beacon Press, 1988), pp. 76, 43-87.

Index